7110 True Crime Library
A member of **Avery Press**
New York • London

Burning Shield:

The Jason Schechterle Story

Burning Shield: The Jason Schechterle Story

This book is a work of nonfiction. References to real people, events, establishments, organizations, products, or locales are intended only to provide a sense of authenticity. Certain incidents and dialogue are drawn from the author's imagination, as needed, and are not to be construed as real.

Cover design: Brandon Stout
Cover photographs: Troy Aossey (www.troyaossey.com)
Editors: Susan Campbell, Lisa Fontes, LeeAnn Kriegh and Jim Moore
Author photograph at back: Troy Aossey

ISBN: 0988651947
ISBN 13: 9780988651944
Library of Congress Control Number: 2013921150
Avery Press, Phoenix, AZ

7110 True Crime Library, an imprint of Avery Press
Manufactured in the United States of America

Burning Shield:

The Jason Schechterle Story

LANDON J. NAPOLEON

Praise for *Burning Shield: The Jason Schechterle Story*

"A maimed cop fights to regain his life in this inspiring true story… Author [Landon J.] Napoleon scrupulously guides readers through Schechterle's teen years, spent absorbing the sounds of REO Speedwagon, excelling at golf and falling in love—and into his laudable career in the Air Force. Faithfully documented is every bump and nook on his road toward achieving his childhood dream: wearing a Phoenix Police Department badge. As the enthusiastic rookie got his bearings in the routines of police work—which involved more picking up shoplifters at Wal-Mart than high-octane shootouts—his future fate was darkly foreshadowed by events elsewhere. All across the country, police officers were dying in exploding Ford Crown Victorias, and attorney Patrick J. McGroder III— "the legal equivalent of The Terminator"—aimed to make Ford pay. Schechterle would be crucial in helping him. Napoleon, the author of several crime novels, is skilled at painting a scene in slangy strokes while balancing plotlines… this true story reads like a novel."

—*Kirkus Reviews*

"Sad, exciting, life-changing and emotional, *Burning Shield: The Jason Schechterle Story* is an amazing story of one man's triumph over tragedy with the support of an entire community."

—Jack Ballentine, former homicide detective and author of *Murder for Hire*

"Jason Schechterle's life has been one of joy, tragedy, love, and hope. In *Burning Shield: The Jason Schechterle Story,* he motivates us with the power of positive thinking and living his life with optimism and gratitude. We learn the importance of chasing our dreams, but more importantly, overcoming our nightmares while touching and impacting lives all around us. This man is an inspiration and his story must be read and shared."

—Derrick Hall
President and CEO, Arizona Diamondbacks

"*Burning Shield: The Jason Schechterle Story* is an incredible testament to the human spirit: You will never look at life the same after reading this book. Jason is one of the most positive and uplifting people you will ever read about, and his ability to convey the power of a positive attitude, along with its healing benefits, is unparalleled. Very powerful!"

—Larry Hayward
Chairman and Chief Executive Officer
Leslie's Swimming Pool Supplies

Praise for Landon J. Napoleon:

"Briskly told and well-drawn, *The Rules of Action* does what many courtroom-based novels and television shows do not: It stays true to the actual practice of trial law... A fast-paced tale of justice in action and a remarkably accurate portrait of a trial lawyer's daily grind. ... Prospective law students are frequently encouraged to read law-student memoirs or legal hornbooks, but for a realistic view of litigation and a great deal more action, they'd do well to add this legal thriller to their reading list."

—*Kirkus Reviews*

"*The Rules of Action* is one of the most compelling and entertaining books I have ever read on the strategy and gamesmanship of the legal process."

—Grant Woods
Former Arizona Attorney General

"Weird, funky, and offbeat—Landon J. Napoleon's writing is a harrowing, hysterical, and ultimately life-affirming romp through America's dark and desperate underbelly. His prose reads like you would imagine a road-rocker's elegy sounds—gritty, jagged, and full of passion."

—David S. Goyer
Writer of *Batman Begins, The Dark Knight,*
and The Dark Knight Rises

More praise for Landon J. Napoleon's debut, *ZigZag*:

"*ZigZag* is one of the boldest and most original first novels to appear in a long time. It's also very funny, in a way that only the raw street-song of truth can be funny. Landon J. Napoleon has written a gem."

—Carl Hiaasen
Best-selling author

"A remarkable debut portraying the inner life of a disturbed ghetto teenager as he attempts to grow up in the frightening world he's inherited. ... An unaffected, moving, astonishing insight into the heart of a troubled, silent genius."

—*Kirkus Reviews*
(starred review)

"This mixture of comic adventure and paean to the values of volunteerism is a vivid read and impressive debut novel."

—*Library Journal*
(starred review)

"[An] affecting first novel that explores the survival of the human spirit in an atmosphere of deprivation and cruelty."

—*Publishers Weekly*

"Landon J. Napoleon's first novel is an affecting work."

—The *Dallas Morning News*

"Like a portrait of Huck Finn in negative."

—*The Times* (London)

"A refreshing debut novel... this is more than your average 'tale from the hood.' It has a stylish, assured quality... highly entertaining and highly recommended."

—*Pride Magazine*
United Kingdom

"A highly colorful tale. ... Along the way the reader is exposed to the strangeness, the magic, and the wonder of ZigZag's imaginary powers... emotional strength and genuine passion."

—Amazon.co.uk

Books by Landon J. Napoleon

Nonfiction

Burning Shield: The Jason Schechterle Story

Novels

ZigZag
Deep Wicked Freaky
The Rules of Action
The Flatirons

Foreword

IT HAS BEEN MORE than a decade since March 26, 2001, the night I was burned alive and, by all measures, should have died. Few people, if any, have survived fourth-degree burns, which are burns that leave nothing except bone; all the skin layers, muscle, tissue, and tendons are vaporized. That I'm here to write about such trauma is inexplicable. As I would discover, something intervened for my larger purpose. It was simply not my time to go, and the unlikeliest collection of circumstances had to transpire to save my life.

Since I was 16 years old, in 1988, all I'd wanted was to be a Phoenix police officer. (Well, that *and* a professional golfer, as you'll see.) When I was in high school my older brother Michael graduated the police academy and was a full-authority Phoenix police officer. I can still remember seeing him in his uniform for the first time, being completely in awe and having my own dream put into motion: *That's who I want to be.* The overall effect was almost too much for a teenager to process: the uniform, the polished badge, the crisp utility belt with sidearm and other tools of the trade, right down to the black tactical boots with a high-gloss shine. I wanted all of it, and the larger duty and responsibility.

Naively, I figured someday I'd stroll down to the Phoenix Police Department at 620 West Washington, apply for the job, take a test or two and be immediately ushered into the next available academy class. If only things were really that simple: In this book you'll learn about my long, labyrinthine journey and all my missteps in trying to become a cop, which was anything but easy. And, truthfully, the dream was dead more than once.

In spite of the many challenges on that long road, on January 7, 2000, in an auditorium in downtown Phoenix, I sat with Academy Class 333 at graduation. That was the night my life as a police officer began. Let me repeat: My *life* as a police officer. It's important to understand the distinction between a job to collect a paycheck and an occupation chosen as a way of life. Being a police officer is the latter: It is who you are down to your core being, a noble calling. If not, I would never have made it through the rejection, eventual hiring process, and the academy. If not, if I somehow got that far, I wouldn't have been around long before moving on to some other more suitable occupation. Being a cop is an all-in prospect. It's a commitment.

So my dream had become real. Not just the dream of being a police officer, but a Phoenix police officer. Even today when I write or say those words they are pure poetry to me. I had a goal, and I achieved it. I'm not a college graduate, so I put every ounce of who I am into this singular career track and profession. That night at academy graduation, my brother Michael pinned my polished new badge on my chest. My parents were there, too, and my sister and her family, along with some friends from high school. Of course my wife, Suzie, and our two kids, Kiley and Zane—ages 6 and 1, respectively, at the time—were there with me. I had achieved my overarching life goal. The feeling when you step into your dream is almost indescribable.

Amid the camera flashes, tears, and proud congratulations, I was overwhelmed by it all. In these pages, you'll learn why, and what I had sacrificed and endured to be on that stage with Class 333. I knew that night I belonged in that uniform, and I wore it with pride, honor, and integrity. Driving home afterward with my wife and kids, I felt as much peaceful serenity as one man can hope to find in this lifetime. All was right with the world.

The thing about goals and dreams is that they often change—whether by choice, design, or destiny. I found that out in a big way just fifteen months later when my police cruiser exploded into a horrific fireball. I was about to learn an entirely new scale for defining the words "sacrifice" and "endure."

The subsequent journey has taken me to some remarkable places emotionally, mentally, physically, and spiritually. I needed these intervening years to recover, rebuild, and mentally process everything that had happened and was happening in my life. I had to relearn how to live in a disfigured body, including my horribly damaged hands and eyes, the latter of which continue to provide daily challenges. Time has given me new perspectives. Only now am I ready and able to share my story.

My message here is simple: We all face challenges in this life. Call it the hazards of living, but from normal hurdles to all-encompassing adversity—a cancer diagnosis, the loss of a loved one, getting laid off, financial calamity, and all the other smaller and daily grinding annoyances—we are all being regularly tested in this journey. And, unfortunately, the tests never end. Fabulously rich, poor, or somewhere in between as most of us are, there is no destination where all our problems magically disappear.

So in spite of it all, how do we get out of bed and face another uphill day? How do we slog forward when the urge to just quit is so appealing? Ultimately, how do we let our human spirit shine brighter than we ever thought possible?

We all get to make one simple choice, day by day, when yet another roadblock gets dropped in our path: to quit or to keep going. In retrospect, our life becomes the story of how we overcome the adversity we face. It is never easy, and we never do it perfectly. But the important stuff—our determination, integrity, honor, loyalty, love, and family—is ours to keep. It is a bad cliché, but there's one tenet I try to follow: Life is 10 percent what happens to you and 90 percent how you react to it. Being burned alive was my 10 percent; how I reacted has been my ninety.

It is my fervent desire that no one ever needs to experience what I have in order to construct a new model of living. If this book inspires you to live better in some small way, to keep out of self-pity and focus instead on living each day in a meaningful way, then my mission will have been fulfilled. And as long as we're going to spend some time together, we should start with another key tenet of mine: Roll Tide! Yes, you will learn all about that obsession, too—for Alabama college football—as I peel back the layers and invite you to know who I am and how I came to be here to share this story with you.

It's all connected in the grand scheme: everything that happened and everything that did not. Collectively, all the twists, turns, ups, and downs—the joy, pain, suffering, and small triumphs—brought me here to this new place where I'm still living and breathing. In this space, I have found a new peace and purpose that transcend anything I might have ever imagined. Once you've been burned to within seconds of death, just about anything else in life gets retrofitted with a new perspective.

In the end, when we drop pretense and posturing and admit our rawest fears and vulnerabilities, we are each just a human being, moving one step forward at a time, toward some unknown, magical, mysterious destiny. We're all headed somewhere, but the destination might be unexpected and, as in my case, might surprise us beyond imagination.

I hope that reading about my journey is enjoyable and, most important, gives you something meaningful to take forward on your own quest.

—Jason Schechterle
November 2013

For everyone—especially those injured or killed in the line of duty—who has heard and followed the noble call to serve and protect.

"The purity of my intention is my protection."
—The Dalai Lama

Prologue

Phoenix, Arizona, March 26, 2001, 11:17 p.m.
500 Precinct, patrol unit 513 Henry

THE WARM SPRING NIGHT was in full city shimmer when the hot call popped at 11:17 p.m. and lit the fuse that would change everything.

Clock ticking: four minutes.

Finally something to dead-end the monotony of paper calls and endless reports. Phoenix Police Officer Jason Schechterle, 28, felt the adrenaline surge of anticipation as he listened to the female dispatcher. *Talk to me.* Most of the city's 3,000 uniforms knew each dispatcher after just a few words. But this voice was unfamiliar: The call was a wider alert from a different patrol area in Schechterle's assigned precinct.

He steered with one hand, leaned forward, and instinctively reached for the black microphone. The night so far had been nothing but paperwork; just maybe proximity and providence were about to clash and—mercifully—ice the rolling steno pool. Two other officers riding solo and nearby in their own rigs, Bryan Brooks, badge 6635, and Kevin Chadwick, badge 6763, also listened intently.

Brooks and Chadwick were partners, but patrolling in separate units on this night.

"Unknown trouble," the dispatcher said. "Twenty-Seven Thirty-Five East Thomas. Possible casualty. All available units, code 3."

Bingo on action: code 3. Some manner of crime, violence, and mayhem.

Schechterle was minutes away: The numbered streets in Phoenix ran north–south, with Central Avenue downtown as the zero line and the numbers increasing eastward. The numbered avenues did the same heading west. Schechterle had just rolled through a nearby intersection and would likely be first on scene.

Schechterle went cop-mode: "Five-thirteen Henry. I'll start up."

With the afternoon and midnight shifts overlapping at this hour, roughly eighteen available patrol cars were in immediate proximity. Because the call wasn't in his beat, Schechterle had no obligation to respond. He could have simply continued talking to his wife—who was waiting for her husband to return to their conversation via cellphone—for a few minutes and let any one of the other officers respond. If he'd simply let someone else take the call, the rest of his life would have unfolded following a completely different trajectory. But that was not to be: Jason Schechterle was always on point and ready to respond. Schechterle never did anything halfway.

Schechterle picked up his cellphone. Before the 11:17 hot call cracked, he and his wife Suzie had been chatting, the nightly on-duty ritual they'd started when he joined the Phoenix Police Department fifteen months ago. The conversation always included some banter about their two young children— Kiley, Suzie's daughter from a previous marriage, and Zane, their son together.

"Baby, I need to go. I'm en route." They each said *I love you,* and ended the call.

Dammit, Schechterle thought. *Chapman's going to miss it all.* Bryan Chapman, his regular partner and best friend from the same academy class, was enrolled in the investigator classes Schechterle had just completed. Classes were Mondays during shift, *tonight*, so their sergeant had split them up for the night. Schechterle had argued the point—*Sarge, please, he'll only be out a couple hours. Let us ride together tonight*—but the boss held firm. Schechterle and Chapman would each patrol solo on this night. That way Chapman wouldn't be stuck cooling out after class if Schechterle was hung up on a call. Their not being together was the first in a long series of strange coincidences on this eerie night—a coincidence that may have saved Chapman's life.

Earlier, Chapman had sent a message to Schechterle over the mobile data terminal (MDT), the in-car computer that chewed data—license plates, names, addresses, DOBs—and issued answers on suspects long before everyone was carrying supercomputers in the form of smartphones and tablets. Schechterle responded that he'd been mired in "paper-call hell" all night. Paper calls were the bane of police work: Some lower-priority crime had been committed— broken car window, stolen bicycle, spray-paint graffiti on a block wall—and the perpetrator was long gone. Still, a police officer had to interview the victim, conduct an investigation, and write a police report; paper calls meant no action and lots of time writing reports. Depending on the day, the backlog of paper calls often carried over, shift to shift. So when Schechterle climbed in his cruiser to start his 3 p.m.-to-1 a.m. shift, there might be ten paper calls stacked up on the MDT.

Knowing what his partner was up against, Chapman offered to pick up Taco Bell at the Third Street and McDowell restaurant, which was police-safe by collective reputation. Eating out was another consideration on the job, because cops who went through fast-food drive-ups and sat in restaurants in uniform ran the risk that some maladjusted punk would do sick (phlegm burgers) and dangerous (shaved-glass sandwiches) things to the food behind the scenes. Without a collective reputation as police-safe, all fast-food lanes and restaurants were to be avoided.

On that night, Chapman would have actually preferred a Burrito Supreme along with Schechterle, but he'd given up fast food for Lent and instead picked up a sandwich at Subway, one of the only establishments that afforded a uniformed cop on-view observation of the food preparation: *Yeah, that's right: I'm watching your every move, so keep it clean.*

With food in hand, Chapman and Schechterle went "10-25," darkened cruisers parked driver's-side door to door at the fire department at 150 South Twelfth Street. The fire station was a popular break spot for cops in CCP (Central City Precinct), which was headquartered farther south on Sixteenth Street just north of I-17. They carried their food inside to eat in the quiet and well-appointed break room and carve out some peace. They joked and made bets about who would get the next OV action: "on-view," when an officer rolled up on a crime in progress.

Schechterle also continued to berate Chapman about the debacle that had begun the day before. On that shift patrol Sunday night, they had rolled up on their academy class buddy Shayne Tuchfarber (pronounced *too-farber* with a silent *ch*), who was working off-duty at the Food City parking lot at Twentieth Street and McDowell. As the confab began, Schechterle tucked a massive wad of Skoal that was, according to Tuchfarber, "The biggest chew I've ever seen a human being put in his mouth." Indeed, Schechterle had traded smoking for "smokeless" right after the academy when he first hit the streets in uniform, and now he was packing wads like a big-league utility player in a doubleheader. Chapman confirmed plans for a special operation the next day with his two friends.

"Yeah," Tuchfarber assured him, "I'm in and will be there by eight."

When Sunday shift ended at one o'clock early Monday morning on March 26, 2001, Schechterle, per the plan, followed Chapman east to his new house in the far-flung town of Gilbert, a dusty Phoenix suburb with a distinct smell of cow manure.

Chapman's plan was for Schechterle to spend the night at Chapman's place to get an early start the next morning on installing an irrigation drip system and sprinklers. Rookie cops on rookie salaries cut corners where possible: Schechterle and Tuchfarber would be the needed free muscle.

This grunt work included digging trenches through sun-hardened Arizona clay of a concrete-like hardness. In other words, Chapman was calling in major favors. Tuchfarber was on the second shift in the South Mountain Precinct, so it was a good opportunity for the three academy pals to get together. On Monday morning, as the three assembled in Chapman's yard and began plotting first steps in the bright sunlight, Chapman's cellphone rang. He answered, said little, hung up, and looked at his two pals sheepishly.

"What?" Schechterle said.

"I just got called in to testify at a DUI trial downtown." From where they stood, downtown Phoenix was thirty-five minutes west, and that was if there was no traffic.

"You have got to be kidding," Tuchfarber said.

"That was city court."

"That was Dawn, wasn't it?" Schechterle said. "You're going to have brunch with your wife."

Chapman could only shake his head. "I gotta shower and go. I'll barely make it as it is."

"All right, Big Head, you go enjoy your mimosas and eggs Benedict while your two migrant workers dig your trench lines," Tuchfarber said.

"You believe this guy?" Schechterle added.

Chapman showered, put on a suit and tie, raced downtown, and promptly learned that one of the lawyers in the case had been granted a continuance. No court appearance for Chapman. He walked back to his car, drove back to Gilbert, and arrived late morning, just as Schechterle and Tuchfarber had finished the worst of the digging.

At the fire station later that night, on "lunch" break with Chapman, Schechterle was still shaking his head as he tucked into his Taco Bell. "I know you went for brunch with Dawn. You are an evil snake." Tuchfarber wasn't there to concur, but he hadn't bought it either.

Chapman rose from the table, laughing. "You know what? Maybe I did. And you two fell for it hook, line, and sinker." It was 10:30 p.m. They'd balled up their paper wrappers, but Schechterle was still surrounded by handwritten accident reports spread on the table at the fire station. This was common, cops chilling at the fire station while the firefighters were mostly sleeping. Because of the sprinkler mission, Schechterle hadn't seen his wife and kids since he left for work at two o'clock on Sunday afternoon for his three o'clock shift. Although it was only a twenty-minute drive to work, Schechterle was never late. His motto: *On time is late—fifteen minutes early is on time.*

"I'm going to go look for stolens," Chapman said. "You're gonna be here all night doing that."

"Look at all this paperwork," Schechterle sighed. "Because you were at your stupid class."

Looking for stolens was near the top of the list of "Fun Things to Do" for the rookie duo, and had turned into something of a competition. The game involved riding patrol, running plates, and trying to hit a bingo: stolen vehicle. When it came back hot, the initiating officer got to orchestrate a felony stop complete with helicopter and spotlight, multiple backup units running parallels, and an eager K-9 unit ready to chomp wide-eyed suspects. Some stolens turned out to be cracked-out cars, a vehicle "loaned" to a dealer in exchange for drugs. But when the car never came back to the drug user, the criminal reported the car stolen.

In the 513 beat Chapman and Schechterle patrolled—roughly west to east from Seventh Street to Sixteenth Street and, from the north, Thomas Road one-and-a-half miles south to Roosevelt—stolens and the felony stops they triggered happened with amazing regularity. In just fifteen months, Schechterle had already been a part of thirty felony stops, guns drawn, multiple units, and tense moments until the call went code 4, arrested persons (APs) in custody. Their buddy Tuchfarber was pulling similar duties patrolling 42 Frank.

Finally, after eleven o'clock and just minutes before the hot call, Schechterle sent his partner a message over the MDT: *I'm done.* Paperwork hell had ended, at least for the moment, and Schechterle was back to 10-8 status: in service. Then Chapman wheeled away on a domestic-violence hot call. Schechterle responded too, but as he rolled on scene Chapman nodded him off. Code 4: no assistance needed.

Again, goose eggs on action for Schechterle. But then the 11:17 p.m. hot call cracked, and Schechterle was rolling. He'd rib Chapman hard on that one. Schechterle smiled, gripped the wheel, and thought: *Wrong place, wrong time: story of Chapman's life. That guy's always a day late and a dollar short. And, of course, he can't shoot for shit.*

TEN minutes before Schechterle was calling in that fateful hot call, a taxicab had wheeled curbside and picked up a fare who'd just walked out of the county jail. Rogelio Gutierrez was behind the wheel. Lawrence Tracy, still dressed in jail-pink pajamas—courtesy of local lightning-rod Sheriff Joe Arpaio—carried a sack of groceries. He climbed in the back seat and gave Gutierrez a destination: Twenty-Fourth Street and Thomas Road. Then he settled back and savored the fresh air of freedom.

FOR Schechterle, code 3 also meant red and blue lights and squealing rubber. All the stuff for which he'd signed up. Replacing the handset, he flipped on the party lights but not the noisemakers. Late at night, with a long way to go, he would keep the lights on and only squawk the siren at intersections. He took a brief moment, in those days before touch screens and GPS, to run the fastest route in his head. He was working solo in the Central City Precinct, one of eight such precincts covering the entire department's unfettered urban-sprawl beat of 516 square miles. Brooks and Chadwick, too, were 500 Precinct, Central City. When the freaks came out at night here, they prowled these wide, six-lane boulevards crisscrossing a giant grid punctuated with fluorescent-lit Circle K convenience stores, beige block walls, palm trees, and a thousand corner strip malls that ran the gamut from flourishing and profitable to floundering and papered with AVAILABLE.

Clock ticking: Three minutes.

Schechterle had the map in his head: east on Thomas Road and beneath the freeway overpass at Twentieth Street. It was easy to conjure the grid: He was an Arizona native and grew up in the west part of the city near Phoenix International Raceway. After graduating high school in 1990, Schechterle had joined the Air Force with one burning mission in mind: follow in his brother's footsteps by becoming a Phoenix police officer. It was a plodding and almost decade-long road he'd traveled to fulfill the vision—from wrangling Haitian refugees to being rejected by the Phoenix Police Department on his first *two* attempts and having to settle for a rent-a-cop post as a stepping-stone—but by the fall of 1999 he'd been making $13 per hour as a recruit at the Arizona Law Enforcement Academy. Law enforcement was what he was born to do; he knew it in his bones and loved every minute of the job. He planned to one day make detective. *Miscreants beware: You're going down. We will find you. And we will squeeze hard until justice is served.*

AS Schechterle sped eastbound on Thomas Road toward the hot-call destination, Fire Engineer Rebecca Joy stood truck-side in Phoenix Fire Station 5, pushed a button, and heard one of the three bay doors rattling upward. As the engineer, her duties included prepping and then driving the fire truck to each call. She unplugged the cord that charged the fire truck's electrical systems and hoisted herself into the shiny cab. She put on her seatbelt, flipped the battery switch and depressed the starter button. As the 1993 E-1 Cummings 8V 92 engine rumbled to life—with almost 400 horsepower and 1,200 foot-pounds of torque—Joy didn't notice the thick diesel rhythm as she glanced at the computer to double-check the destination.

The same call Officer Schechterle had received had come in code 2—no lights, no siren—so there was not a sense of urgency as Captain Michael Ore climbed into his assigned spot in the front passenger seat. On code 2 calls in the middle of the night, the firefighters' motions were done in a state of half-sleep. There was rarely any talking, the only sounds the rumble of the truck's engine and brief chatter from the radio.

Darren Boyce, senior firefighter, climbed into his seat directly behind Engineer Joy. He pulled on rubber latex gloves, put his head back, and closed his eyes. When the rear passenger door still hadn't opened, Joy turned in her seat and broke the silence with, "Where's Henry?"

Even in his sleep-deprived state, Boyce knew exactly where to find their missing crew member. On a more urgent code 3, Joy would have just left minus the new kid. But rookies—called "booters" in the firefighting world— needed training, so they took the extra time to fully round out the crew of four, a mild annoyance that would only delay the crew's response time by about thirty seconds.

As she waited and replayed the day in her mind, Joy concluded it had been a weird one: in and out of the truck for check-welfare calls and Dumpster fires. But nothing she would remember specifically a month later, especially in a firefighting career that spanned more than eighteen years. She yawned and figured this call would be another non-emergency and that, by midnight, she would be backing the truck into this exact position and readying herself again for some shuteye. The mindset of the entire crew was that this call was at the bottom rung of the ladder of urgency and risk.

Two fire trucks and separate four-person crews shared space at Phoenix Fire Station 5: Engine 5 and Engine 705. The eight firefighters on each shift shared one bunkroom with small, individual sleeping quarters separated by lockers and curtains. Throughout each twenty-four hour shift, every call for either engine crew emitted the same dispatch tone and then call specifics, which on this call had been: "Engine 5 check welfare, code 2 response."

The lights always went on automatically, both crews woke up, and everyone eyed the indicator bar to see which engine was being called out for duty. Each time it was a coin-flip proposition: four got up and dressed while the other four drifted back to sleep.

On this call Darren Boyce woke up, glanced at the indicator bar, and heard someone snoring loudly. *Somebody slept through the dispatch,* he thought as he pulled on his duty shorts and T-shirt. For his entire career Boyce slept in a sleeping bag, because at six-foot-four his feet always hung over the edge of the twin-mattress bunk.

As a single-level fire station, there was no pole to slide down. Instead, assuming the sleeper was someone on the other crew, Boyce sleep-walked to the truck in the adjoining bay.

Now Boyce walked back into the dark room and pulled the curtain back. The booter, Henry Narvaez, was face down, his heel sticking out from under the sheet. Boyce slapped an ankle and said, "Henry. Get up. We've got a call."

From a dead sleep, the booter flew into motion and was dressed and moving so quickly that by the time Boyce had walked back to the truck the two firefighters climbed in on opposite sides at the same time. Narvaez might have verbalized his apology then—none of the members of his crew were awake enough to notice or care at that moment—but what no one could have known then was the short delay caused by the oversleep would turn out to have a platinum lining. Just like football, life was a game of inches and seconds. Destiny turned on the most minute detail or change. In this instance, unbelievably, the booter's screw-up was about to save a man's life.

Joy pulled the truck out of the station and headed eastbound on Cambridge Avenue, a quiet residential street with clusters of apartment complexes to the north and west and a vacant field to the south. Because of the fire station's location on a secondary side street rather than a main thoroughfare, Joy would have to stop at three stop signs to reach the main thoroughfare, which was the 51 freeway northbound. As the driver of a fire truck on a code 2 call, by regulation she had to bring the massive truck to a complete stop at every empty intersection, even in the dead of night.

Less than one minute.

No one spoke: Routine and interrupted sleep coalesced into efficiency minus any inane chit-chat. The booter took a few deep breaths to steady things and mentally kicked himself for the oversleep. As the truck ghosted eastbound along Cambridge to the first stop sign, the sweep of the halogen headlight beams lit the vacant field to the south, revealing a homeless wanderer and sagging palm trees that would never get trimmed. At the end of Cambridge, Joy stopped at two more stop signs as they drove under the freeway overpass and then turned north onto the access road along the 51 freeway. She moved to the far right of five lanes.

As she approached Thomas Road, to her left was the 51 freeway overpass extending north-south over Thomas Road. From the fire station to this location, the crew had only traveled about one-third of a mile. Suddenly, to their left, each of the four firefighters heard a startling impact crash and loud explosion, like something from a Hollywood blockbuster.

JASON Schechterle's thoughts weren't on his nascent fifteen-month law enforcement career—nor on how quickly it could all end. Every cop learned to compartmentalize the danger, squeeze it up tight, and stuff probabilities inside a sealed container, and then pull on the dark uniform every night to do the job. Play the odds that you'll be with the majority: career blues who log enough years to pension out without ever discharging the Glock on the streets. Trigger tight groupings through range paper, and that's it. Especially with the Taser jolt as the new preferred ass-plant. The holstered .40-caliber, polymer-frame pistol rode on one hip, the jolt joy-toy on the other. Schechterle had never discharged either in the field, but in the life of a cop that first could come on any shift, at any moment. Tonight could be that night.

As he approached the intersection at Twentieth Street, he slowed to clear the intersection. *Never fails.* The protocol for cops was 15 miles per hour over the posted limit even on the mostly empty, six-lane boulevard. Even with lights blazing and sirens blaring, distracted and dumbfounded civilians still littered intersections like cats looking for higher ground in a flash flood. It was all in play at that moment—all Schechterle's training and the near-decade of anticipation and the intensity of racing toward a serious crime scene—so much so that with all his attention focused on the intersection, Schechterle failed to see the taxicab roaring up from behind.

Zero minutes.

And then it was too late. The rocketing taxicab, full frame in the rearview mirror, hurtled into the back of Schechterle's Ford Crown Victoria at 115 miles per hour, a speed determined later by crash-scene investigators and debated by lawyers. The wrenching impact destroyed the rear half of the police cruiser into instant scattershot. A fierce fireball lashed out and then skyward in a menacing swirl, licking up against the concrete of the freeway underpass.

The fierce impact snapped Schechterle's head back against the metal cage and knocked him unconscious. The devastated car hurtled 271 feet before stopping. Schechterle was instantly engulfed in a roaring 700-degree inferno. If he hadn't already been unconscious, the smoke, searing heat, and toxic fumes would have done the same job. Imagining the horror of being trapped and burned alive, other cops would later wonder why Jason hadn't used his own sidearm to quickly end the inhumane suffering; Schechterle never had that option.

Instead, and mercifully, the imminent cloak of death was enveloping and would likely soon be balm in releasing him from the unimaginable white-hot hell. It *had* to: There was simply no way any human being could survive being swallowed up by such a ruthlessly intense blaze. Within seconds his trapped body was already blackened and indistinguishable as the interior of his patrol car melted around him.

Already, by any rational or emotive measure, a swift death was the single and only humane possibility that remained for Jason Schechterle.

Part I

Man in Blue

CHAPTER 1

The Buffalo Kid

AS A KID growing up in Buffalo, New York, in the 1950s, Patrick J. McGroder III had no desire or intention to become a lawyer. But that is exactly what he was destined to become, and perhaps that same disinterest is what later gave him an uncommon edge in court. From the outset, McGroder had a layman's disdain and impatience for arcane legal minutiae. Instead, his common-folk approach, street smarts, sense of humor, and personality imparted an uncanny connection with his clients. The long and successful legal career all started with a key role model in McGroder's life: his father.

Patrick J. McGroder II had built a looming hometown legacy by helping Buffalo land its beloved football team, the Bills, in 1960. The senior McGroder would then serve as a longtime team executive until his death in 1986, with his name forever etched on the team's Wall of Fame at Rich Stadium. The template for the younger McGroder was set early: a blue-collar Buffalo work ethic coupled with an unrelenting dedication to serve others six days a week. Sundays were set aside for two sacred rituals: church and Buffalo Bills football. The arctic fury that was winter in the northeast further solidified the town's collective tenacity and spirit. It all had an undeniable impact and influence on shaping young McGroder's future.

With those values in mind, the senior McGroder had dictated that his son would go to Notre Dame for undergraduate studies and then on to a law school to be determined later. The father's reasoning was that licensure of some kind—accountant, doctor, lawyer—was a lifelong hedge against the low-class stigma of being Irish Catholic. And the way he said it had left no room for discussion: "I don't care how you do it; just do it."

No shouting matches or defiant stand-downs erupted between father and son, nor any real communication about what the son might or might not want to do. This was a logical path, if originally uninspired, and aside from grumbling to his best friend John Moore, McGroder acquiesced to the track his father had laid out.

But by his own admission, McGroder was not Notre Dame material. He'd gleaned his savvy and smarts not under the roof at Saint Joseph's Collegiate Institute—a college preparatory school for young Christian gentlemen—but in Buffalo's dark taverns and with back-alley denizens. This was a place and a time—the late 1950s and early 1960s—wherein blue-collar ideology infused boys early, and by age 14 each could find a stool at the bar and get served with a wink. McGroder's edification, therefore, had evolved equally from these odd parallel tracks of studying schoolbooks and prowling frozen streets through late-night haze. He and his buddies went across the tracks, literally, and into the nooks and crannies of Buffalo's vibrant and smoky hideouts.

So while he really didn't have a singular purpose in mind—become a priest, perhaps?—he did sense what and who he was: a fun-loving kid with a thirst for adventure. Even under the Victorian clamp-down of the waning Eisenhower years, McGroder had cast himself as bon vivant. But a lawyer? That, he feared, might slowly suffocate and eventually kill whatever visions he could conjure as an adolescent. The steady guidance and pressure from his father loomed, however—mostly unspoken and never heavy-handed, but squeezed down on McGroder like some mysterious force, a force he would later thank as key in helping him rise to great heights.

With that backdrop, in the fall of 1963, Patrick J. McGroder III trudged off to South Bend, Indiana, like a prisoner in heavy chains sent to the gulag. He began his freshman studies at Notre Dame, hated it at first, then hated it more and never stopped hating what was essentially, in the mid-1960s, a monastery. Time and nostalgia would later dim this dislike, and McGroder went on to carry the Notre Dame banner as one of its proudest alums. But at the time, he couldn't get out of icebound and dreary South Bend fast enough. Law school followed at the University of Arizona in Tucson, and in 1970—two years before Jason Schechterle was born—McGroder had hung his lawyer shingle in the same sleepy desert metropolis of Phoenix, Arizona.

CHAPTER 2

The Hidalgo Kid

JASON SCHECHTERLE came of age during the last, long rays of the sunset of America's innocence, the 1980s, a decade of ebullient optimism, hair bands, parachute pants, and Members Only jackets. He was 7 when the decade began, and a freshly minted high school graduate when it ended. On the larger national stage during those years—and in his wonderful, dusty corner of the universe on the rural fringes of the big city—there were no dark nights of the soul. No major traumas, overt or otherwise. No disconnect between parents and child triggered a descent into dark places.

By his own choosing, Schechterle stamped his destiny early without struggle or soul-searching: a career in uniform, first military and then as a cop. With that neatly squared, he went to work stacking up what would be a deep reservoir of fond childhood memories. Not perfect by the markers of wealth, material accumulation, or elite social standing, but one of long days filled with strong family bonds and being outdoors: riding BMX bikes and prowling the open desert parcels on excursions that, for a curious boy, equaled Lewis and Clark's incursion into untamed wilderness. Two other early interests, shooting (a Daisy

Red Ryder BB gun) and golf (taking awkward 5-year-old whacks with his dad's full-length clubs) would become steady and prominent threads in his chosen career and life pursuits.

This was a time when the troublesome ghosts of Nixon, Vietnam, and the Iranian hostage crisis had faded in the rearview mirror. And the watchwords of a darker chapter were not yet imprinted onto the national psyche: Osama Bin Laden, WMD, and the war on terror. In between, Schechterle became a young man with the soundtrack of the era pumping out carefree anthems about girls, parties, fun… and girls. His childhood decade was the modern-day 1950s, an era recalled with selective reminiscences, when the innocence of youth wasn't tainted, jaded, and hurried along. Instead, looking back, childhood seemed to stretch and linger just a bit longer than today. The music of his time reinforced who he was becoming—Pat Benatar's *Hit Me with Your Best Shot*—and who he would have to be to survive the night of March 26, 2001: Journey's *Don't Stop Believing*.

THE family moniker "Schechterle" has lineage back to the mid-1880s in Germany. It was Jason's great-great-grandfather who brought the name stateside when he immigrated to America with his wife. Jason's great-grandfather and great-grandmother were born in the United States: Frederick Everett Schechterle and Elizabeth (Brauner) Schechterle. Jason's paternal grandfather, Frederick Schechterle I, was born October 23, 1915, in New Jersey and dubbed "the first" although his father had had the same name. He married June Alberta Specht, born June 16, 1920, in Neptune, New Jersey. Her mother, Anna Diehl Specht, was born in the United States, and her father, Frank Specht, in Frankfurt, Germany; he'd been orphaned and later joined his sister in the United States.

On February 22, 1942, Jason's father was born in Asbury Park, New Jersey: Frederick Everett Schechterle III. In August 1966, he moved to Arizona after joining the Air Force and being stationed at Williams Field. He served in Europe during the Vietnam War and retired after seven years to pursue a career as an engineer. In October 1970 he married Jason's mother, Bette Karen Oliver, who was born March 31, 1947, in Florence, Alabama.

Her mother, Jason's grandmother Bette Earl (Clark) Oliver, was a traditional Southern girl from Alabama who believed, "If it ain't fried, it ain't fit to eat." Her fried chicken, biscuits, and gravy rivaled the best.

It was her husband, Jason's maternal grandfather—George Edward Oliver, born July 23, 1924, in Madisonville, Kentucky—who would have the most influence in shaping Schechterle's personality, demeanor, and life track. George was the second son of John R. and Lola (Gentry) Oliver, and when he was born his mom proclaimed, "This is to be my little preacher boy." Both his parents were from Kentucky; his father died at 72 and his mother at 92.

George grew up in coal country, where his uncle owned Gentry Painting, a one-man house-painting operation conducted from a covered wagon pulled by a horse. George would tag along and fetch brushes and supplies as they labored under the heavy cloak of summer humidity and light dustings of snow in the winter.

From there, George's family started a due-south migration following the I-65 corridor, first living in Nashville, Tennessee, and then settling in Florence, Alabama. With a temperate climate and lush greenery, the region was a fisherman's paradise, with the scenic Tennessee River cutting a gentle swath through Florence, Lauderdale County, and The Shoals, including a series of dams and three different lakes: Pickwick, Wilson, and Wheeler, all loaded with trophy large- and smallmouth bass, catfish, crappie, salt water stripe, sauger, and bream.

In these new surroundings George discovered not only lazy afternoons along the riverbank with a cane pole dipped in the smooth waters, but a new religion that he would live, breathe, and one day pass on to his grandson Jason: Alabama Crimson Tide college football. Just two and a half hours south, by squiggly state routes, was the cathedral known as Bryant–Denny Stadium, which opened in 1929 and has been annually minting young new believers ever since. In the 1930s, George was among those dizzied new converts.

During the tenth grade, George was bored with the plodding pace of things at school, especially with World War II in full swing. But at 17 he was too young for the draft, so he enlisted. George was an engineer-gunner on B-24 missions over the Dutch East Indies, the Philippines, Borneo, and French Indo-China (which later became Vietnam). The young airman logged thirty-five combat missions before his twenty-first birthday. When his grandson Jason asked years later if he'd been scared, George replied: "What do you think was in the seat of my pants?" Again, that sense of humor would imprint early on grandson Jason.

For George, the worst part of combat was enduring the fierce anti-aircraft fire from Japanese ground forces. Strapped into his gunner seat on the B-24, all he and his fellow crewman could do was watch helplessly as shells burst all around them. The closest explosions rattled the airplane and elicited rapid prayers for mercy.

After his service in the South Pacific, George returned to Kentucky and attended Bowling Green University, studying shorthand to become a court reporter. He married Bette on June 2, 1946. In 1949, George joined the U.S. Air Force and moved to a new outpost in Columbus, Ohio. He was then stationed in Japan for fourteen months; Waco, Texas; and Luke Air Force Base in Phoenix, Arizona, in March 1961. He then shipped off to Vietnam, where he did four tours.

George survived Vietnam and was next stationed on a Portuguese island in the North Atlantic, followed by Langley Air Force Base in Virginia. He returned to Phoenix and finished out his twenty-five-year military career at Luke Air Force Base. George earned an Air Force Medal with two oak leaf clusters, combat ribbons for the Atlantic-Pacific Theater and Philippine Liberation Campaign and—surprisingly, he said—a Good Conduct medal.

George had seen and experienced the horrors of combat, involving human suffering most cannot fathom. Yet he was an eternal optimist who always looked on the bright side of every situation. George never met a stranger, and always had a quick joke. He brightened the room when he walked in with his laughter and smile. From personality to career choice and life outlook, George would have a profound influence on his youngest grandson, Jason.

Jason Scott Schechterle was born November 3, 1972, at Maryvale Hospital in Phoenix. The youngest of three, he has an older brother, Michael, nine years his senior, born in 1963, and an older sister, Alissa, born in 1967.

His mother Karen and father Fred had arrived in Arizona in 1961 and 1966, respectively. Before Jason was born, his mother had divorced her first husband, with whom she had Alissa and Michael. When she married Jason's father, the family set up in a modest house on the west side of Phoenix. Fred Schechterle then raised all three children as his own. While technically his half-siblings, Jason has never considered Alissa and Michael anything other than his sister and brother.

Mom stayed at home to tend the children while Dad worked as an engineer. Until Jason was 4, the Schechterles lived on Marconi Street near Fifty-Ninth Avenue and Bell Road, in a northwestern suburb of Phoenix called Glendale. Then the family moved south to a house at 12808 West Hidalgo, in another outlying part of Phoenix called Tolleson. Perched on an acre-and-a-half lot in a sparse neighborhood with only a few dozen houses, the house was at the end of Hidalgo, where the pavement turned to dirt, surrounded by open fields cut through by the Salt River and the canal system that brought water to the desert. It was here that Jason came of age, outside, riding his bike and exploring with friends—where he became the Hidalgo Kid. It was also here that he first tried golf, at age 5, and took whacks with his dad's full-length clubs. By high school Schechterle was good enough that he began considering the sport as a full-time profession.

WHEN Jason Schechterle was 5, Ford Motor Company recalled its Pinto model, which had been erupting into flames upon rear-end impact with alarming regularity. A few months after that famous recall, in October 1978, Devary Durrill and Bonnie Watkins were struck from behind while in a 1974 Ford Mustang II, which also exploded into flames. Ford engineers built the Mustang II from the same vehicle platform as the Pinto, including a fuel tank mounted rear of the axle. Although similar in this fatal design, the Mustang II wasn't included in the Pinto recall. Durrill's father had given Devary the Mustang II for her birthday; the dealership had assured him it was safe and not part of the recall. A bystander pulled Durrill from the flaming car. Durrill was burned so badly that the male bystander couldn't tell whether she was male or female, black or white. The inability to identify the fire victim's race was a macabre scenario that was to be repeated on the night of March 26, 2001. In Durrill's case, she lived for seven days in excruciating pain before succumbing to the burn injuries over 90 percent of her body. Her parents were able to touch her only on the top of her head. Tragically, Durrill had no other major injuries, broken bones, ruptures, or body penetrations, which meant she would have likely survived the collision minus the fire. Bonnie Watkins, too, had tried to extricate herself from the burning vehicle, faltered, and died at the scene. This case would later go to trial.

That same year, 1978, Ford Motor Company introduced a new platform for its full-size passenger cars code named "Panther" by company insiders. This new platform included full-sized Ford-, Mercury-, and Lincoln-branded vehicles. The Panther platform, which was a body and chassis design rather than a unibody design, would remain in production for more than 30 years; by the early 1990s it would underlie the Ford Crown Victoria Police Interceptor (CVPI).

Two characters in this emerging story—car and driver—were now on an ominous twenty-three-year march to an explosive intersection in the new century.

ON March 5, 1981, Officer Ted Villemaire, too, became a part of the Crown Victoria narrative. He had just ended a suspect pursuit in Dearborn, Michigan; it was time to approach the stopped vehicle and make the arrest. As he was stepping from his Crown Victoria Police Interceptor, manufactured by Ford Motor Company, a second vehicle smashed into the cruiser from behind with the horrific sound of crumpling metal.

"The last that I remember of the accident before waking up in the hospital is that I heard a screech, and then that's it until I wake up in the hospital," he said.

After that screech of rubber, Villemaire was pinned beneath his Ford cruiser. Gasoline soaked his uniform as the car burst into flames and burned the officer over 70 percent of his body. He would spend the next four months in a hospital. Villemaire later retained an attorney and sued Ford Motor Company, claiming the Crown Victoria's fuel containment system was defective. Attorneys for Ford settled before trial, but admitted no fault. Although Villemaire had the unfortunate distinction of being the first police officer to be horribly burned inside a Crown Victoria, he would not be the last.

Plaintiff and defense lawyers, at least, were already formulating the key questions: Were Ford designers and engineers negligent for some inherent design flaw in the company's vehicle platform? Or was it unreasonable to expect any vehicle to withstand high-speed rear impact and not explode in at least some instances?

The answers, unfortunately, wouldn't come any time soon. And as the two sides debated their points in court and in settlement conferences behind expensive doors—for decades through the 1980s, 1990s, and into the 2000s— more police officers would be burned and more bodies stacked up.

CHAPTER 3

The Asphalt Jungle

GROWING UP, Jason Schechterle's three closest compatriots were Dale, Rex, and Sheldon. The foursome attended Littleton Elementary; by the time they were 8, they were living the boyhood dream. Schechterle prowled by BMX bicycle, a silver and black Diamondback Viper that was the envy of his pals. Together they were forever riding bikes, building ramps to jump, and then building higher ramps to jump. Dale, Rex, and Sheldon each took turns holding cherry bombs in an open palm while another lit the fuse. Even at 8 years old, Jason already had a sense that this wasn't a good combination, and passed.

Not to be outdone, Schechterle proudly displayed the Red Ryder BB gun his older brother had bought him, and the foursome took turns plinking cans and birds. Some of the older kids in the rural neighborhood had full-on adult firearms. By the time he was 9, it was nothing for Schechterle to wander down to the Salt River with a .410 shotgun or a .22 rifle to shoot at cans, bottles, doves, and snakes.

Around the same time, Schechterle went through a series of rites of passage. He kissed his first girl, Phyllis, and kept that and their ongoing play a secret from his friends. He tried chewing tobacco for the first time, with his sister chasing him around the house so he couldn't spit it out. (He hated it then, but would later return to the habit as a police officer.) He joined Little League and thrived, with a natural swing similar to his growing golf prowess.

Before school, he congregated with Dale, Rex, and other friends at Sheldon's house, which featured a pool table and bar setup. There he tried cigarettes for the first time and discovered the soundtrack of the era. Eventually, at 15, experimental puffs, burning lungs, and nasty coughs gave way to an official daily smoking habit he wouldn't kick for more than a decade.

As the kids laughed and shot pool and looked cool with cigarettes dangling, REO Speedwagon, Pat Benatar, and Journey played in the background. Then it was Def Leppard and John Cougar (the original iteration before John Cougar Mellencamp and John Mellencamp). To this day, the songs take Schechterle back to that innocent time: *Jack and Diane, Keep on Loving You,* and *Take It on the Run.* It was a freewheeling and fun time, and everything seemed possible.

Another rite of passage for the golf prodigy was his first birdie when he was 8, playing with his dad and his dad's friends. It was a par three at Estrella Mountain Golf Course: the fourth hole, 130 yards. With the group playing in front still putting and a lake guarding the green, his father told his son to go ahead and hit. No chance the kid posed any danger to the golfers on the green. Using a driver, Schechterle put the ball on the green on the fly, and it rolled right up into the group, six feet from the cup. It was a nervous putt, but Jason sank it dead-center and at the perfect pace.

During the year Jason turned 11, 1983, the carefree years at the Hidalgo house were unknowingly winding down; the family would soon move north to Glendale. But one final milestone was crossed during that special era: baptism. One weekend morning, friend John Walston invited Schechterle along to the First Southern Baptist Church. At the end of the sermon the preacher asked if anyone in the congregation felt the calling to be saved. The Schechterles had never been particularly religious, or anti-religious for that matter; they just never got around to going to church.

"Something moved me that day to just walk up there by myself," Schechterle said. This wasn't a few sprinkles of blessed water. Rather, this was the full-immersion variety, with three dramatic dunks in the big tub. Then he went home and the next day picked up where he'd left off: REO Speedwagon, riding his bike, shooting guns, and thinking about girls.

As 1983 drew to a close, two events were unfolding worlds away from Schechterle's innocent youth, each with a thread that would eventually connect to the kid from Phoenix. The first occurred in Texas, on November 22, 1983, as native Texan David Perry stood before a jury arguing that Ford Motor Company designed, manufactured, and marketed a defective, dangerous vehicle.

BORN November 7, 1942, in Austin, Texas, Perry grew up and started school in nearby Liberty Hill, where his family had a farm. He was interested in sports as a kid, but quickly realized his talents were more suited to the realms of academia, reading, and public speaking. He had a razor-sharp intellect and a calming and easy demeanor, and was a natural orator.

His upbringing was decidedly middle-class, and by his early teens he was working—whether flipping hamburgers, jerking sodas, pumping gas at the corner station, or delivering newspapers. He bought his first car, a 1949 Studebaker, in high school in 1959 for $100, and then lost the car six months later because he couldn't afford the insurance.

"I had a rural outlook on the world," Perry said. "Somewhere along the line I learned a little bit about the law, although no one in my family was a lawyer." With that, he decided he'd become a lawyer himself. His hardscrabble upbringing helped shape and hone his iron will, laser focus, and tenacity—traits every trial lawyer needed when taking on corporate goliaths. He attended University of Texas for both his undergraduate schooling and law degree and, in 1967, was admitted to the Texas bar.

By 1983, it had taken his groundbreaking case five years to reach a jury: It was *Durrill v. Ford Motor Company*. The case centered on the Ford Mustang II that burst into flames during that 1978 rear-end collision, severely burning and killing two occupants. Perry argued that Ford engineers used the same faulty fuel tank in the Mustang II as that of the Ford Pintos recalled when Schechterle was starting kindergarten. The lawyer presented evidence that Ford employees knew about the dangerous design flaws from Ford's own crash tests. Perry produced evidence that Ford representatives had sought to delay or water down safety standards. To corroborate this bombshell allegation, Perry admitted into the proceedings transcripts from the Watergate tapes detailing conversations between then-chief executive officer Henry Ford II and President Richard Nixon, with the CEO arguing against new safety requirements.

Perry focused the jury on a key fatal design defect in the Pinto. Upon rear-impact collisions, the fuel tank would crash forward into the rear axle and puncture on sharp components located on the axle, including the bolts surrounding the differential cover. When Ford executives had recalled the Pinto, they installed a plastic shield between the fuel tank and the rear axle to protect the tank from puncture.

Perry argued that Devary Durrill's Mustang II was a Pinto with sporty sheet metal, which failed in precisely the same way: The fuel tank was punctured by sharp bolts on the differential cover. The Pinto shield would have prevented the punctures in the fuel tank on Durrill's car.

The plaintiffs prevailed: The jury awarded $6.8 million in actual damages and an eye-popping $100 million in punitive damages, which at the time was the largest-ever wrongful death award in U.S. courts. Under the settlement terms, the recovered punitive damages went to a charitable Devary Durrill Foundation to support community projects in and around Corpus Christi. Ford attorneys appealed the record verdict; Ford's liability was upheld on appeal, although the amount of the verdict was reduced during the appellate process and later settled.

Concurrently presiding in a nearby courtroom was Rene Haas, recently elected as one of eight district judges in Corpus Christi. Haas had "read law" and passed the bar exam without attending law school, served as both prosecutor and criminal defense lawyer, and then ran against and defeated an incumbent district judge the year before the Durrill trial. She and David Perry had known each other for years, and they married in January 1985. When Haas' four-year term expired two years later, they became law partners.

Nearly twenty-five years later (2001), Perry and Pat McGroder would argue the same failure pattern resulted in the fire in Jason Schechterle's Ford CVPI: sharp components, including the differential bolts, puncturing the fuel tank.

THE second event would eventually hit even closer to home for Schechterle. On December 17, 1983, in Georgia, Cobb County Police Department Officer Drew Haynes Brown was running radar while parked in the median of U.S. Route 41, which ran north–south and paralleled I-75 all the way from Tennessee to Florida. Brown patrolled the small stretch of the route through Cobb County; nearby Marietta was the largest city, with Atlanta just to the south. Nabbing speeders along this stretch was regular duty for Brown.

But on this day, his new Crown Victoria Police Interceptor was hit from behind and exploded. Brown was trapped inside the raging inferno, and died of severe burns and smoke inhalation. Later, the accident report documented that Officer Brown would have survived the crash if not for the fire. Brown's family retained counsel and sued Ford Motor Company, claiming Ford engineers designed a defective and dangerous fuel system on the CVPI. Corporate attorneys for Ford were now facing the second case of an exploding Crown Victoria and subsequent burning of a police officer. In the first, in March 1981, Villemaire had at least survived.

Now Ford attorneys had a death on their hands. Ford representatives could be given a pass on the first case as an aberration, but with two similar incidents in less than three years, a full recall and/or redesign of the Crown Victoria Police Interceptor seemed reasonable to the trial lawyers clamoring for such action. Instead, lawyers for Ford settled the Brown wrongful death case before trial and continued to roll out Crown Victoria Police Interceptors with no design changes to the fuel tank system.

INITIALLY Jason was crushed when, in 1984, the Schechterles moved to Glendale from Tolleson. The dusty suburb had been a kid version of the Wild West—strolling out the front door with a .410 shotgun underarm and a thick chew packed, meeting friends at the riverbank to smoke, throw rocks, and laugh—but Glendale, just twelve miles away, was Bright Lights, Big City. Welcome to the asphalt jungle.

He'd had to leave his friends and the area he loved and start a new school, his beloved outdoor spaces gone and replaced by pavement. The new house was at 5409 North Sixty-Fifth Lane. Schechterle picked up at Mensendick Junior High. Along with golf, he was getting decent at basketball. From his new house he could walk over to O'Neill Park and always find a pickup game. He graduated eighth grade in 1986 and began high school at Independence.

But all was not lost in the move to Glendale: On the first day of high school, freshman year, he saw a beautiful girl named Kim McQuistion. The available pool of girls had expanded commensurately with the move to the big city, an improvement he hadn't previously factored into the move. For all his shyness, somehow he mustered the courage to ask the stunning beauty to go out with him, which by the freshman doctrine meant she'd officially be his girlfriend. She said yes.

Awkwardness aside, Schechterle had at least one big thing going for him during these formative years. Amid the "Karate Kid" craze, Jason Schechterle was Ralph Macchio's identical twin; Schechterle *was* Daniel-san. As the new kid, being good-looking was a powerful trump card and equalizer. But the jumbled insides didn't yet match the suave exterior, so the mere presence of Kim McQuistion sent Schechterle into a panic, the wheels of rumination spinning wildly in his head: *Why did she agree to be my girlfriend? Now what do I do? Oh boy; maybe this was a bad idea.* At a football game one week after she'd agreed to be his girlfriend, Jason broke up with her, saying he thought they should just be friends.

"What the hell was I thinking?" he said. "I have no idea."

His lanky awkwardness continued: During sophomore year another cute girl with blond hair, a senior, asked him to prom during geometry class. She was the senior teacher's aide in the class, and she'd broken precedent and social code by inviting a sophomore. This bold move was the equivalent of a rookie cop breaking chain of command by going straight to the police chief with some low-level beef.

So what did Schechterle do amid this history-making turn? In the span of a few seconds, a random barrage of *What if* anxiety bombarded him: *Whose car will I take? What if my tux isn't back from the cleaners? What if there are locusts? What if I run out of gas? What if someone else wants to ask me? Where would we go to dinner? How much is that going to cost? Why's she asking me, a sophomore? Is there something wrong with her? Is this a joke? Do I have something in my teeth?* As the cute blonde smiled at her own Daniel-san, Schechterle simply said, "No, thanks." To this day, he's as puzzled as anyone about that answer.

He had the parachute pants, the Members Only jacket, and the good looks to complete the ensemble, but he wasn't making much headway through the high school social hierarchy. He went to the high school parties and had a few beers. He tried pot a few times. But as a Type A person, as most cops turn out to be, he never much cared for being drunk or high, without his full set of faculties.

Mostly he was a tall, lanky, introverted kid. The one bright spot was his best friend Krissy Hamm, hands down the hottest girl at Independence High School. From the moment they met in seventh grade, they had a brother-sister bond, a special connection and friendship that precluded any possibility of romance.

Schechterle was growing quickly, which helped his basketball game but also led to problems with his knees. The growth spurt and pounding on the court beset him with a condition called Osgood Schlatter disease, the formation of painful lumps just below each knee. At the start of high school he was five feet flat and 100 pounds; by graduation he'd be six foot three inches, 160 pounds. With the condition, basketball was less an option. Instead, he channeled all his focus, and introversion, into the sport he loved, which demanded the ferocious perfectionistic drive that came to him so naturally: golf. Trying to hit a small white ball into a small hole 500 yards away is the simplest of games that no human has yet perfected. Hence, the athletic, dedicated, focused, overachieving, and tenacious Schechterle had a sprawling canvas onto which he could paint the rest of his athletic days.

By sophomore year, his entire universe and being—mind, body, and spirit—revolved around golf. After school he'd head straight to the golf course, and then play again on Saturday and Sunday. By junior year he could consistently shoot in the seventies—rare turf, as anyone who has attempted the game knows. He sneaked out of class to watch the touring professionals play at the Phoenix Open. There before his eyes were all the golf luminaries, including Jack Nicklaus, Greg Norman, and Lee Trevino.

He picked up a part-time job his junior year at Super Saver Cinema, where Krissy also worked. After work he'd sneak into her room, where they talked for hours. Krissy's mom knew he'd crept in through her daughter's window, but she didn't care because she knew it was a harmless and platonic friendship.

Between school, golf, and Super Saver Cinema, there wasn't much time left for anything else. As much as he'd already decided he was going to be a Phoenix police officer like his older brother, Jason's passion for golf was unbridled. He set a new goal: to get a golf scholarship at a Division I university and, eventually, play professionally. He had the sweet, fluid swing that made the notion more than a passing pipe dream.

During his senior year, his dad bought Schechterle a silver 1982 Datsun king-cab truck. It was used and had almost as many dents as miles, but for $1,600 it ran like a charm. It wasn't nice by any standard, but it was transportation.

THE golf dream continued to flourish into the fall of 1989, when Schechterle found himself in the thick of the Arizona high school state championship. Obviously, winning the state championship would bode well for his plans to land a scholarship to a top-tier university. On the first day he shot 72. On the second and final day, Schechterle was neck and neck with Bryan Kontak as they approached the eighteenth green at Willow Creek Golf Course in Sun City. Schechterle bettered his score from day one by two strokes, shooting 70, and finished one stroke out of a playoff with Kontak and one other golfer. Finishing third was a disappointment, but didn't seem cataclysmic at the time. There'd be many other high-profile tournaments, qualifying school, and, if things went right, paid tour events. A golf professional who finished near the top consistently could carve out a handsome living without ever winning a single tournament.

But it was a turning point: Kontak would later turn pro and play golf professionally on one of the smaller tours. As Schechterle would discover, shooting par was impressive on one level, but the skill gap between where he was and the touring pros was actually a chasm full of talented scratch golfers.

Instead, less than two years later Schechterle would be bundled like an Eskimo and stationed in Grand Forks, North Dakota, guarding nukes.

CHAPTER 4

Man in Uniform

IN THE SPRING of 1990, Schechterle was in the last months of high school and feverishly pursuing his dream of playing golf professionally. The law enforcement career track was still in play, too, simmering on the back burner. Fortuitously, one day while practicing at Maryvale Golf Course, the Phoenix College golf coach tracked down Schechterle and offered him a scholarship on the spot. He'd start fall semester in August and be on the golf team.

"OK," the lanky youth said, figuring that while it wasn't exactly the bright lights of Division I college athletics, it would be a start. He'd also more likely be a bigger fish in a smaller pond, golf-wise, rather than vice versa at a larger university.

In May 1990, high school graduation came and went without much fanfare. Schechterle was still working at Super Saver Cinema, playing golf seven days a week, hanging out with Krissy, and dreaming about life as a golf pro: a typical 18-year-old kid's life. Then in August, right before school began, Schechterle got a phone call from the new golf coach at Phoenix College, who was replacing the coach who had recruited Schechterle. It wasn't an auspicious beginning to a college sports career. The coach said, "Jason, you need to come down so we can see where you'll fit in on the team."

For Schechterle, it seemed an odd thing to say; he thought, *Where I'll fit in is being the number-one golfer on the team.* But he said nothing and agreed to come meet the coach, and they both hung up. This was the first fissure between recruit and coach, and the gap quickly widened and deepened. Schechterle went and played a round, with the coach hovering over every swing and scribbling copious notes like a driving instructor about to deny his student driving privileges. Schechterle found the entire process odd and unnecessary. At the end of eighteen holes, the coach started his assessment by studying his legal pad and saying, "You said the f-word ten times today." He then nodded gravely as though his new recruit had committed a Class 1 felony. The coach said nothing about Schechterle's obvious talent for the game.

"Yeah," Schechterle said, thinking, *Sounds about right for eighteen—not even one per hole. Not bad, actually.*

Without saying much else, it was already obvious to both that their chemistry was not making magic. From the first phone call, the coach had rubbed Schechterle the wrong way. He seemed to Jason an old, crabby know-it-all. To the coach, Schechterle was some kid his predecessor had recruited, meaning there'd be no credit for him if the kid proved successful; more important, Schechterle took up a slot the coach could use for one of his own protégés. Two months later, mid-term, Schechterle walked up and said, "Coach, I'm done." The cool vibe had turned frosty, and the coach did nothing to try to convince Schechterle to stay.

Quitting the Phoenix College golf team didn't have to be the death knell for his professional golf career, but Schechterle sensed where his ability placed him in the rarified hierarchy of touring professionals. He was a damn good golfer, with a beautiful fluid swing, who could shoot par and below and beat 99 percent of the frustrated hacks out there. Even so, he wasn't good enough to beat the 1 percent in the elite ranks, let alone the one-tenth of 1 percent, the 150 or so top-echelon pros who play the PGA Tour events each week.

Almost immediately, Schechterle's earlier vision came back to the fore: He would be a Phoenix police officer. Seeing his older brother Michael Adams in his Phoenix Police Department uniform for the first time, two years earlier, had left a powerful impression. Michael had joined the U.S. Army in 1982 and tested for the Phoenix Police Department four years later. Up against 1,000 other applicants, he didn't make the cut. Two years later he tried again and landed a spot in the academy.

Wow, Jason had thought. *Normal people can do that!* The teenager had put his brother and every other officer in uniform on a special pedestal. Especially those who made the cut in Phoenix, the big-city metropolis with all the big-city problems and criminals that had to be confronted and resolved hour by hour, day by day. Schechterle went on ride-alongs and to the station to see it all unfold. His brother was working the Maryvale Precinct, one of the rougher sections of Phoenix, on the west side of the city.

One of Michael's admonishments about becoming a Phoenix cop was simple and direct: *Keep your nose clean and stay away from trouble.* Post-high school, that was getting harder and harder to do as Schechterle's friends struggled with the transition to full adulthood. Passing a joint here and there. Staying out too late and looking for things to rattle the monotony. A few beers at a friend's house, and then a drive home. Nothing was overtly criminal, nor was Schechterle partaking. But there was also no structure or discipline to keep him on track—the potential to slip into some of the same routines seemed dangerously imminent. Schechterle was pining for a change of scenery, too. In the balmy lower desert, he'd never experienced snow or a change of seasons. He was hungry to get out of his boyhood hometown and see some of the world. His classes at Phoenix College were also setting a new standard for boredom. The military and the police world would provide the structure, discipline, and camaraderie Schechterle craved. Driving home late one night, the soundtrack of his youth came on the radio with *Roll with the Changes* by REO Speedwagon. The lyrics and the moment spoke to Schechterle. Yes, he was tired of the same old story, ready to turn some pages.

It was time. Without consulting his grandfather or father—who'd each served in the Air Force—or his brother, who'd served in the U.S. Army, Schechterle decided to enlist as a cop in the military, which would get him out of Phoenix and pave the way for his eventual return and hiring by the Phoenix Police Department. Surely a military veteran with policing experience would have a leg up when he applied to the department. Schechterle was very proud of the military tradition in his family, but he didn't want to tell his grandfather, father, or brother, for fear they'd try to talk him out of joining. He, too, wanted to wear the uniform and serve his country.

In January 1991, Schechterle drove to the U.S. Air Force recruitment office in Glendale. He went with Todd Williams (who later became a Scottsdale firefighter) and signed up. The procedure to completely reorder his life was ridiculously quick and painless.

"I want to be a military police officer," Schechterle told the recruiter.

"Great," the recruiter said, smiling. "You will be a cop in the United States Air Force. Sound good?"

"That sounds perfect," Schechterle said, not realizing that two distinct tracks existed under the banner of military police: law enforcement and security police. The first was what Schechterle envisioned as he sat filling out the paperwork. Just like his older brother, he'd be in a police car with a red and blue light bar on top—except on a military base, to patrol the gates, check credentials, respond to on-base crimes, and arrest troublemakers as necessary. Schechterle might have had a vague idea about the second track, the security police detail, if anyone had asked. But security guard duty—standing watch over airplanes and weapons— was certainly not why he was signing on the bottom line. Security guards didn't arrest people and take them to jail, conduct investigations, or perform most of the other police work that fascinated Schechterle.

Schechterle finished the paperwork, scheduled a physical, and shook hands with the recruiter. Just like that, he was a new Air Force recruit. He went home and told his parents. As usual, they were supportive and easygoing, although a bit surprised. Two weeks later, Schechterle passed a basic physical. He received his orders: On May 14, 1991, he'd report to Lackland Air Force Base in San Antonio for basic training.

The next few months leading up to basic training were nervous ones. Schechterle continued his part-time job at Super Saver Cinema, hung out with his friends and Krissy, and played golf once a week with his dad.

On May 14, 1991, Krissy drove Schechterle in her maroon Chevrolet Camaro to the military processing station in downtown Phoenix. Schechterle went through a final round of medical clearances and sat through a debriefing of what to expect once he arrived in Texas. Around 4 p.m., he boarded the plane with several packs of Marlboro Reds stowed. His parents had no idea he was a smoker. Even to his best friend Krissy, watching him board the plane that day, Jason had always been a unique amalgam. Tall, lanky, and rail-thin at 165 pounds, Schechterle was equal parts: gun-toting, Marlboro-Man cowboy who had grown up on the dusty outskirts of Phoenix; accomplished athlete and golfer who could play and converse alongside well-heeled scratch golfers on country club courses; and straight-up late-'80s preppy, with Ralph Macchio good looks and the maroon Members Only jacket, thin at the elbows but still serviceable.

"I was an old soul who saw myself as a cowboy," Schechterle said. "I was a dork."

On the ground in San Antonio, Schechterle sat in the airport terminal surrounded by other 18-year-old recruits with the same look on their faces: abject terror. Schechterle burned through a pack of Marlboros in the first hour. He didn't say much to anybody, just sat quietly taking long drags on his cigarettes and nervously wondering what these next days and weeks would be like. Finally, at 11 p.m., the recruits filed onto a bus to the base. The drive was thirty minutes, quiet, and cut straight through the warm, muggy Texas night toward their destination.

The bus was waved through the gate by armed guards in berets. On the base grounds, the bus slowed to a stop. No one said a word or moved from his seat. Up to this point, joining the U.S. Air Force had been a relaxed and pleasant journey with a lot of time to smoke Marlboros and reflect. However, the boot camp experience everyone on the bus had been nervously fearing and anticipating in the weeks and months prior was about to begin in earnest. The sound of the bus door opening sent everyone's heart rate up a few notches.

Here we go, Schechterle thought. The first thing he saw was the crisp Smokey the Bear-style hat rising from behind the divider at the bus steps, followed by a perfect physique, in Air Force dress blues, that looked like it had been chiseled out of granite. The officer's voice perfectly matched his intimidating demeanor and presence: "Get your suitcases and get off this bus!" Forty teenagers leaped out of their seats, pushing, jostling, and colliding as they all attempted to exit the bus simultaneously.

"Line up," the drill sergeant boomed. "You will not speak. You will not start crying because you miss your mama. You will stand at attention and do whatever the hell I tell you to do." Then a long pause for dramatic effect, followed by, "Holy mother of God. I wanted military recruits, and *this* is what they send me? I have to take *this* and turn you into something useful and worthwhile. That will be a tall order indeed."

Schechterle, tall and lanky, felt insecure and awkwardly out of place. His prototype golfer physique, long and lean, had imparted the natural physics of a beautiful swing, but also the constant unease of sticking out in a group. The generalized yelling and nonsensical commands continued for some time: *Pick up that suitcase, recruit. Why are you holding your suitcase? Put that down! Didn't I tell you to pick up that suitcase? Do you have rocks for brains?*

Schechterle, to his great relief, was spared any personalized verbal beat-down. The Air Force version of boot camp was the shortest and least intense— less *Officer and a Gentleman* "steers and queers" and more *Full Metal Jacket* Lite —than any of the other branches of the U.S. military. But it was still a branch of the U.S. military, and was presently unraveling the nerves of the wide-eyed teenagers.

Around midnight, the drill sergeant ordered the group upstairs to their dorm and new home for the next six weeks. A row of beds lined each side of the room. Everyone grabbed a bunk, received his two sets of dog tags, stripped down to skivvies, slipped under the single blanket, and stared into the darkness without a word. No one got much sleep that first night, which ended a few hours later with a different drill sergeant walking into the room banging a metal trash-can lid with a small club.

"Get up, get up, get up. On your feet, line up, attention!"

The blinding lights clicked on, and Schechterle squinted to see his new charge. This one looked similar to the first—perfect physique, perfect crisp BDU (Battle Dress Uniform), impeccably polished boots—but was somehow even more menacing. He marched the group down the main street of the base in their street clothes for the first rite of initiation: haircuts. If each haircut took twelve seconds, the barber was off his mark. Clumps of hair fell to the tile floor in a frenzy of buzz-cutting. No one was allowed to touch his head. Then they marched off to get their uniforms, the standard green camouflage BDUs. Those who survived boot camp would get their dress blues later, for graduation day.

Schechterle quickly fell into a groove and adapted well to the structure, discipline, and routine of boot camp. He wasn't getting a lot of sleep, nor did he have any free time. But the regimented march and careful lockstep of each day was exactly what he'd craved. Each day started in darkness, at zero-dark-thirty, and was an endless blur of drills, marching, following orders, and the never-ending grind of PT (physical training): running, sit-ups, push-ups, and pull-ups. After the first week, Schechterle called his parents collect. When he heard his mom's voice, he was overcome by emotion and could barely speak.

"It was so good to hear her voice," he said. The conversation lasted about one minute before the drill sergeant was yelling in his ear to get off the phone.

At meals everyone fell into four lines, led by squad leader Airman Wardell, a bodybuilder from Tennessee who looked like he'd been blasted out of a block of Appalachian Mountains granite. He was in his late 20s and was always first, followed by the recruits lined up by height. That meant the gangly Schechterle was number two. Before any recruit touched his food, he had to down two glasses of water. *You will stay hydrated! If you become dehydrated you are of no use to the United States Air Force.* When Airman Wardell was done eating, then everyone was done eating. Some days Schechterle and the others were able to get most of their meal put away, but other days they might only grab a few frenzied shovelfuls before Airman Wardell was up and moving. In the military, Schechterle learned the fine art of clearing a plateful of syrupy French toast in five seconds flat.

He also learned to iron and fold a T-shirt into a perfect six-inch square. Same thing with underwear and socks. If the sergeant didn't like the way he'd folded and arranged the clothes in his drawer, the entire contents got dumped. To get perfect hospital corners on the bed, Schechterle used straps to hook the blanket at each corner. Then he carefully crawled in without disturbing the tight snap of the blanket, and slept in that position.

"Pay attention to detail," Schechterle said. "That's what I learned in the military and what I needed in life." Although he didn't realize the full scope and importance of this first lesson, it was a critical one that would be similarly beat into his head in the police world.

While the experience of boot camp wasn't exactly an all-inclusive resort arrangement, it wasn't insurmountable. He knew that of all the branches of the U.S. military, he'd drawn the easiest card. Schechterle was grateful he wasn't grinding out thirteen weeks of sweltering hell, mosquitoes, and fury with the Marines Corps at Parris Island, South Carolina. He wasn't in Cape May, New Jersey, for eight weeks with the Coast Guard, where he would suffer swimming one hundred meters without goggles, without touching the sides or bottom of the pool, and then tread water for an additional five minutes.

In contrast, he had only to endure six total weeks before progressing to Tech School. He got one weekend off after basic training and started Tech School the next Monday. During that weekend off he bought his first pack of cigarettes, since he'd not been allowed to smoke during basic training. Consequently, the first drag off the Marlboro Red had his head spinning. His dad had smoked Marlboro Reds, so it was a family tradition, not unlike soldiers from World War II: military service and smoking cigarettes was the American way.

Schechterle had gone through basic training thinking he was going to stay at Lackland Air Force Base for the thirteen-week Air Force Police Academy. But the first nine weeks were at Lackland, with the final four at Fort Dix, New Jersey. Then he'd be a cop just like his brother. However, he still didn't understand the distinction between military law enforcement—military cops who drove a police car on base to respond to crimes—and the security police, aka security guards, who stood watch over airplanes and weapons. All along he thought he'd signed up for the former.

"Those are LEs," one of his fellow recruits informed him at the start of Tech School. "We're SPs." Law Enforcement or Security Police—no one had told him there was a difference.

"I want to be an LE," Schechterle said.

The other recruit stared at him for a few seconds and said, "Well, I don't know how to tell you this, but you're not."

Schechterle was surprised, but quickly realized he'd also chosen to walk into the recruiting office on his own with no guidance. He could have taken his brother or father, both veterans, but he hadn't. Schechterle was disappointed, but not one to dwell on missteps. There was simply nothing he could do now.

With seventy recruits in his class, Schechterle went to work learning new tactics, including how to conduct building searches, and search and arrest suspects.

"I was playing soldier," he said.

He learned his standard-issue M-16 weapon backward and forward, and could break it down and reassemble it in the dark. He took frequent written tests about threat levels, weapons terminology, military codes, and M-16 specs. Schechterle also learned that the clawing humidity of south Texas was quite different from the bone-brittle firestorm of Arizona. One morning he woke up in the back of an ambulance after collapsing from dehydration during PT. After two intravenous bags of fluids, he was back at it.

Recruits had a little more leeway with their time once they were in Tech School, including the chance at night to play cards and call home. Schechterle shared a room with his high school buddy Todd Williams. It was a big surprise, since Williams had joined as an open-assignment recruit. The first morning at Tech School, Schechterle looked to his right and there was Williams. Schechterle also got his first tattoo: a Special Police beret stamped with "USAF."

Finally, it was time to get his assignment. All the recruits assembled in a room at Lackland Air Force Base for the moment of truth.

"All right," the sergeant said. "I will read your name and assignment. We need warm bodies in every post, but if you want to switch assignments it has to be right now, in this room, before we leave."

Nervous anticipation rippled through Schechterle. Where would he be stationed? There were many great possibilities. *Maybe Italy, like Dad? Dover? Washington, D.C.? Southern California?*

Instead he heard, "Airman Schechterle. Incirlik, Turkey."

What? You have got to be kidding me. I don't know where Turkey is, what's in Turkey, or why anyone would want to go to Turkey. Once all the assignments were issued, without any further thought, Schechterle said, "Does anybody want to switch with me?"

A female recruit said, "I will."

Schechterle didn't know the destination she'd been handed, but it didn't matter because he knew it wasn't Incirlik, Turkey, wherever and whatever that was. "I'll take it," he said. "Where am I going?"

She looked at him, smiled, and said, "Grand Forks, North Dakota."

Grand Forks, North Dakota.

Suddenly Schechterle wasn't sure if he'd traded up or down. At least he knew, generally, where North Dakota was, and that it was part of the contiguous United States. But beyond that, his doubts expanded rapidly, and all he could see were endless miles of flat, frozen tundra. A random moose meandered into his vision, which he'd have to shoo away from the fence line. And then more endless miles of flat, frozen tundra. He felt a little clammy and lightheaded as his new reality fully registered: *Grand Forks, North Dakota.* He flashed back to the night he'd been driving home in the wee hours and had decided to join the military. The song came back, too, and seemed even more apropos now: *Roll with the Changes.*

CHAPTER 5

Nothing but Wind

AS TECH SCHOOL ENDED in August 1991, Schechterle was still pondering the idea of life in the northern latitudes—the name repeated in his head for days: *Grand Forks, North Dakota.* Before shipping off to the hinterlands, however, he still had four more weeks of Air Base Ground Defense training at Fort Dix, New Jersey.

With nervous excitement, Schechterle immersed himself in this final phase of security police training, including playing war games in the humid and bug-infested woods with fellow recruits as well as nasty chiggers and ticks. Schechterle and his brethren hauled their M-16s everywhere they went, humped sixty-pound rucksacks, and ate MREs (Meals Ready to Eat).

Since leaving his suburban city life in May, Schechterle had changed a lot. Despite his ongoing affection for Marlboro Reds, he was in the best physical condition of his life. He was never a distance runner, but he was skinny and could knock out long bursts of push-ups and sit-ups.

He was energized by the structure and clear, steady accomplishment of military life. He had a focused sense of direction, purpose, and discipline. He felt different about himself in a way that went deeper than the obvious surface changes such as his buzz cut. While he'd always looked up to his brother, father, and grandfather—all police officers and military veterans—Schechterle finally had his own understanding of what it meant to serve in uniform.

"I liked playing soldier," he said. "I wanted to know how to use my M-16 and use it correctly in case I ever needed to in the field."

Shooting came naturally to Schechterle. Growing up around guns and shooting regularly with friends at the Hidalgo house in Phoenix had built his proficiency. His larger mission was still in play: He wanted to be the best shooter in his unit and eventually carry that skill into the police academy back in Phoenix. True to that goal, he sat in a bunker on test days with his M-16 and plinked pop-up targets that varied from nearby to 100 yards. He only missed one, scoring 49 of 50, and received an award of Expert Marksman.

During that summer of 1991, Jason's father came to his home state to visit his son for a weekend. Together they went to the boardwalk and ate taffy pulled the old-fashioned way from the machines. They visited Asbury Park, New Jersey, and hung out at the beach. It was a perfect father-son weekend. Once his four weeks were up in late September 1991, Schechterle left Fort Dix, went straight to Newark Airport, and took a commercial flight home to Phoenix. He had a little R&R before reporting for security police duty October 10, 1991, in Grand Forks, North Dakota.

While October heralded the onset of autumn in most corners of the United States, in Phoenix the desert sun still burned bright, with daytime highs in the upper 90s. When Schechterle stepped from the airplane in Grand Forks on October 10, snow covered the ground—a sight he'd seen only once in his life, on a trip to his grandparents' beloved Alabama.

This is going to be interesting: Welcome to North Dakota.

"Not a tree in sight," he said. "Nothing but wind."

Schechterle would be working six shifts on, followed by three days off. Each shift was 2100 to 0700, which meant 9 p.m. to 7 a.m. His security responsibilities included two main areas of "overwatch." The first was the flight line, where a couple dozen enormous C-130s and B-1 bombers sat at the ready. The other was WSA, the weapons storage area, a sprawling compound of fifteen or so buildings rigged with ground sensors and barbed wire. Another security police guard always patrolled during the same shift, while a third manned the tower. A small response team was always on standby if a hot call went out. Other than that, Schechterle was primarily alone in his Chevy Blazer or on foot patrol in and around the various buildings.

Like most law enforcement jobs—from federal posts to city cops and county sheriffs—long stretches of each shift were mind-numbingly boring. During the long lulls, Schechterle walked the buildings, tugged on padlocks, and turned knobs to make sure doors were secured.

Lather, rinse, repeat. Ten hours at a stretch.

A television with five channels, and card games with the other SPs, entertained during breaks in the non-action. A battery-operated transistor radio pumped out a 60/40 mix of music and static. The former, music, was a vital part of his survival. He had a boombox with a single CD player, and every two weeks he'd head to Target to buy a stack of CDs. His mainstay was the country music he grew up listening to in the 1970s and 1980s. For the rest of his days, if Schechterle could only listen to Johnny Cash, Merle Haggard, and Conway Twitty, and nothing else, he'd die a happy man. His collection also included Alabama, Alan Jackson, Paul Overstreet, George Strait, Randy Travis, and Travis Tritt. He branched out into pop and light rock during the 1980s, and during his Grand Forks Target runs he'd return with CDs by Def Leppard, Journey, and REO Speedwagon.

Schechterle sat on his rack in his base dorm room; his cook roommate was always gone. With the tunes spinning, he daydreamed as the music triggered memories of home. The weather outside, of course, was abysmal and brutal for the kid who grew up in the desert wearing shorts twelve months a year. The snow he first saw on October 10 only got deeper and dirtier with each passing month. The frigid wind stung and chapped his face, and often had him wondering if that female recruit was still laughing somewhere on a sun-splashed beach in Incirlik, Turkey. Schechterle had never checked the map, but he was certain that no place on Earth could be worse, weather-wise, than Grand Forks, North Dakota.

The days and weeks inched by with nothing to break the monotony of duty. On New Year's Eve 1991, Schechterle was on shift and patrolling with Sergeant John Golinsky, who, as the senior officer, was driving. Golinsky rolled the official duty sport-utility vehicle to a stop where a number of padlocks needed to be given a yank. High-level security detail stuff, North Dakota style. The wind outside was blowing steadily, which put the wind-chill temperature at minus-40 Fahrenheit. Without saying a word, Golinsky gave Schechterle the look that spoke volumes.

You're the one-striper, Airman Schechterle, and you know what that means. Get your skinny ass out there. I'll keep the heater running.

Dressed in his parka and snow boots, and with his M-16 slung over his shoulder, Schechterle pushed open the door and winced when the cold punishment hit his face. It was a feeling he never fully adjusted to—WHAM!—and one that had already inspired a new mantra: *I have to get out of North Dakota.* What was about to happen next only further solidified that position, and his resolve.

Schechterle slammed the SUV door shut, took a few steps, hit a patch of black ice, and promptly fell flat on his backside. Although the fall was sufficiently embarrassing on its own, even worse was that he landed on his M-16, which promptly snapped his collarbone like a strand of uncooked spaghetti. Schechterle knew immediately he was hurt badly and, with the ferocious Arctic wind numbing his face, he simply had no interest in getting up. Perhaps he could just lie there until the ice thawed in June.

Schechterle spent the first two weeks of 1992 laid up in his barracks to recuperate. The 19-year-old used his time to feverishly plan his escape from North Dakota. He went back on shift with his arm in a sling, reduced to a glorified errand boy with the call sign Lima One. He'd put in food orders, run paperwork, and bounce back and forth to Central Command as gofer. The overnight shift was bitter cold and dead quiet; the day shift was slightly less bitter cold with a little more activity. Working overnights, Schechterle had enjoyed a small battery-powered radio covertly strapped to the visor in his truck, where he could usually pull in an AM country station to help pass the hours.

Schechterle's collarbone healed nicely, and winter finally eased its grip. The summer in North Dakota brought a bonus: Schechterle could finally play golf again on the nine-hole course on the base. The summer weather in North Dakota was better than the winter in the same way a horse bite on the finger is better than a shark bite to the torso. Horse-bite summer in North Dakota brought temperatures in the high 80s along with suffocating humidity and mosquitoes large enough to pluck small furry prey from the prairie. And while the golf course was serviceable, it left a lot to be desired for someone who grew up in the Sun Belt playing decent public courses. Schechterle would get off duty at 0700, change clothes, play golf, and then go to bed at 2 p.m. to be up at 8 p.m. that night for work at nine o'clock.

In the fall of 1992, Schechterle filed his transfer paperwork with only one caveat: *Anywhere but here*! He was allowed to list his top eight choices, and included Korea, where his brother had been stationed. In October his official orders came through: Airman Schechterle was to report February 1, 1993, at Osan Air Force Base in Korea, seventy miles south of the DMZ. He was also given thirty days of leave to go home to Phoenix prior to deployment. The final months in Grand Forks were a slow, tedious, daily countdown to freedom. The snow was back, the wind was howling, and all he could think about was leaving.

AS Schechterle dreamed of new possibilities, 1,600 miles to the east Auxiliary Trooper Edward W. Truelove, 73, of the Connecticut State Police was helping the occupants of a disabled vehicle. It was Friday, November 13, 1992, and Truelove directed the driver and passenger of the disabled vehicle to climb over the guardrail and onto a nearby embankment to stay out of harm's way along I-84 in Cheshire. Truelove safeguarded the scene with strobe lights while sitting in his Ford Crown Victoria Police Interceptor to radio a tow truck. Several minutes later, a tractor trailer plowed into the vehicle from behind. The cruiser burst into flames, and Truelove suffered the same horrible fate as Officer Drew

Haynes Brown had in 1983: trapped and burned alive in a Ford CVPI. Truelove perished, but his orders to the driver and passenger to move off the roadway had likely saved their lives.

Back in Michigan, in the gleaming offices at One American Road in Dearborn, Ford Motor Company executives now had a serious problem: three exploding police cruisers, three horribly burned law enforcement officers, and two dead bodies in eleven years. Or did they? Was this simply the macabre reality for a fleet of vehicles that were driven harder than any other—on duty and on the road 24/7 every day of the year—and then plowed into from behind at exceedingly high speeds? In other words, could any vehicle short of an armor-plated military tank be expected to withstand such abusive forces of physics and combustion?

Or was there some fatal flaw in the Crown Victoria's engineering, design, and production that was causing these horrible deaths by fire?

Corporate attorneys for Ford were in the former camp; the plaintiff's attorneys in the latter. With each side dug into their respective trenches, the litigation battles were underway to determine cause and assign blame. Each side marshaled their respective experts to espouse equally articulate explanations on both sides of the argument.

Either way, whatever was being discussed or not being discussed within the walls of Ford, at depositions, and in settlement mediations, the Ford Crown Victoria Police Interceptor continued to roll off the assembly line and into service with no design changes to the fuel tank. Trooper Joyce Roberson-Nowak, who graduated seventh in her academy class before joining the Ohio State Highway Patrol, might have hoped Ford executives had ordered *some* safety improvement attempt, anything, because she was next on the burn list. Just twenty-five months after Trooper Truelove, on December 28, 1994, she would be trapped and severely burned in her Ford CVPI after a rear-end impact. She was the fourth such victim, and the first woman, burned inside a Crown Victoria police vehicle.

ON New Year's Eve 1992, Schechterle piled into his reliable blue 1986 Ford Ranger pickup. He had a box full of cassette tapes for the almost 1,800-mile drive to Phoenix. As he rolled through the gates at Grand Forks Air Force Base for the final time and into the night, the headlight beams illuminated a light flutter of snowflakes. Ice, snow, Arctic fury... it didn't matter: Airman Schechterle was going south. He pushed a well-worn cassette into the deck, *American Fool* by John Cougar, and drove out of Grand Forks tapping the dashboard to *Hurts So Good*. By the time the second song started, *Jack & Diane*, Schechterle was surrounded by the frozen darkness and cutting through the silent snowstorm along the narrow strip to Fargo. He'd never felt happier, as he cracked the window, barely, and lit a Marlboro Red.

At six o'clock the next morning, Schechterle rolled into Fargo and stopped for breakfast. In the diner, he studied the map of his route. Because he planned to visit a friend in Pocatello, Idaho, he was taking a more westerly tack, cutting across Montana and into neighboring Idaho. From there, it would be a straight shot south through Utah and then back into his home state. Schechterle ate quickly, paid his tab, and was back on the road twenty minutes later.

By the time he crossed the state line into Idaho on New Year's Day, after seventeen hours behind the wheel, Schechterle was having trouble staying awake. He kept the music loud and the flow of nicotine steady, but it wasn't until he drove straight into a white-out blizzard that he was fully alert again. Crawling along the freeway at 5 miles per hour, Schechterle finally found his exit; he stepped into his friend's living room during halftime of the 1993 Sugar Bowl between Alabama and Miami. Schechterle was thrilled that his beloved Crimson Tide was leading 13–6, but nervous that the game was that close. But the second half was all Alabama as they rolled to a 34–13 victory to claim their twelfth national championship. North Dakota was already gone from the rearview, and Alabama lorded atop the college football universe: All was right in Schechterle's world.

Two days later, Schechterle was back in his Ford Ranger for the final push to Phoenix. At eleven o'clock that night, he was in Flagstaff, Arizona, and just two hours from home. But as he stood pumping gas he noticed a bubble starting to protrude from the front right tire.

Damn, he thought. *That doesn't look right.*

It was, potentially, an understatement of epic and potentially fatal proportions. However, Schechterle had no spare and zero interest in spending the night in a Flagstaff motel when he was so close to home. People who wanted to be cops were known risk-takers, too. And in less than three hours he'd be snug in his own bed. He decided to take a chance, climbed back in the truck, and merged onto I-17 headed south.

After 1 a.m., in early January 1993, the headlights from Schechterle's headlights were illuminating his parent's house in Glendale. He'd made the final stretch on the gimp tire without incident.

During the month Jason was home, he caught up with friends and played golf a couple times a week. On the day before his deployment, Schechterle was standing in the street with his brother in front of their grandparents' house. He'd be in Korea for one year, and he worried that Grandma or Grandpa might not be there when he returned. Tears flowed from Jason's eyes as his brother embraced him.

On February 3, wearing his dress blues and polished black shoes, Schechterle left for the airport; his dad had offered to take him. As Dad drove, he grabbed his cigarettes and asked his son, "Want one?"

Schechterle, 20, was surprised. And then he realized that his "secret" habit had been discovered long ago by his parents. He nodded and took a Marlboro Red from the pack. They stopped and had breakfast together and then drove to Sky Harbor International Airport. At the curb, Dad gave his son a hug and said, "I'll see you in a year."

CHAPTER 6

700 Refugees

IN EVERY WAY POSSIBLE, being stationed in Korea was everything Grand Forks was not. Finally, Airman Schechterle was living the overseas military life he'd envisioned when he enlisted. His job duties were similar to the Grand Forks experiment: Schechterle guarded airplanes, A-10 warthogs, and other expensive military craft and weaponry. Schechterle worked three shifts, had one day off, and then had three shifts on again. He patrolled the flight line stacked with a couple dozen A-10s and F-16s each. He also worked in a "Priority A" area replete with cameras and alarms. He worked out at the gym every day, played softball on the SP team, and played on the dart team. Every other facet of his existence, however, was 180 degrees from North Dakota.

For starters, Schechterle had a Korean girlfriend named Jumi. Like the city of Songtan, she was beautiful, exotic, and gave Schechterle the confidence boost he'd never quite mastered in the high school social hierarchy. Every night after work, Schechterle went to a small upstairs bar called The Romance Club, which occupied a space about ten feet wide and thirty feet long. It was so small it had only two booths, with the disc jockey Mr. Lee crammed in one corner spinning vinyl, including old Merle Haggard tunes, on a turntable.

Are you kidding me? Merle Haggard! The adopted Alabama kid was right at home.

Another bar, called Phoenix, he frequented at first solely because of the name. Once he was a regular, each time Schechterle walked in that DJ played "Turn the Page" by Bob Seger (Jason's all-time favorite song to this day) and "Time for Me to Fly" by REO Speedwagon. With the soundtrack as an anchor, and the mood and spirit of things in Korea, Schechterle might as well have been coming of age at the Hidalgo house again, or transitioning to adulthood at Independence High. Finally he was energized, on purpose, and things made sense again.

Unfortunately, the weather in Korea wouldn't let Schechterle shake North Dakota, just in case he was feeling homesick: cold as a blue steel revolver on ice in winter, and in summer hot as a piece of scrap sheet metal left in Satan's front yard. Korea, at least, was absent the nonstop piercing wind that howled down through every layer of insulating clothing. But with the weather as the only element tipping the scale downward, Schechterle was happy as could be otherwise.

At The Romance Club, overlooking the busy street below, Schechterle drank OB (oriental beer) and learned the art of throwing darts. Mr. Kim owned the place and let Schechterle stand in as DJ whenever the mood struck, which was often. He turned 21 while in Korea, but it was somewhat uneventful because the drinking age was 18.

Like his post in Grand Forks, Schechterle's work life was largely uneventful. He went through two different training exercises, one three-day and one ten-day. On one occasion an American F-15 pilot had to eject from his plane, which crashed into a mountainside in the Korean outback. Schechterle was on duty and immediately dispatched to the crash site by helicopter so that he and two others could stand guard over the wreckage through the night. It was a nerve-wracking flight, his first on a helicopter, above the mountain treetops. Then it was a chilly fall night standing watch, but the adrenaline of the situation made it easy to stay awake.

Other than that, his year in Korea sped by in a dizzying blur of nights with Jumi, spinning records down at The Romance Club, and perfecting his dart form. Suddenly Schechterle was at another decision point. He'd already been assigned to Luke Air Force Base, which put him in hometown Phoenix as his final assignment, a synchronous arrangement that would be the perfect capper to his military career. Proximity would also place him perfectly to begin planning and preparing for his next move: to become a Phoenix police officer. Schechterle already had transfer orders to leave Korea February 10, 1994. He was riding a high of adrenaline, excitement, and new possibilities when, two weeks before leaving, a dispatcher called Schechterle over the radio as he patrolled in his short-bed truck. The brief words spoken by the dispatcher were oddly ominous: "You need to go to Outbound Assignments."

This can't be good, he thought. He already had his outbound assignment. Schechterle found the office on base and stepped inside. "Airman First-Class Schechterle."

The clerk shuffled through a pile of paperwork. "Your orders to Luke have been cancelled," he said. "Fill out a request for a follow-on." The clerk broke the bad news with all the emotion and empathy of someone reciting items on a grocery list.

"My kit and gear are already outbound for Phoenix," Schechterle said.

"Like I said: Put in a new assignment."

"What if I want to stay here?"

"You can't." The clerk scowled and looked down. "Your transfer form says here you want to leave."

"Right, to go to Phoenix. Which has already been approved. But if I can't go there, I'll just stay here."

"Look, I'd like a goose that lays golden eggs, right?"

"What?" Schechterle said, his head spinning from this major wrench being jammed into his life plans.

"Goose. Golden eggs? You know."

Schechterle was dumbfounded, less by the inane references—which he understood—and more by the shock of what he was being told.

"'If wishes and buts were candy and nuts...' Anyway, it ain't gonna happen, Airman Schechterle. You have to go back to the continental U.S."

"What? Why?" These were fruitless single-word queries being lobbed into a vast canyon of indifference and military protocol. The net effect would be the same if he were reciting a particularly beautiful haiku in Japanese: *zilch*!

"You put in for a transfer. All the Osan slots are already filled. Put in for a new assignment."

The inflexible march of the bureaucratic military machine was just what Schechterle had craved at the outset of this adventure, but at times the illogical circular traps were inflexible and maddening. By now he'd also learned that expending any more energy on the matter—and using reason, common sense, and diplomacy—had the same sum total outcome as unzipping and pissing into a hurricane to change its course. Invectives coursed through his brain, and Schechterle left without saying another word.

Later that night he looked at all his options for U.S. Air Force bases, and one in particular went right to the top of his list: Eglin Air Force Base in Valparaiso, Florida, aka the Sunshine State. The map showed the base was flanked by the temperate waters of Choctawhatchee Bay. Schechterle pictured palm fronds swaying in a light breeze and bikini-clad girls glistening under glorious rays. His drop-dead, night-sweats worst horror: being shipped back to Grand Forks. It would be a tense waiting game until the new orders came through.

Within a week, Schechterle got a letter via interoffice mail: Eglin—the baby-oil bikini vision had trumped the nightmare. Schechterle had one final detail to address. A month prior, Jumi's mother had married an American and moved to the United States. Although Schechterle and Jumi had said their official goodbyes and it had been a clean, amicable break, the young airman was feeling lonely and stung by not being able to return to his hometown. His next move, in hindsight, was ill-advised. One night as he readied himself to ship out, Schechterle called Jumi and invited her to move to Florida. She said "Yes" without hesitation.

BACK in Phoenix before heading out to Eglin, Schechterle bought a 1994 Plymouth Sundance, brand-new, for nine grand out the door using an Air Force credit union loan. He went shopping at the mall with his best friend Krissy, who told him he should buy Jumi a ring. Not an engagement ring, but just a piece of jewelry as a show of affection. Schechterle said she was crazy, but somehow fifteen minutes later the duo was at the counter of Helzberg Diamonds, where Schechterle opened a line of credit.

In early February, Schechterle and Jumi left Phoenix in the Plymouth and drove to Florida. For this trip, he wouldn't even need a map: 1) drive west on I-10 until reaching destination; 2) exit freeway and unpack. Schechterle and Jumi lived off base and settled in a one-bedroom apartment in Fort Walton Beach, on the second floor of three. Uncle Terry, his dad's brother, lived nearby in Panama City. He and Schechterle became regular golf buddies.

In June 1994, around nine o'clock one night, Schechterle got a phone call from one of the tech sergeants.

"Schechterle: Get your A-bag together. We're leaving at midnight."

"Is this a drill?"

"No, real world."

"Where we going?"

"Don't know. And even if I did—"

"Right. I know. OK. I'll mobilize."

Schechterle hung up the phone and looked at his petite Korean girlfriend sitting on the couch. She was listening to their new stereo, which Schechterle had just bought from Sears that day. The system had two tower speakers and a six-disc CD changer. He didn't quite know how to tell her what he needed to tell her. The fact that she didn't speak English very well didn't help the communication process.

"I'M—LEAVING," he said, as though talking to an 81-year-old woman with one bad ear and dementia: loud, slow, and clear. "I—DON'T—KNOW—WHERE—I'M—GOING. OR—WHEN—I—WILL—BE—BACK."

Jumi could only respond with a quizzical look and then a smile and nod. Without saying anything else, Airman Schechterle went into the closet, found his A-bag, and started packing. One hour later he was at the base and then aboard a C-130 with forty-three other soldiers. During taxi, the senior officer stood and yelled to be heard above the rumble of the engines.

"We are deploying to Guantánamo Bay, Cuba, to assist with the Haitian refugee crisis. We will receive our specific assignment upon arrival. I do not know how long we will be deployed, nor the specific nature of our mission. Any questions?"

There were, of course, lots of questions, but no answers.

After landing, when the forty-four-man team walked down the ramp at the back of the plane, they were each ordered to relinquish all weapons, an unexpected and odd order at the outset of a military mission. Each man gave up his M-16 and a 9mm sidearm—it looked like a police agency weapon buyback, but instead they were stepping onto Cuban terra firma, unarmed. There were whispers and concerns about what a bizarre way this was to begin deployment. Almost from Day One of boot camp soldiers had been trained to eat, breathe, sleep, and function with weaponry as a constant companion—teacher, mother, secret lover—and an integral element and tool. Decommissioning the soldiers was the equivalent of taking Superman's red cape and boots. The de-smocking was also the first and most obvious indication that the mission was going to be a wacky one for the books.

The 1991-to-1994 Haitian refugee crisis was the culmination of twenty years of the tired and poor, the huddled masses of Haiti, seeking asylum in the United States. Years of political tensions, cruel dictatorships, and harsh treatment by military governments finally exploded in the early 1990s when a coup in Haiti in September 1991 opened the refugee floodgates. Within six months, U.S. Coast Guard personnel had intercepted almost 40,000 Haitians floating on hand-lashed crafts—basically flotsam and jetsam—on the open sea. Meanwhile, other Haitians fled into the country's mountains and another 30,000 crossed into the Dominican Republic during the mass exodus.

Establishing camps at Guantánamo Bay, Cuba, was the U.S. political response, to process and detain refugees as different presidential administration policies played out (first those of the senior George Bush and then Bill Clinton). The exodus of refugees from Haiti finally slowed and then stopped altogether with the September 1994 invasion led by U.S. forces. But as Schechterle arrived at Guantánamo Bay in June 1994, the detention camp was teeming with seven hundred hot, tired, pissed-off, and displaced Haitians (with hot, tired, and pissed off being the operative words). As part of the forty-four-man team, it was Schechterle's job to keep order among the camp detainees—at a ratio of fifteen refugees to every one U.S. airman.

Just like the Haitians he was charged to monitor, Schechterle lived in a (hot) tent and slept on a (back-wrenching) folded cot that overlooked a fifty-foot cliff and the bay. He worked twelve hours on, twelve off, seven days a week. The Haitians were largely miserable and disgruntled, and, to vent their anger, began fighting in the afternoon when the heat intensified the foul mood and general pall of the place. The Haitians fought each other as well as the U.S. service members sent to babysit. Since no one had weapons, the fights were quelled with shields and sticks until the next one broke out.

Lather, rinse, repeat.

Somehow amid the melee Schechterle crossed paths with a fellow airman, who had gone to the same high school back in Phoenix. *Holy shit*, Schechterle thought. *What are the odds?* The two started working out together, providing mutual support, commonality, and laughter through the withering haze of madness.

"It was like the film *Groundhog Day*," Schechterle said. "We'd feed them breakfast and then fight. Then we'd feed them lunch and fight some more. They were good people, just frustrated by the conditions and slow political process."

In August 1994, as the crisis reached the crescendo that led to its eventual resolution, Schechterle received a "Dear John" letter from Jumi. Racked out on his cot one night in the sweltering heat—with his Sony Walkman playing George Strait and a warm Budweiser in his hand—Schechterle pondered the letter. His reaction was a mixture of anger and passive-aggressive relief, *good riddance*, followed by a few choice adjectives describing the female sex in the pejorative. In that time and place he was like a heckled Haitian with a pounding headache: not in the mood to deal with any more crap.

In mid-October 1994, an imposing Army captain, a six-foot-six Citadel graduate, gathered the troops under his command, including Schechterle, and addressed the all-male group with, "Ladies, I have good news and bad news. Which do you want first?"

"Bad," everyone said almost in unison.

"Today is your last shift here."

There were murmurs—*Last shift, how in holy hell could that possibly be the bad news?*—which triggered nervous laughter. *Last shift, then where on God's green*

Earth are they sending us now? A cruel thought and twist of fate flashed through Schechterle's mind: *I'll tell you bastards exactly where we're going: Incirlik, Turkey. Just watch*, he thought. That'd be the proverbial icing on this ass-backward cake.

"Now the good news, ladies: You're going home in two days."

Thank God, Schechterle thought as he let out a long sigh of relief.

Two days later, after the short flight back to Eglin AFB, the C-130 landed, and Schechterle was stateside. He picked up his bag, walked straight to his car, and drove to his apartment. When he opened the door, he saw that Jumi had cleared out her things as promised. Except she'd left a set of pink sheets on the bed and pink curtains on the window, which he ripped off and threw in the Dumpster. Aside from that, he was elated to be back in his apartment, out of the sweltering melee in Cuba, and eyes forward on the next step: police work.

On November 3, 1994, his birthday, Schechterle walked into an office on base to talk to a recruiter. His enlistment officially ended in six months, on May 15, 1995. Instead he asked for early release, signed the requisite papers, and was granted an honorable discharge two months later on January 3, 1995.

"The Air Force, for me, was four years of fun," Schechterle said. "It was peacetime and a great experience. But it was time to pursue my dream. And all I could think about was being a Phoenix police officer."

CHAPTER 7

Cop Dreams

ON DECEMBER 16, 1994, Schechterle left Florida for Phoenix to be home for his first Christmas in four years. Jumi, whom he'd not seen since June, was living in El Paso, Texas, which was right on the way along I-10. Before leaving the Sunshine State, Schechterle played golf one last time with Uncle Terry, loaded up the Plymouth Sundance, and then headed home. In El Paso, he called Jumi and took her to dinner at Red Lobster, where he tactfully retrieved the ring he'd given her.

On December 19, a Thursday, he was back in metropolitan Phoenix and drove straight to Krissy's house. He knew his dad played golf every Friday afternoon, and he wanted to stay out of sight until then, for a surprise. The next day, Schechterle hid in a corner of the kitchen and emerged when his dad came home.

"You going to play golf?" his mom asked. "Someone wants to play with you."

He saw his son: "What are you doing here?"

"I wanted to surprise you for Christmas. I'm out of the Air Force. Let's go play golf."

Two days later Schechterle was at Cheyenne Cattle Company with Krissy, in downtown Phoenix at the Arizona Center, for a night of revelry. Krissy now worked for the U.S. Postal Service and had made a new friend who'd be joining the duo. When that friend walked into the bar that night, Schechterle's life changed forever.

Whoa, he thought. *Who is that girl?*

Her name was Suzie Hiett, her married name, and the man at her side was her husband. At home was their 1-year-old baby girl, Kiley. It was a moment that would change everything for Suzie and Jason, but neither knew it at the time.

SUZIE KNOWLES was born January 28, 1971, in San Fernando, California. Her father was a mortician, which was the early foundation of Suzie's later ability to find solace in dark humor. An only child, when she was 2 years old she entertained herself on one occasion by hiding in an empty casket.

"I was smart enough that I knew to take my shoes off," Suzie said. "I was a very old soul at a very young age."

At age 3, she and her parents moved to Phoenix. When she was 7, Suzie tagged along with her father when he drove back to California on some official mortician business. He drove a hearse *sans* prostrate passenger, and they returned with a dead passenger named Mr. Lively. Suzie wasn't too young to fully appreciate the hilariousness of the name of the deceased, and without flinching she rode all the way back to Arizona right next to the black body bag containing Mr. Lively.

In 1979, when she was 8, Suzie's father had a stroke, which left him paralyzed on one side. Within two weeks, he was dead from an aneurism. The void left by her father's absence was cataclysmic to the young girl. Suzie's maternal grandmother, who'd also moved to Phoenix, helped raise her. Suzie's mother never remarried, so with no one at home to kill roaches and fix things, Suzie stepped up.

One time the toilet chain broke, and all Suzie's mom could do was cry, because she didn't have enough money to hire a plumber. So Suzie took paper clips and fashioned a serviceable chain. Even before she was a teenager, Suzie's personality and traits were forming. She was resolute, independent, smart, determined, and a problem solver. She was a caretaker, too, for her mother, a role that would serve her well later.

"I didn't have a bad childhood, but my mother was always sad and seemed very lonely," she said. "Something always seemed to happen. All the adversity I've had in my life helped prepare me for Plan B, and there was always a Plan B."

Suzie hated being an only child, and was determined to have a big family of her own someday. That resolve, in combination with the early loss of her father, led her into a marriage in her twenties that was doomed from the start: She'd met an older man who she thought was her knight in shining armor. Her daughter Kiley was the one and only silver lining from the relationship. After that experience she was even more resolute, and realized that not only did she not *need* a man in her life to be happy... she swore them off completely.

In many ways, Suzie was everything Schechterle was not: extroverted, boisterous, and a fun-loving crazy girl. Like many things in Schechterle's life, the route to his union with Suzie would prove to be circuitous.

IN January 1995, an oncoming car turned in front of Jason, who was driving his Plymouth Sundance. Unable to avoid the collision, Schechterle hit the full-size van head-on.

This is going to hurt, and I may die right now.

It was one of the first times in his life that he felt the complete emptiness of not having control. In the confused aftermath of the crash, when Schechterle saw the Phoenix police officer arrive, he felt better. His brother had been on the same force for five years, so an immediate bond and kinship kindled whenever Schechterle saw a uniformed cop on patrol—especially one from the Phoenix Police Department.

But then Schechterle panicked when he remembered the small pile of weeks-old empty beer cans littering the car floor. And the loaded historic revolver his grandfather had given him, tucked under the seat. He hadn't been drinking, but he was terrified at how it would all look to the responding officer. A two-officer unit had witnessed the entire incident.

"Do you know Michael Adams?" Schechterle asked, desperate for some friendly support.

"Yeah."

"He's my brother. Can you call him?"

Schechterle was pinned in the car with a broken arm. His brother did arrive; the empties became a nonissue, as did the historic weapon. Firefighters spent thirty minutes cutting Schechterle out of the demolished car. He was hospitalized for four days with a broken ulna; the orthopedic surgeon inserted a steel plate with nine screws into his forearm. One week later, against the advice of his doctor, Schechterle tried to tee off at the golf course, and the pain was so intense he dropped the club and started crying. As bad as the car crash, his first ever, had been, it was nothing compared to what was in store for him in his next car crash, six years hence.

MEANWHILE, Schechterle was living at home again, with no bills, but no immediate job prospects either. It was time to start his application process with the Phoenix Police Department.

Within months, by February 1995, Suzie and her husband had separated, and she and her daughter were living with Suzie's mom in Glendale, about five blocks from her future husband. She and Jason were becoming good friends, with Krissy as the link. One day Suzie called Krissy to ask about her cowboy boots that Krissy had borrowed. Schechterle was the designated delivery person.

Suzie knew of Jason through Krissy; their paths just hadn't officially crossed yet. Suzie had often heard from Krissy how much she thought of Jason Schechterle. Because Suzie respected Krissy so immensely, the endorsement of Jason carried a tacit gold stamp. When Suzie and Jason finally met, everything Krissy had said was spot-on.

"Eventually I had interacted with Jason enough that I knew he was a good, nice man," Suzie said. "I was very protective of Kiley, but he had earned the right to at least meet her. Of course the last thing I wanted was to get married."

The first time Jason saw 14-month-old Kiley, who was sleeping in her crib, he felt something profound that he'd never experienced before. The feelings stirred something inside and took him to a place he'd never been. He resolved to get his application in with the Phoenix police and get his life and career on track.

To those ends, he filled out his application and took the written test in March 1995. He passed the physical agility test, background interview, and polygraph examination. Schechterle's application was rejected, however, after his oral board examination, conducted by two officers and a civilian. They asked questions, role-played, and presented scenarios. They provided no clear explanation, other than that he'd been eliminated from consideration.

It was a shock to Schechterle's system, but his first thought was that he'd try again. The crushing disappointment presented a reality for which Schechterle had not planned: He needed to find a job. He alternated between shock, anger, depression, and sadness: it just wasn't possible that he'd been rejected, because being a Phoenix police officer was the only dream and career path he'd ever conjured. His four years in the U.S. Air Force had all been carefully orchestrated as a precursor—almost a guarantee, or so he'd thought—to becoming a cop. He had no Plan B, C, or D. Being a police officer was the one and only Plan A, so rejection meant he had no job, no career, and no other options. Schechterle was lost. He played the oral board examination over and over in his mind. Maybe he'd been too aggressive. Maybe he wasn't mature enough. Maybe he just wasn't cop material. He never did sort out where it had gone wrong.

Ultimately, he realized that the Phoenix police representatives hadn't said he couldn't apply again, which is what Schechterle planned to do. No way they'd reject him twice, because now he better understood the process. Plus his brother was already on the force, an officer in good standing with an impeccable record. There was no way they wouldn't at least strongly consider the younger brother, too. And, of course, he was a military veteran in good standing. How could they *not* hire him?

What Schechterle didn't consider was that *thousands* of eager young recruits-to-be were applying for what might be twenty to thirty officer positions with the city of Phoenix. The hiring staff at the Phoenix Police Department could therefore pick and choose the best of the best candidates. A college degree, which Schechterle didn't have, certainly didn't hurt one's chances as hiring agencies looked for the diamonds in the rough. Similar to lawyers who had to attempt the bar exam more than once to pass, Schechterle had gained some key knowledge on avoiding certain bureaucratic traps in the process. He was certain he'd succeed on his second attempt to become a police officer.

For income, Schechterle had taken a job doing deliveries and working in the warehouse at Arizona Electrical Services, a residential electrical supply company. He liked his work peers, and it was a steady paycheck until he got on with the PD. And by that summer, in 1995, Schechterle knew he'd found the girl he wanted to be his wife. Suzie was the one, the real deal.

"At some point during our friendship I realized he was fantastic," said Suzie.

Suzie's divorce was finalized by October, and everything was falling into place. By the next summer, in June 1996, Schechterle had proposed and he, Suzie, and Kiley were living together in Suzie's house in Glendale. Suzie was as surprised as anyone that she was going to marry for a second time, but she also knew in her bones that she and Jason Schechterle were soul mates. For better or worse, in sickness or in health, Suzie would stand by her man.

To keep his possibilities open, Schechterle began applying to other police agencies in the Phoenix metropolitan area, including those in the suburbs of Mesa and Peoria, along with the Arizona Department of Public Safety (DPS), the state highway troopers. But after taking the written test for DPS, Schechterle decided roaming the state's freeways doing traffic stops—as other motorists sped by at 75 miles per hour—wasn't the stripe of police work he wanted to pursue.

At each police agency, the process of hiring officers began with the basic minimum requirements for sworn officers, established by Arizona's Peace Officer Standards and Training (POST) Board. From there, agency representatives could add more stringent requirements and tailor the hiring and screening process however they deemed best. What might be acceptable by state standards, such as number of lifetime marijuana usages, might be too high at a specific police department. Each department's brass had wide latitude in determining its own agency's standards.

The good news in that for Schechterle was that, while he'd been bounced out by the Phoenix police, he was free to pursue employment with other agencies too. In fact, he did just that for the city of Mesa by clearing another long process: application, physical agility test, background screening and interview, polygraph, psychological and medical examinations, and drug screening. But then he died on the list, which meant he'd been cleared to be hired, but no positions became available within the allotted time designation. Once the time limit was up, he had to reapply, go back to the beginning, and start the entire hiring and screening process again with all those long and intrusive steps, including the hundreds and hundreds of questions.

How many times in your life have you smoked marijuana? Ever tried cocaine? Methamphetamine? Steroids? Christmas trees? White crosses? Ever taken a prescription pill for which you did not have a prescription, including that of a boyfriend/girlfriend, spouse, family member, or friend?

Why do you want to be a police officer?

Have you ever had sex with an animal?

If required to shoot and kill someone in the line of duty, would you hesitate?

Have you ever stolen anything from an employer? This would include Post-it Notes, paper clips, pens, and other office supplies.

Have you ever indecently exposed yourself in public, which would include sex on the beach, in a vehicle, or outside your home, as well as urinating in public?

Have you ever driven while intoxicated or otherwise impaired? If so, how many times? When was the most recent time? Any time within the last five years? For each incident of driving while impaired, describe the exact circumstances of the impaired driving, including intoxicant ingested, how and when ingested, with whom, how you obtained the intoxicant, how far you drove, and how the situation resolved.

And hundreds and hundreds of other narrow screening questions.

For the city of Peoria, in early 1996, Schechterle had made it through the process to another oral board examination. Then he made a key blunder when he told the hiring department he wanted to do patrol for ten or so years and then move on to working for a federal agency, perhaps become a deputy U.S. marshal. Not wanting to be Schechterle's springboard to bigger and better things, the department ousted him from consideration.

But in Schechterle's mind, really, all roads led back to the original vision: If he was hired by another city, his entire focus and purpose would be a lateral transfer to the only agency that mattered in the contiguous United States: the Phoenix Police Department.

AS Schechterle pursued his dream, on February 9, 1996, Vincent Julia rolled out for his regular shift with Delaware River and Bay Authority Police Department, where he'd been an officer for two years. During his shift, dispatch sent him to assist the driver of a disabled truck. Julia parked his 1996 Crown Victoria Police Interceptor and went to work closing the lane on the Delaware Memorial Bridge. While on scene, Julia was in his cruiser when a dump truck rear-ended the police car. Flames engulfed the patrol car and truck, and Officer Julia died on scene.

Amid all his attempts at other agencies, Schechterle reapplied to the Phoenix Police Department and began the process for a second time. Once again, he went to the back of the line: application, physical agility test, background check and interview, polygraph test, medical and psychological examinations, and the dreaded oral board examination. He was nervous going in because that's where it had ended on his first attempt, but he was also ready to redeem himself and move past the stumbling block. Within a week, his background investigator called with the news: Schechterle had passed the oral board examination. The only hurdles remaining were the psychological and medical evaluations, including a drug screen, all of which seemed mere formalities at that point. And since he'd already been given an academy start date for late fall 1996, it seemed he was on the downhill side of realizing his dream. The lengthy process required that he drive to the academy every few weeks and repeat the physical agility test to ensure he was staying fit. Every marker looked good: Schechterle would soon be a cop. He'd step into his dream and fulfill his destiny. Life was good again.

Schechterle underwent the medical evaluation and the next day sat for the psychological examination. He knew he had no medical issues or drugs in his body, so all that stood between him and his dream was a standardized test: the Minnesota Multiphasic Personality Inventory, commonly called the MMPI. The test was purported to identify personality structure and uncover potential psychopathology. Again, Schechterle was at ease and without worry: He knew he was sane and stable and ready to start the police academy. Many law enforcement and other agencies—the Department of Defense, the Central Intelligence Agency, and the Federal Aviation Administration—used the same test to screen applicants and to establish security clearances. Well, Schechterle had also served in the U.S. military, so how could he *not* pass this test? If anything, the 567 true/false questions were fun and ran the gamut from silly to odd, reasonable and logical, to flat-out bizarre:

- *I have a good appetite.*
- *I think I would like the work of a librarian.*
- *My hands and feet are usually warm enough.*
- *There seems to be a lump in my throat much of the time.*
- *I have diarrhea once a month or more.*
- *No one seems to understand me.*
- *I would like to be a singer.*
- *Evil spirits possess me at times.*
- *At times I feel like smashing things.*
- *My soul sometimes leaves my body.*
- *It would be better if almost all laws were thrown away.*

For putative cops such as Schechterle, the correct answers seemed obvious: FALSE – laws are generally helpful, and sort of important to the job of policing; might be good to keep those. Every question followed that same logic, which made the test easy.

He finished the MMPI—evil spirits *did not* possess Schechterle, his soul had never left his body (at least to his knowledge) and, yes, his hands and feet were just the right temperature—and awaited the results. Again, given the questions, the test seemed nothing but a bureaucratic and final formality before Schechterle was sent off to the academy as a shiny new recruit. He was relieved the arduous process was all but over. He drove home and thought about his station: He was getting married soon, he'd made it all the way through the long, tough screening and interview process—again—and he'd soon get his dream job. Life couldn't be any better. A few days later his background investigator called with the MMPI results and started by asking, "How do you think you did on the test?"

"I think I did great." Schechterle replayed a few of the MMPI Greatest Hits:

- *I have had no difficulty in starting or holding my bowel movement.*
- *I do not read every editorial in the newspaper every day.*
- *I have often wished I were a girl.*

Duh, duh, and more duh. True, True, False: How hard can this test be for any sane person?

The background investigator then explained the 1-to-5 scoring scale; to be hired by the Phoenix Police Department, potential recruits had to score "4" or "5."

A score of "1" or "2," apparently, meant you were Abby Normal—a brain in a jar—and obviously *not* going to be a cop; the 4's and 5's were reasonably stable people with no Hannibal Lecter longings for liver with fava beans and a nice Chianti.

"So how did I do?" Schechterle said.

"You scored a 3."

Smack-dab in the middle of the scale: equidistant from sane-and-steady at the top and, at the bottom, time-to-get-fitted-for-your-straitjacket-Mr.-Schechterle. This didn't make sense, and Schechterle's head was spinning. After a slight pause, he asked the million-dollar question: "So what does this mean?"

"Unfortunately, this means the process stops here."

• *Do you hear or see things that are not there?*

Gut shot. Schechterle winced as the air left his lungs. This was cataclysmic: Failing the oral board examination was something from which Schechterle could learn and therefore overcome. Being told he was a half-bubble off level, a mouth-breather from a shack by the swamp, was completely out of his control. Without saying much else, Schechterle hung up and stared at nothing in particular. Internally, he was livid. But he remained silent.

• *At times I feel like smashing things.*

He'd worked so hard, and now all he'd planned had been ripped away right before getting married. Schechterle was apoplectic and wanted to lash out.

• *I am sure I get a raw deal from life.*

But instead he stayed calm and started pondering a question he'd stopped considering: *Now what?* That night, he grudgingly accepted the harsh truth: He'd never be a cop. The sting lingered for months: *How could some stuffed-shirt psychologist reading a standardized test result take this away from me? You know what? The Phoenix Police Department can kiss my ass.* The next string of thoughts included more f-bombs than a riot in D Block.

At 23, nothing had ever affected him so intensely. Schechterle had no college degree and no training other than his Air Force service guarding bases, which wasn't even really police work. The reality hit hard as he focused on taking care of family; he didn't have the time or the luxury to wallow in self-pity and sadness. Late one night, with tears welling up in his eyes, he told Suzie, "For whatever reason, I'm not cut out to be a police officer." The dream was officially dead.

ON April 26, 1997, Jason and Suzie married in Schechterle's brother's backyard in Peoria, a Phoenix suburb, with a hundred guests in attendance. The young couple paid for the ceremony themselves, and so kept it simple. Suzie was soon pregnant with a son, to be named Zane; he arrived the following year, on June 2.

Right after getting married, in May 1997, Schechterle took a job as a security officer at the Palo Verde nuclear plant operated by Arizona Public Service, one of two major utility companies in the Phoenix metropolitan area. At $14 per hour, it was decent pay with one of the premier employers in the city. Even at that starting rate, he was already earning more than he would've as a new police recruit. Mentally he'd moved on, too: This was his new life.

The job entailed guarding a nuclear plant through foot and vehicle patrol. The high security at the facility included cameras, a command room full of monitors, and heavy doors with electronic access codes. As he had in the military, Schechterle, and the other forty-five or so guards on duty at any given time, patrolled the grounds with a 9mm sidearm and an M-16. It was all hauntingly familiar, like his Air Force duties, and not necessarily in a good way. He felt trapped in a limbo that refused to release him to the greater vision he'd nurtured for so long. But there was no sense in ruminating: What was done was done.

The job might as well have been Grand Forks II (minus the freakish frigidity). But make no mistake; it was equally boring. One of the best aspects was the plentiful benefit package for his young family, including health insurance. Schechterle's new career was a serviceable one, but not inspired. For the first six months, he took the rookie shift: 1800 to 0600, which put him back on overnights. Then he switched to days: 0600 to 1800. After two failures with the Phoenix Police Department, Schechterle pushed the entire notion out of his mind. Fanning an ice-cold dead ember was simply too painful.

Sometimes on Friday nights after work he and Suzie went to his brother's house to play volleyball.

"I was the one who, after a few beers, would ride the tricycle around on the patio," Suzie said. "Jason would just shake his head. Life's too short; I was never afraid to make a fool of myself and just have fun."

While Suzie and Jason had different personalities, they also shared key traits: They were each level-headed, dedicated, and wholly committed to their pursuits. Neither could have known the extent to which their marriage vows and bond would soon be tested, and how their shared core values would, ultimately, inspire each to keep walking through the darkness for the other.

Invariably, since almost all of Michael's friends were also cops, Jason was immersed in police shoptalk about life on patrol, the crazy arrests, the bureaucracy machine at a three-thousand-officer operation, and all the rest. It was interesting, but Schechterle kept his guard up so that being around the life didn't lead to his pining once again for police work. He drew the line, and stayed on his side of that line without much struggle.

If anything, his exclusion from the force soured him a bit on the once-hallowed world of law enforcement. Growing up, just seeing a cop in uniform gave Schechterle a jolt of enthusiasm during which he'd extend silent reverence and respect. But now, that instant and automatic respect was gone, the shiny allure tarnished.

Even so, career-wise Schechterle needed a change. He flat-out didn't like the security job at Palo Verde nuclear plant, located in the boondocks west of Phoenix in a nowhere-ville called Tonopah. But more critically, the job was beyond boring, in the time before domestic terrorism added a whole slew of other responsibilities and possibilities. During the entire time Schechterle patrolled the nuclear-plant grounds, there hadn't been one single eventful incident, minor or major, of any type. This was, of course, wonderful news, but carried with it the numbing reality of spending twelve hours at a stretch doing absolutely nothing.

So in June 1998, Schechterle and a work friend applied for the lineman apprenticeship program at Arizona Public Service. No security officer at Palo Verde had ever moved from security patrol duties directly into the highly sought position. But in this case both did, and they began in August 1998.

"That was a great job," Schechterle said. "I'm a redneck, blue-collar guy who likes to be in jeans and boots and be outside. That's why being a cop was always so appealing: I couldn't stand the thought of going to an office cubicle every day and doing the same thing. Plus the APS job paid a great salary. I accepted that everything had worked out for the best."

The new position was a four-year apprenticeship working on overhead and underground power lines. The beginners started as grunts—driving trucks, fetching tools, and cleaning job sites. It would be months and months before Schechterle was cleared to set foot in an elevated bucket for high-wire work or climb up poles, which was good: He was actually terrified of heights. It was an element of the new job he hadn't entirely considered.

Schechterle went to work and was content. He had a beautiful young wife, two kids, a mortgage, and a job earning $60,000 including overtime. It hadn't all played out as he'd planned—Schechterle knew his childhood dream of wearing the badge was over—but he'd always embodied the easygoing spirit of his grandfather: Life happens. If the glass was always half full in his world, which it was, then his life situation was good going into the 1998 holiday season.

ABOUT a hundred miles south of where Jason Schechterle was learning his new trade as lineman, highway patrol Trooper Juan Cruz, 48, was already living the dream Schechterle had been forced to abandon. Like many police officers, Cruz was a quiet and anonymous American success story. Growing up poor in a rural Arizona mining town, he'd worked hard in school and had the same early vision as Schechterle: a career in dark blue. Cruz eventually graduated from junior college and joined the highway patrol, Arizona Department of Public Safety, as badge 3111. Like hundreds of thousands of police officers in the United States at the time, he patrolled his beat in a Ford Crown Victoria squad car.

On December 9, 1998, Cruz took a dispatch call and raced toward an accident along I-10, the southernmost transcontinental highway in the U.S, which cuts east–west through the lower portion of Arizona, including the connecting link between Tucson and the Phoenix metropolitan area. By December the brutal summer reign of heat had finally fully relinquished its grip, replaced by days and nights downright frigid to desert dwellers: lows in the 40s meant long sleeves and puffy jackets.

The accident scene was not unlike the dozens Cruz had helped manage, document, and eventually clear before returning to patrol his District 8 beat. Along with two other DPS officers, Cruz used his 1996 Ford CVPI cruiser to block the high-speed left traffic lane while officers and rescue crews worked the scene. Cruz, sitting in his vehicle, didn't have time to react to the speeding Nissan Altima rapidly approaching westbound from the rear. Marissa A. Rodriguez, 21, struck the rear of Trooper Cruz's parked vehicle. She was inebriated in celebration of her twenty-first birthday, and she plowed into Cruz's parked patrol car at 66 miles an hour. Later, according to Pima County Sheriff's Office investigators, the young female driver logged a blood-alcohol content of .168. She walked away relatively unscathed physically.

Upon impact, the now-familiar horror repeated: The fuel tank ruptured, sparks ignited fuel vapors, and the Crown Victoria burst into flames with Cruz trapped inside. The tow truck driver on scene ran to help and could see Cruz still alive through the partially open window. The trapped officer was writhing and pushing on the door, which had been jammed shut by the impact. He screamed out for help, yelling *Get me out of here*, but there was nothing the panicked tow truck driver or other officers could do except watch Cruz burn alive and die.

The day after the crash, Schechterle watched the local TV news and the report of Cruz's death. *That's horrible*, he thought, but unfortunately also part of the job. Schechterle reacted with empathy and concern for Cruz's family, but didn't process the event any differently than if the deceased had been a civilian. It was simply a horribly sad story that left five children fatherless.

At the time, lawyer Pat McGroder wasn't involved in any Crown Victoria cases. A Tucson lawyer referred the Juan Cruz case to him, neither lawyer realizing how the case fit into the larger history and pattern of the Crown Victoria. But once McGroder began his initial investigation and due diligence, it didn't take long to piece together the dark history of the Crown Vic.

As a first step, McGroder went to Tucson with Mark Arndt, an automotive design engineer, to investigate the crash. When they put the damaged police cruiser up on a lift, Arndt almost immediately found a hole in the fuel tank that matched the size and shape of a bolt. That moment began a six-year odyssey for McGroder, an odyssey that would eventually connect him to a Phoenix police officer named Jason Schechterle.

One of the first people McGroder contacted was legendary anti-Ford crusader and lawyer David Perry in Texas. In 1983, Perry had gone to trial by himself against an inveterate corporate team of Ford lawyers and won the landmark $100 million jury verdict in the Durrill case. Similar to the Crown Victoria, the Mustang II defect was a faulty vehicle platform with the fuel tank located in the rear overhang of the vehicle, behind the rear axle. Over the next fifteen years, Perry handled another two dozen similar crash cases against Ford, which all settled before trial. At every occasion Perry spoke with his distinct Texas drawl and, except when in court before a judge, wore his trademark blue jeans and custom-made Lucchese cowboy boots from San Antonio. Right down to his affable manner and dress, he represented the common man's plight against corporate greed and indifference. So by the late 1990s, it was no secret that documented issues existed with Ford's design platforms.

"Ford executives obviously knew about the problem," said Perry. As early as the mid-1960s in Dearborn, Michigan, in fact, Ford president Arjay Miller was driving a Lincoln Continental that was rear-ended on none other than the Edsel Ford Freeway. The car caught fire, but Miller escaped the flaming wreck and survived. In his testimony to a U.S. Senate subcommittee on auto safety legislation, he said, "I still have burning in my mind the image of that gas tank on fire."

With the 1979 model year, Ford debuted a new platform for their full-size cars, which was essentially the previous Galaxy platform, downsized and named the Panther platform. Manufacturers typically create a vehicle platform—the automobile's underbody, suspension, axles, underfloor, engine compartment, and frame—onto which they can build several different models. The models on the Panther platform were Crown Victoria, Lincoln Town Car, and Grand Marquis. This process allows manufacturers to share common design, engineering, and production efforts across several models, thereby reducing manufacturing cost per vehicle. To change any single element of a vehicle platform, such as a fuel tank position or design, requires shutting down production and reengineering everything—an extremely expensive proposition costing tens of millions of dollars. Morbidly, it was more cost-effective to settle cases as they arose than to redesign an entire vehicle platform.

"By the early 1990s, there was a clear track record of the Panther platform having a defect where the fuel tank would be punctured by the differential," Perry said. "The behavior by Ford executives was heinous and callous. There are no words to describe the suffering that burn victims go through."

McGroder knew of Perry's expertise and successful track record. He contacted the Texas lawyer and asked if they could co-counsel on the Cruz case; Perry agreed. The pairing created a formidable team: the automotive-products-liability tactician Perry, and the equally talented litigator and negotiator McGroder.

Not surprisingly, the autopsy results confirmed what the two lawyers had already theorized: Juan Cruz did not have a single broken bone or any other injuries. Fire, not the crash, killed Cruz. The following year, on April 12, 2000, Rodriguez entered a plea of guilty to manslaughter and two counts of aggravated assault, but that did nothing to help Juan Cruz.

For the two attorneys, McGroder and Perry, the pileup of horrible burn injuries and charred, uniformed corpses was negligent, cruel, inexplicable, and shameful. Their case theory was that Ford engineers designed the Panther platform with the fuel tank positioned directly behind the rear axle, within each vehicle's crush zone. According to the lawyers' experts, after a high-speed rear collision crumpled the back of the car, the impact pushed structural metal and trunk contents (such as jacks) into the tank, thereby puncturing it. Sparks from the collision ignited gasoline vapors. Further, the force of the impact often jammed the doors shut, trapping occupants in a hellish and fiery tomb. The fundamental design of the car, according to McGroder and Perry, created an egregious perfect storm. The lawyers had other strong evidence to support their cases.

During the 1970s, positioning the rear axle behind the fuel tank was commonplace for all manufacturers. Over time, however, manufacturers of passenger cars in North America changed this fuel tank position, because engineers deemed it too dangerous. By 2000, Ford Motor Company was the only manufacturer still using the design, on the Panther and Mustang platforms. In 2005, Ford engineers changed the Mustang platform design, leaving the Panther as the only vehicle platform still being manufactured and sold in North America with the fuel tank behind the rear axle.

EIGHT miles west of lawyer Pat McGroder's tony Biltmore office, on March 26, 1999—exactly two years to the day before Schechterle would be burned alive—

Phoenix Police Officer Marc T. Atkinson had dropped in behind a suspicious vehicle with three occupants. Following protocol, and his rapidly rising reasonable suspicion, Atkinson radioed the plate. Near Thirty-First Avenue and Thomas Road in west Phoenix, the driver led Atkinson into an industrial area at Thirtieth Avenue and Catalina Drive. Atkinson followed and was soon immersed in an ambush by gunfire. Atkinson died almost immediately. A private citizen on scene drew his own weapon, engaged the suspects in a gunfight, and seriously wounded one of the suspects. The suspects were all later arrested. Atkinson, 28, had been an officer for almost five years and left behind a wife and 7-month-old son.

Schechterle, a self-professed news junkie, came home from his power company job March 26, plopped onto the couch, and turned on the local evening news. The lead story was about Marc Atkinson, who had patrolled in Maryvale Precinct, which meant Schechterle's brother Michael most likely knew the fallen officer.

"I should be doing that job," Jason said aloud as he watched the news coverage.

It was the moment everything changed again for Jason Schechterle. His response to the news of Atkinson's death was not the same as most people— police officers and firefighters have different genetic wiring. Those who choose the professions run opposite the direction of everyone else: *toward* gunfire and *into* burning buildings. The other 99 percent of people watch that same news coverage and think, *I'm sure glad I'm not doing that job: Look how dangerous it is.*

Learning of Marc Atkinson's death imparted a strange sensation and moment of clarity for Schechterle. Before, he'd merely *wanted* to be a police officer, but in that moment, he knew being a police officer was his calling. He didn't say anything to his wife, out of fear she'd think he was crazy, which he was according to the Minnesota Multiphasic Personality Inventory. For the next few days, the life and death of Marc Atkinson consumed Schechterle's thoughts and internal monologue. *The call of duty. The nobility of policing. First on scene. The New Centurions. To protect and serve.* Thoughts of policing bombarded Schechterle. Not the tortuous hiring process he'd have to undergo for a third time if he made such an attempt, but simply *being* a police officer.

A few days later, Schechterle was working with a crew at the northwest corner of Fifty-Ninth Avenue and the 101 Freeway. Schechterle and three others had been tasked with installing a large transformer at a new shopping center. They'd been talking all morning about the Marc Atkinson funeral procession, which they knew from the news coverage would be passing within view of their job site. The plan was to take a short break, remove their hard hats, and pay their respects to the fallen officer whose story had dominated the local airwaves and print media. Eventually, one of the crew noticed that all eastbound traffic had stopped on the freeway. They continued working until the first flashes of red and blue came into view. Schechterle and the others put down their tools, walked across the access road and right to the fence along the freeway. No one spoke as each removed his hard hat.

The first element of the procession was a string of police motorcycles, followed by police cars that seemed to go on forever. Schechterle watched the proceedings with rapt attention. Although he'd long accepted he'd never be a cop himself, he felt that old familiar tingle flash through his body, one he'd not experienced since getting bounced out of the hiring process a second time.

Odd, he thought. Then goose bumps rippled across his arms. Something stirred inside and clicked. He knew this was his calling, just as he'd always known: He had to try again to become a cop. And oddly, somehow, he had no doubt he'd now succeed in that endeavor.

He'd never seen a police funeral. Something about all those clean and shiny motorcycles, in tight rows two-by-two, inspired awe. He began counting and stopped at eighty-two rows of motorcycle cops from different agencies across the state. The hearse drove by, and then limousines. The procession was eight miles long.

I have to go do this, he repeated to himself. *I should not be standing here wearing these clothes: I should be down there wearing that uniform.*

Schechterle, of course, understood the dangers of the profession and had just watched a funeral procession for an officer killed in the line of duty, yet he was still undeniably enamored by and pulled toward the very same duty. For the men and women who earn and wear the badge, the profession, at its highest form, is a calling to serve. For those who don't feel the pull and sense of duty and obligation to do the job, there's a long list of other ways to draw a median paycheck—minus gunfire.

At that moment, feeling the call, it didn't occur to Schechterle that he'd already been bounced out of the stringent screening process not once but *twice*, so the odds of passing on his third attempt were slim and none. Nor did it occur to him that he was pulling down $60,000 in his job at APS and that as a police recruit he'd start at $26,000 while also facing a nightly barrage of bullets, blood, spit, and verbal vitriol from angry, bewildered, and drugged suspects. Schechterle didn't ponder that his young wife might not share his enthusiasm for such a career change, at a deep cut from his current salary, with two young children at home. None of these realities clouded Schechterle's vision as he watched until the silent flashing lights of every police motorcycle and car in Marc Atkinson's funeral procession had long passed into the high glare of the Arizona sun. Schechterle was simply born to serve, and did not really have a choice in the matter. The full power and force of the mantra, temporarily diminished, had never been completely silenced. Whatever it took, Jason Schechterle simply had to be a police officer.

CHAPTER 8

Police Academy

LIKE JASON SCHECHTERLE, Bryan Chapman was born in 1972, came of age during the 1980s, and knew from a young age he wanted to be a cop. He was a leap-year baby, born February 29. As a teenager in Bettsville, Ohio, a one-stoplight outpost surrounded by endless neat rows of corn, Chapman's singular vision was law enforcement. To that end, the only uniform he wanted to wear was that of the proud and mighty Ohio State Highway Patrol. Separated during their youth by 1,900 miles of high desert, grassy plains, and American heartland, Chapman and Schechterle were nonetheless linked by destiny and their parallel passion to pin a badge. But Chapman's journey began at a decidedly different point of origin.

Chapman's high school class totaled nineteen people, and Bettsville had more bars (three) than stoplights. Immediately upon turning 18 in 1990, Chapman marched down to the Ohio State Highway Patrol building, submitted his application, and was summarily denied with no explanation. With a lifetime rule that applicants could only apply twice, Chapman would only get one more shot at his dream post. Suddenly and without warning, he was already walking the cliff's edge. On his next attempt, Chapman convinced his twin brother Ryan to come along and apply as well. Ryan made the cut and to this day is still with the Ohio State Highway Patrol as a staff lieutenant. Bryan, the elder twin (by five minutes), didn't fare so well. Instead, he was once again bounced out of the hiring process, which meant his dream of roaming Ohio's highways in uniform was officially dead. Like Schechterle, Chapman had whiffed on two straight pitches and was down 0-2 in the count. Also like Schechterle, the sting of cold rejection would trouble Chapman for months: He was dazed and frustrated, with an empty void in his gut that lingered and roiled.

Eventually Chapman recovered, moved on, and attended community college. In 1993, still dreaming of a career in law enforcement, he became a police officer with the Bettsville Police Department. It was a start, but wasn't exactly the Ohio State Highway Patrol: by joining the Bettsville police "force," Chapman doubled the size of the uniformed staff—two was all a town of six hundred people needed. The other half of the police department was a gruff, old-school police chief sent straight from central casting. Mack, who had an eighth-grade education, followed the classic good ol' boy approach to law enforcement. And in the bustling metropolis known as Bettsville, that style worked just fine, thank you very much. So while Chapman was in blue and officially a cop, he was in for a sleepy introduction to Police Work 101 with Mack as boss, teacher, and mentor. Trying to nab a few speeders along State Street, the Route 12 main thoroughfare—the gateway to Lake Erie—was the highlight of action on each shift. Said Chapman, "The radio never cracked." And "never" was not hyperbole: The radio *never* cracked.

Knowing the Bettsville Police Department was not his life's calling, Chapman concurrently pursued his education at the University of Toledo and, in June 1995, got a bachelor's degree in criminal justice. He also applied and was accepted as a recruit to the police department in Bowling Green, a university town thirty miles west of Bettsville with a population of 30,000. Chapman made it through the academy, joined the much larger force at Bowling Green, and spent the next four years in a dream police job. As part of the Toledo metropolitan area, the Bowling Green Police Department employed fifty officers who dealt primarily with college town issues—Bowling Green State University had an enrollment of about 18,000 students on the main campus—and little serious or violent crime. Chapman had his own assigned car and a department that paid to have his uniforms dry-cleaned regularly. The police department facilities and equipment were all shiny, clean, and immaculate. After the shift ended at 11 p.m., Chapman and his fellow officers hit the bars in plain clothes to mingle with cute coeds. It was a comfortable gig and a great start to his law enforcement career. But as far as police work, Bowling Green was still a little too uneventful for Chapman. He handcuffed lots of drunk college kids and intervened in fights among fraternity kids. But after four years on the job, Chapman had his eye on something more, a big-city force where he might even get to break leather a little more regularly. "Break leather" was cop lingo left over from the days of all-leather holsters and duty-belt gear, and meant removing one's weapon (today's modern holsters are almost exclusively rigid, molded plastic, form-fitted to each pistol make and model). In four years of patrol in Bowling Green, Chapman had only unholstered his .40-caliber Smith & Wesson a handful of times and had never fired his weapon on duty. Not that either of those facts were bad things; every night a cop went home safe and without incident on shift was itself a victory. Stringing together an entire career like that was just as righteous and noble as any cop's career on a big-city force in New York, Chicago, or Los Angeles. Even so, Chapman just wanted to be in a bigger metropolitan area where he could apply all his police training.

The life-changing epiphany that would put him side by side with Schechterle came in the brutal cold of February 1998. If Schechterle had despised winter in North Dakota, Chapman's disdain for the gray bleakness of Ohio in February was equal, if not greater. One bone-chilling Midwest winter night, Chapman spent the first three hours of his shift doing nothing but pushing stranded motorists out of deep snow. Each time invariably meant stepping from the cozy warm confines of his cruiser, slipping and sliding on the ice, and getting blasted in the face by stinging wind-driven flakes. Shoulder to bumper, he was blasted by tire-propelled black ice and sludge. Nowhere during his academy training had this integral investigative duty been discussed. For the remaining five hours of that shift, the only other traffic on the streets was snowplows rumbling through the mist of white flurries with flashing yellow lights. To Chapman it felt like he was patrolling the dark side of the moon as he ghosted quietly down snow-padded streets. That's when the mental epiphany rang out in his head: *There has to be more to police work than being a snowplow operator with a badge.* The seed of his own manifest destiny and eventual westward migration was planted.

Later that year, in August, Chapman met an intriguing woman named Dawn, which put his big-city move on hold temporarily. Then as the months ticked by, another Midwest winter loomed. Hearing the alarm bell, Chapman began researching other options for police work. He triangulated three factors: 1) a large metropolitan area; 2) police departments hiring recruits; and 3) a temperate climate 100 percent devoid of snow, sludge, black ice, and road salt. Two possibilities matched his triumvirate of requirements: Las Vegas and Phoenix. By the spring of 1999, Chapman was arranging trips to the two desert cities to take the initial written examination and physical agility test for each police department. Then he returned to snowplow duty in Bowling Green and waited.

According to the U.S. Constitution, does one require probable cause to push a car out of a snow drift? No, Chapman said to himself, *one does not, making this current duty something other than police work.* The urge to head west intensified. At home, Dawn, now Chapman's fiancée, was already onboard with the idea and fully supportive of any move Chapman needed to make for his career. Now the matter was in the hands of larger unseen forces—an unlikely mixture of providence, timing, municipal budgets, bureaucratic machinery, and a little luck, all of which might or might not ever coalesce. Chapman shuddered at the thought of being 43, six months out from retiring on a full pension, and still idling around sleepy Bowling Green in his regulation police snowplow. Like Schechterle, he couldn't have a stronger desire for what he wanted, but that desire alone wasn't going to manifest the dream. All he could do was disperse the next drunken mob at the next college kegger, and break up the next fight between Alpha Tau Omega and Sigma Nu members.

The Midwest freeze thawed, turned to spring mud and, eventually, the heavy humidity and dancing fireflies of summer returned. No word from either department; Chapman wondered if he was slated for another brutal winter in his police-issue motorist assist vehicle. Finally, in July, as Chapman stood in his apartment's small kitchen holding the telephone, a background investigator with the Phoenix Police Department said the magic words: "If you want the job, we can get you in the next academy class."

Hallelujah, mothball the snowplow! The kid's going west.

Chapman was giddy beyond words, but he wouldn't be able to start that next academy class, which began in two weeks. He needed a little time to close things out properly in Bowling Green, get his life packed, and make the cross-country move to the desert Southwest. Instead, he'd start in Phoenix on September 21, 1999, with academy class 333.

BY the time Shayne Tuchfarber was a 10-year-old in Alice Springs, Australia, he had only one career goal—aligned, unbeknown to him, with his future cop pals Schechterle and Chapman.

"I knew at an early age I wanted to be a police officer," he said. During cops and robbers with his friends, he always took the role of law enforcement, although he eschewed the traditional regal blue uniform in favor of no shirt, cowboy boots, and shorts, with his six-shooter holster riding low on his hips. If he'd been an Australian citizen, he'd have joined that country's military at the first opportunity when he came of age. But instead he was the kid of an American expat, dreaming of a life behind the badge in the hot, dusty desolation of a 20,000-person town pinpoint in the middle of the Australian continent.

Tuchfarber's father worked for defense contractor TRW, and had made the career move and taken his family to Australia in 1982. Tuchfarber, who had an older brother and younger sister, was born in Santa Clara, California, in 1974. Prior to Australia, his father's job had taken the family to Las Cruces, New Mexico, where the senior Tuchfarber worked at the White Sands Missile range.

"My family members are all top-secret weirdoes, and I'm a dump cop," Shayne said. His grandfather worked at Area 51 and Los Alamos lab along with other aunts and uncles. As a youth, in preparation for his career, Tuchfarber had numerous unplanned direct contacts with the local police.

"I would introduce myself to the Alice Springs Police Department quite often," he said. Usually it was for off-roading, fighting, or, sometimes, on particularly wild zeniths in the blistering outback, both. Even as he was being reprimanded by the local cops, Tuchfarber was in awe of them.

"I love and appreciate what you do," he'd tell the responding officers, like some precocious kid who had a knack for making adults admire him even as he was getting the heavy hand. "Yes sir," he would proudly tell the police, "someday I'm going to do what you do."

On his seventeenth birthday, in 1991, Tuchfarber returned to the United States with his mother and sister. His brother had previously moved back, and his dad stayed Down Under to work, a long-distance family arrangement that eventually led to his parents' divorce.

"It was tough for me to deal with that," he said.

Back in Las Cruces, New Mexico, Tuchfarber wasn't exactly on the pristine path required for becoming a police officer. Every transgression, from the ridiculously inconsequential to the larger missteps of youth, would one day be pored over, analyzed, documented, and incorporated into the official record of the cop-to-be. Obviously any felonies or major misdemeanors would forever preclude Tuchfarber from the police ranks. But even a long list of minor flubs— smoking pot too many times, dabbling in harder drugs, one too many drunken fights, or a few too many instances of bad decision-making and judgment— could end the career of a potential police officer before it ever began. The files at municipalities across the United States today are bursting with tens of thousands of permanently rejected applicants. By the time a new recruit clears the grueling background process, physical agility test, and various other screening hurdles, he or she is part of the elite 1 percent of all applicants who make the cut; the other 99 percent will never be police officers.

Without fully weighing such long odds and the ramifications of each of his decisions against his future law enforcement possibilities, Tuchfarber promptly dropped out of high school and, for ten straight months, used all his free time to drink too much. Then he snapped out of it, quit drinking, and finished high school in 1993 when he was 18. After a lost year in Virginia—he'd followed a girlfriend who, coincidentally, also worked for TRW as his father had—Tuchfarber moved back to Las Cruces, where he tried to get hired with the sheriff's department. Like Schechterle and Chapman, he too learned the tough lesson of how difficult it actually was to become a police officer. Hiring personnel at the Las Cruces sheriff's department politely took Tuchfarber's application and then didn't return his repeated phone calls, until Tuchfarber accepted that the process had officially fizzled.

Concurrently, there in the Land of Enchantment Tuchfarber met his first ex-wife. She worked in the tourism industry and had an internship slated for the summer of 1994 in Phoenix, Arizona. Tuchfarber made the move with her and began his law enforcement job hunt in earnest.

By September 1995, the Phoenix Police Department was hiring, and the competition was fierce. Tuchfarber went to take written tests in a cavernous lecture auditorium with hundreds and hundreds of other applicants. Ultimately, only one out of every hundred made it to an academy class.

From 1996 to 1999 Tuchfarber repeatedly applied with numerous local jurisdiction agencies in metropolitan Phoenix, including the suburbs of Chandler, Gilbert, Mesa, and the Maricopa County Sheriff's Office. One of his roadblocks was that during his short stint in Virginia he'd smoked marijuana for the second time in his life. Many people smoke weed twice in a day, every day, going back twenty years. But becoming a cop held people to an almost impossible standard of lifetime conduct. The only shoo-ins were Amish girls in their early twenties from small towns, whose worst transgression in life was passing audible gas during church. (Horribly embarrassing, that one, but never documented on official hiring paperwork.)

For Tuchfarber, however, his second marijuana use had been only two years before his applications, which didn't meet the minimum three-year window of drug-free history. It was an annoying hurdle, but one that time would remedy. In the interim, he married in 1997 and divorced in 1998, doing odd jobs through it all to survive. He worked as a janitor mopping laundromats at 2 a.m., as a cook and bartender at Red Lobster, and—like Schechterle prowling the grounds at the nuclear plant—a similar rent-a-cop job doing hotel security. He was desperate to get hired with a police department and didn't have a clue what he would do if his original and longtime dream died on the vine. In January 1999, Tuchfarber reapplied with the Phoenix Police Department, his third attempt.

"There was no Plan B for me," he said. "I fought, kicked, and scratched, and did whatever I had to do to get this job."

By summer, he was feeling dejected and losing hope that it would ever happen. While on a trip to Florida, his mother called and told him someone from the Phoenix Police Department had called looking for him. He was either about to hear the best or worst news of his life. He found a pay telephone and called his background investigator, Claudia Burgess. In a surreal twist, Tuchfarber was standing at Walt Disney World in Orlando, Florida, as he spoke to Burgess back in Phoenix.

Great, Tuchfarber thought. *It's either going to be cupcakes and rainbows—Dreams Come True at Magic Kingdom Park!—or like bad Thai food through Snow White and all seven dwarves: shit through a goose.* Ultimately, the phone call delivered news somewhere in the middle of those two extremes: Burgess told Tuchfarber they'd like him to come in for an interview. At least his dream hadn't been disemboweled under Mickey Mouse's long shadow; that would've been another twisted turn Tuchfarber could do without.

He was so excited and relieved he said Mickey could pound sand (well, not those exact words): that he'd immediately cancel his trip, catch the next flight back to Phoenix, and be at 620 West Washington the next day. Instead, Burgess told him to finish out the trip and call when he was back in town. Tuchfarber's feet didn't touch the surface of Florida for the remainder of his trip. Upon his return to Phoenix, Tuchfarber breezed through the rest of the hiring process and was told to report with academy class 333 in September.

"If I hadn't gone through all that bullshit, we wouldn't have all ended up in the same academy together," he said.

BY the summer of 1999—as an elated Chapman submitted his resignation letter to the Bowling Green Police Department and dreamed of swaying palm fronds, and Tuchfarber took his life-changing phone call at Walt Disney World—Jason Schechterle was on his third and, in his mind, final attempt to clear the stringent process and get a spot in the next academy class for the Phoenix Police Department. He'd filled out his application the first week in April, right after watching Marc Atkinson's funeral procession. His police-officer brother, working as a DARE officer in an unmarked car, drove out to the job site and gave Schechterle the application. Once again, Jason started back at the beginning: physical agility test, background investigation, interview, polygraph examination, oral board examination, medical screening, and psychological evaluation.

The mantra—*I have to go do this*—drove Schechterle through the tedious process. In fact, although he already had much evidence to the contrary, he had a sense there was no way he wouldn't make the cut this time. He was more mature. He had more life experience. And he pulsed with a genuine, heartfelt belief that he was meant to do the job. Like Jake and Elwood from *The Blues Brothers*: He was on a mission from God. Even so, repeating the grueling, invasive, and monotonous process was a complete pain in the ass. Slow and steady, Schechterle was calm and ticked the boxes as he went. Once again he'd have to pass a polygraph examination—the fifth he'd taken, counting his two previous attempts with Phoenix PD and two with other agencies. The night before the test, he told his wife he was never taking another polygraph again: Either he passed and moved forward in the hiring process, or that was it. This was the absolute final attempt at becoming a cop, period.

As Chapman, Schechterle, and Tuchfarber continued their respective quests to join the Phoenix Police Department, on July 26, 1999, sheriff's Deputy Steven Agner, 30, was killed when his Ford Crown Victoria Police Interceptor exploded after being rear-ended by a college student driving a pickup truck in Madison County, Florida. The officer was assisting a road construction crew; his fellow officers unsuccessfully tried to pull him from the burning wreckage. Weeks later, on August 9, 1999, Schechterle's background investigator called as he was driving home from work. He flipped open his cellphone and took the call.

"Hey, Jason; it's Debbie."

"Hi." *OK, here it is. In or out, standing at the door of the Last Chance Saloon.* The next seconds would determine Schechterle's life going forward—cop or lineman—and either validate or destroy his lifelong dream. Had watching a police officer's funeral procession truly been a life-changing moment and an invitation to a higher calling? Or just some sentimental lapse that sent Schechterle off to pound his head against the same brick wall he'd bloodied himself on twice already?

"I'm here with Kathy Van Gordon," she said over the speakerphone.

"Hey, Kathy."

The small talk killed time, but the tension was unbearable. Schechterle stopped at a red light at the intersection of Dunlap Avenue and I-17 in west Phoenix. He could handle whatever they had to say. He prepared himself for the worst and assumed this was the end once again.

Then both women screamed: "You made it!"

"Really?"

The decade-long process had started the day he saw his older brother in a Phoenix police officer uniform for the first time, in 1988. He'd covered a lot of ground and years—from Grand Forks to Korea, Florida, Guantanamo Bay, and back to Phoenix. Not to mention the two failed attempts at joining the Phoenix police force. He was certain she'd said he made it and had a seat with academy class 333 on September 21, 1999. But Schechterle didn't trust his own ears.

"Could you repeat that?" he said. Indeed, he'd heard correctly: Jason Schechterle was going to the police academy! A sense of calm and serenity replaced all the years of angst and longing.

"Thank you," he said aloud and then repeated in his mind: *Thank you, thank you, thank you*. He asked a few questions about his start date and the academy. They told him that as a pre-hire he could come to "620"—Phoenix police headquarters at 620 West Washington, downtown—and do odd jobs. Unlike Chapman, Schechterle didn't need much time to close things out with his current employer: "I'll see you next Monday."

He wanted to eliminate any possible chance of getting hurt at APS. Also, it was August in Phoenix, which meant working outside in 110-degree weather wearing work pants and long-sleeved shirts. That, and the fact he'd discovered that working with and around dangerous and potentially fatal levels of electricity wasn't for him, made it easy for him to say goodbye to APS.

Unbelievably, the dream was back on the front burner and alive with possibilities again. With no college degree, and a wife and two kids, Schechterle had followed his true calling after seeing the Marc Atkinson funeral procession. He took a deep breath: This was his path and destiny, and there was absolutely no way he was going to blow this opportunity now. When he walked into his house, Suzie was napping on the couch. He gently shook her awake.

"Debbie called," he said. "I made it."

Suzie congratulated her husband, but her fears and concerns ran deep.

"It was difficult," she said. "There was a part of me that wasn't pleased. I didn't love that we were cutting our income so drastically, but I knew we'd make it. I felt like I needed to support Jason in the dream he wanted so badly. Yes, he was going to be put in harm's way. But I've always believed that when it's your time, it's your time. Whether it's a gunshot wound or a garbage truck hitting you on that day, your profession doesn't matter. I also know he would support me in the same way."

After five polygraph tests with different agencies, three attempts with Phoenix PD and all the years of anticipation, planning, rejection, and failure, the sum total of their celebration was a quiet hug on the couch.

For the next five weeks, Schechterle drove down to 620 in a polo shirt and slacks. For the way he felt, he might as well have been a billionaire mogul being chauffeured around town in a limousine: There was simply no better post on planet Earth. The official start date of his long-sought police career was August 16, 1999. For those first days and weeks he was a civilian gofer, doing whatever any cop asked: moving furniture, parking cars, putting photographs in an album, filing papers, getting coffee, or doing any other administrative task. When someone said, "I need a pre-hire," Schechterle was at the ready. By any job standard, it was boring, repetitive work, but Schechterle was finally on the inside, literally and figuratively: As his former fellow power company linemen toiled under the August desert sun, Schechterle was sporting business casual in an air-conditioned building. It was easily the best boring five weeks of his entire life.

Then, for one week prior to the official academy start date, Schechterle and the other sixteen Phoenix Police Department recruits attended a pre-academy class together. After that, when the academy officially began, class 333 would expand to forty-plus, to include recruits from cities and police agencies throughout Arizona.

On the first morning of pre-academy week, Bryan Chapman rolled into the dark parking lot in his green Pontiac Grand Am at precisely 4:45 a.m. for the 5 a.m. start. Chapman knew attention to detail was an important trait for a police officer; being on time was detail number one. Be late on the first day, and the entire class would be doing push-ups until Thanksgiving.

When he'd moved from Ohio with his fiancé, Chapman had selected their apartment based solely on its proximity to the academy, at 10001 South Fifteenth Avenue at the base of an outcropping of desert foothills in Phoenix.

"I wanted to live close to the academy so I wouldn't ever be late," he said. With an apartment at Thirty-Sixth Street and Baseline, he'd achieved his objective. "It was picturesque, minus the gunshots at night."

When Chapman arrived he noticed a single vehicle in the parking lot, a white truck backed into a space. Already a cop for four years, he quickly and unconsciously noted the driver was reading a newspaper and smoking a cigarette. *Maybe he's the groundskeeper*, Chapman decided, and didn't give it another thought.

At the appointed start time, the sixteen Phoenix PD recruits (badges 7110 to 7125) filed in wearing the requisite uniform: white shirt with black tie, black pants, and black shoes capable of being polished (no black Air Jordans). Each chair had a last name written on it, in alphabetical order. "Schechterle" was in the second to last row. Written on the grease board:

Sit down.
Don't touch anything.
Be quiet.

For the first exercise, each recruit drew a slip of paper from a hat. Written on each was a speech topic, which the recruit had to present to the class for five minutes. Schechterle could strip down an M-16 and had faced mobs of hot, angry Haitians for months, but nothing was more terrifying than public speaking for the kid who hadn't quite outgrown his shyness. The topic he drew certainly wasn't doing anything to quell his nerves: *How to bake a cake.*

At 26, Schechterle had never baked a cake in his life. But that was the entire point of the exercise: learn to improvise, think quickly, and take command of a situation without losing confidence and presence. Cops do it every shift, every day on the job. Schechterle nervously took his spot before the class and began.

"I'd like to help you learn how to bake a cake," he said, which immediately prompted chuckles throughout the room. Laughing especially loud was Bryan

Chapman, seated in the front row, the one who'd shared that he'd already been a cop for six years. Schechterle, under immense pressure to succeed, had already decided to seek out Chapman's counsel, because he carried himself in a way that demonstrated he knew what he was doing.

"I prefer Duncan Hines over Betty Crocker," Schechterle said, which got another good round of laughter. Somehow he filled his allotted five minutes; in part two his peers could ask questions. The first hand went up in the front row, just a few feet from Schechterle.

"Recruit Chapman," Schechterle said, wincing as he waited for whatever was about to be lobbed his way.

Chapman couldn't disguise his grin, or the ease with which he was already operating in the first hour of the pre-academy class on Day One. In fact he was thinking, *This is fun!* Then Chapman said, "Do you like sprinkles on your cake?"

This got the biggest round of laughter. When the guffaws subsided, Schechterle responded with all the seriousness of testifying in open court: "Yes, I do like sprinkles on my cake."

"Bryan Chapman is a true leader," Tuchfarber would later say. "He's got a very big head on his shoulders, but it's a very good head. We still seek advice from him, and even approval. He will tell you the right thing to do. I've never seen anyone stick to their principles the way he does—except Jason Schechterle."

But on this day in the academy, before the trio had coalesced, Schechterle was nervous and not doing a very good job of concealing his anxiety. Neither was another recruit he'd meet during the pre-week: Shayne Tuchfarber. With the at-ease Chapman leading the way, the threesome would eventually become fast friends. And thanks to Chapman, less than one hour into the most serious and intense process he'd ever endured, recruit Schechterle had a wonderfully horrible new nickname: Sprinkles.

On Day Two, Chapman arrived again at 4:45 a.m. to see the same white truck backed into the same parking spot. It appeared to be the same driver, sitting reading the newspaper with smoke trailing out the open window. Once again, Chapman didn't give it much thought.

But on the third day, with his innate cop curiosity at full tilt, Chapman intentionally arrived a full *thirty* minutes early, at 0430 hours, to gather some intel on the vehicle and its mysterious lone occupant. As Chapman wheeled into the parking lot—*Are you kidding me?*—the white truck was already backed into the same spot, with the same driver reading and smoking. This was too much; time to investigate further. Chapman parked, stepped from his car, and walked over in the darkness holding a foam cup full of steaming coffee.

"Hey, what's up?"

The driver dropped the newspaper. "Hey."

Now Chapman had a positive ID: He recognized the face from class, but couldn't recall the name. The kid who liked sprinkles on his cake. This was no groundskeeper, but rather a fellow recruit. *What the hell?* Even in the darkness, take away the glasses, he had a passing resemblance to that actor from *The Karate Kid*. Cops naturally sought answers, so Chapman asked, "What are you doing here so early?"

"I'm never late."

"Right, me either. But why are you here so early?"

Schechterle took a pull on the Marlboro. "Dude, I have a wife and two young kids at home. This is *my* time."

The unmarried and childless Chapman did not yet fully understand Schechterle's stance. He nodded slightly and gave Schechterle a quizzical look. What he was thinking was, *OK, you're weird*. But what he said before walking back to his Grand Am was, "Enjoy your time."

Sergeant Giles Tipsword, an intense, fit, muscular cop who looked like he'd just walked off the set for a U.S. Marine recruitment-poster photo shoot, was running the new Phoenix police charges through the one-week warm-up: no testing, no screaming, and only some light PT, including short runs. The purpose of the pre-week was to prepare the recruits for the full academy and a career in law enforcement. The full beat-down and intensity would begin at the start of the official academy.

Guest speakers talked about the stresses of the job and the importance of learning to manage that stress on patrol and at home. The recruits learned the average cop's life span, a number Schechterle would never forget: 59 years. The speaker explained that cops regularly experienced an overload of adrenaline, sometimes on the same shift, and that over the course of a career that weakened the body and the immune system. When a cop was a few years removed from the job and died from pancreatic cancer at 56, the death didn't get logged as "in the line of duty." But the dotted line back to the job, the ravaging stress, and the toll on mind and body was all too clear.

Fifty-nine years. That reality settled in and hit home for Schechterle as he sat with rapt attention. The same speaker talked about other stressors, such as memories that can haunt cops long after harrowing incidents. Imagine being on scene, he said, and seeing a fire truck run over and kill a small child. *Things happen on this job that you'll never be able to erase. You have to learn to deal with that, or it will eat you alive.*

Schechterle could barely sit through the full week, he was so full of anticipation. The new recruits were drilled daily with the same admonishments:

You will be on time.

Your uniform will look pristine at all times.

Integrity, integrity, integrity.

Do not be late, or you will hate your life for the foreseeable future.

Schechterle's four years in the Air Force certainly helped him feel comfortable with the routine of structure and discipline, and the philosophy of creating a unified team. But he was also nervous because he couldn't afford a single misstep: He'd walked away from his $60,000-a-year job for this $12-per-hour, four-month training session. All escape routes were closed. He simply had to succeed academically, physically, and mentally. With the warm-up week complete, it was time. The recruits were sent home for a restless weekend and told to report September 21, 1999, at 0500 Monday, when the full wrath of *How bad do you want this?* would be unleashed on the recruits.

On that day, with the full class of forty-four assembled, the room was silent, the same instructions on the grease board:

Sit down.

Don't touch anything.

Be quiet.

Then it began in earnest with a booming roar from behind: "On your feet!" The source of the authoritative command was Sergeant Lauri Williams, a diminutive five-foot-two-inch fireball in a crisp blue uniform.

"I'll never forget the voice," Schechterle said later.

Williams walked the room slowly and looked over her new recruits. She asked them to introduce themselves, which each did.

"Jason Schechterle. Born and raised in Phoenix. My older brother Michael is a Phoenix police officer. I tested twice and failed, so I'm proud to be here."

"Shayne Tuchfarber. I want to put bad people in jail. That's always what I've wanted to do."

"Bryan Chapman. Born and raised in Ohio. I was a police officer there for six years. I got tired of pushing cars out of snow-filled ditches at ten below zero. I'm a lifelong Ohio State Buckeyes fan. Go Bucks."

One of the recruits' first homework assignments was to stencil their last names onto the back of four white T-shirts, exactly four inches below the collar, as instructed. With eleven letters in his last name, the exercise proved challenging for Schechterle. So much so that he was up after midnight trying to get his shirts properly stenciled.

At lineup the next morning Sergeant Williams walked among the recruits to check their work. With a ruler she measured the spacing between letters and the distance from the collar. It might seem pedantic and a colossal waste of time, but the exercise was a simple lesson in following instructions: Cops spend their shifts following rules, regulations, and protocol. It was also a lesson in attention to detail: Cops had to be fastidious in their preparation. Otherwise, someone might die unnecessarily. Sergeant Williams stopped at the lanky kid she'd heard others call "Sprinkles," tipped her head sideways, and scowled.

"Recruit Schechterle: That's not even close."

The other recruits were already snickering. The first few letters were dead level and spaced nicely: S-C-H. But from there the E-C-H started to drift downward slightly. By the end, T-E-R-L-E, it was all wrong.

"It resembled a train that had jumped the tracks," Chapman said.

"He was whining about all the letters in his name, but there's ten letters in my name, and I put it on just fine," Tuchfarber said.

Sprinkles wasn't doing a very good job of avoiding the spotlight in Week One. He even got a call from his background investigator to inquire about his introduction on the first morning.

"You can't tell people that you failed the hiring process twice."

"What? Why? It's the truth."

"Just don't say that." Schechterle never received any further clarification, but he never mentioned his hiring process again.

As one of the group's responsibilities, they created a nickname and roll call for class 333. During a training run, Mark Roach, a former U.S. Marine, yelled "Class" in a way that drew the word out over about ten seconds in a booming, authoritative voice. Then the entire group of forty-four responded in unison with, "First to fight, never flee, Williams Wolfpack 333." The T-shirts they created had "Class 333" with a wolf dressed in uniform.

The full academy included the one pre-week, sixteen weeks of full-time training, and then three weeks of post-training before advancing to the field officer training program. By the second of the sixteen weeks, most of the nerves had subsided for Schechterle, and he was enjoying the rhythm and pace of the academy.

After PT first thing in the morning—running, push-ups, and sit-ups in the cold darkness—all the first weeks were like a miniature law school, wherein recruits began learning the Arizona Revised Statutes for alcohol (Title 4), criminal (Title 13), and traffic (Title 28) offenses. They had courses in the history of law enforcement, criminal justice systems, liability issues, constitutional law, search and seizure, and laws of arrest. Classroom lectures covered defensive tactics and an introduction to firearms. They learned the fine art of determining reasonable suspicion and how to move from that level to probable cause, which was the minimum standard to arrest. The amount of information that had to be processed and assimilated in a short time, with proficiency demonstrated through dozens of written examinations, was voluminous.

"It's overwhelming," said Schechterle. From there, recruits learned how to diagram scenes, clear buildings, and make both routine traffic stops and high-risk felony traffic stops. They practiced hand-to-hand combat training, learning various pressure points on the human body and proper handcuff procedure.

As September turned to October and then November, the recruits learned every phase of being a cop. They spent endless hours on the gun range firing handguns and long guns, and trained at night with a flashlight. They fired thousands of rounds with both dominant and non-dominant hand in case the need ever arose to ward off an attacker from the weak side. For the tactical driving training the recruits spent three straight days at the track learning maneuvers they'd only ever seen in the movies.

Through it all, week after week and month after month, Sergeant Williams and her three RTOs (recruit training officers) were breaking down the individual personalities and bringing everyone together as a successful, cohesive team. Having gone through the process already, Chapman was helpful in dispensing key wisdom to Schechterle and his other new friends, including: 1) know your role and shut your hole; 2) never be first or last: just blend in with the pack; and 3) if you don't hear your name being yelled, you're doing just fine.

Schechterle continued to be especially determined and focused. Failure was simply not an option, not after all he'd given up to be there. He was undergoing a complete transformation, and had his nose in a book whenever he wasn't at the academy. Criminal and traffic law were especially challenging, as the recruits had to read and learn dozens and dozens of statutes—written in twisted legalese—straight from the three-inch-thick law book.

Schechterle studied all day on Saturdays to prepare for the four or five tests he knew were coming the next week. Three test failures and he was out. He had to learn, process, and assimilate an immense amount of material into increasingly more taxing scenarios and field training evaluations, such as K-A-R Day.

No one was told what the training listed as "K-A-R Day" on the schedule involved, or what the acronym meant. Each recruit had to undergo the exercise solo and was called away from the group to begin. A willing cast of hairy, disheveled, grimy undercover cops played the roles of bad guys with aplomb worthy of a Broadway stage.

"Schechterle. Now. You're up."

In scenario number one, a maniac ran toward Schechterle screaming nonsensical gibberish. Schechterle had to draw his sidearm—always a non-operable red gun during training—and handcuff the suspect. Then the sergeant relayed scenario number two: "You just got a call for a tripped alarm at a building. As the responding unit, you need to clear the building and come give me a report."

In the exercise, the gymnasium doubled as "the building." Schechterle drew his weapon, slowly opened the door, and saw immediately the room was pitch-black. He took one step inside and felt a hard object pressed against his face.

Shotgun barrel.

Hot blast.

Officer down.

K-A-R Day was designed so that no recruit could pass. The lessons were many: *Never enter an unknown building alone and without first calling backup units. Always establish a perimeter to head off potential escape routes. Always expect the worst and be prepared.* And most important: *Behind every closed door is a gun with a chambered round marked "To whom it may concern."*

In scenario number three, a six-foot-seven-inch beast, in a leather vest with a beard to the middle of his chest, was Schechterle's suspect. The role player's sheer size and potential to inflict physical harm represented every cop's worst nightmare. But in this scenario, the suspect was compliant and handcuffed without incident. More lessons learned.

Never assume anything.

Don't judge people by appearance alone.

Maintain poise and presence regardless.

Fight, flight, or freeze? Cops can never choose the latter two.

Those who wear the badge are the line between chaos and civility. But authority has to be balanced with tact.

After weeks of running, PT, sweating, and washing and drying his shorts and T-shirts, speculation began to circulate through class 333 that Schechterle only had one pair of shorts. The class collectively drew this conclusion in locker room whispers based on visual evidence that Schechterle's shorts were faded and considerably higher and tighter than on day one. Chapman and Tuchfarber wondered why Sprinkles made it so easy, but that didn't mean they eased up for one second:

You smuggling grapes there, Sprinkles?

Looks like the forecast calls for another cold morning at the academy, with a high probability of shrinkage.

Bumble Bee tuna: Your balls are showing.

John Stockton called: He wants his shorts back.

Not every recruit got every reference, but regardless the laughter induced actual tears and bellyaches. The faded, tight shorts became such a sensation that "Sprinkles" lost favor as the chosen moniker, toppled by "Schechter Shorts."

"He was always the first one at the academy every morning," Tuchfarber said. "We'd just say, 'There's Schechter Shorts.' Just ask him: To this day he still has them and wears them to bed every night."

"I loved those shorts," Schechterle said. "But they were a little short and a little tight." In his defense, the family cookie jar was especially barren during the autumn of 1999. He simply didn't have the money to buy more pairs of shorts, especially with his perfectly serviceable go-go pants. Besides, Schechterle could hold his own in dishing out the abuse, and Chapman had a new nickname, too: Big Head, which derived from—according to Schechterle, Tuchfarber, and their class 333 compatriots—Chapman's enormously disproportionate pumpkin head. The recruits rode each other like carnival barkers working on commission.

Ladies and gentleman, behold the human bobblehead in all his freakish wonder!

Chapman, your head looks like a cantaloupe on a straw, a gargantuan cranium with its own weather system.

How many moons orbit your head, Chapman?

Poor Chapman: He'll be crying himself to sleep tonight on his huge pillow.

They also called the veteran cop Lousy Shot because for all his six years of law enforcement experience, during range qualifying Chapman looked like a drunk on codeine cough syrup trying to thread a needle in a dark theater: He could not hit the mark.

"I'm not a great shot," he said.

"But he can hold his own on the street," Schechterle said. "And he has the gift of gab like nobody else. He's a great cop."

In the politically incorrect world of police academy recruits, Tuchfarber also had several choice nicknames used equally and interchangeably by his fellow recruits: Fat Ass, Fatty, Fatso, and Man Boobs.

The abuse was tribal behavior that would carry on into their careers: When cops like one another, the slapstick derision never stops. However, if cops turn on one of their own, for various unforgivable breaches of duty or honor, they simply shun the offender, like the herd turning its collective back on a sick calf. So insults were pure love, and silence the coldest dagger form of estrangement in the police world. "You're cool" and even "I love you" came in the form of getting more abuse than the fleet of rental cars at the Detroit airport.

Early on for Chapman and Tuchfarber, their classmate Schechterle was a fascinating contradiction of oddities. He was the most determined, focused recruit they'd ever seen, yet he couldn't stencil his surname straight across a T-shirt. And despite smoking more Marlboro Reds every week than ten cowboys on a thousand-mile cattle drive along the Chisholm Trail, Schechterle always held his own on training runs. It didn't make any sense—and then, just when they thought they'd figured out the inner workings of Schechter Shorts, he would pull another trick from his bag.

"Let's go play golf," he said to Chapman one week during academy. Chapman unwittingly agreed, so on a Saturday morning he and Schechterle walked to the first tee at Estrella Mountain Golf Course, which Schechterle had played hundreds of times. Never once in the months he'd known Chapman had Schechterle mentioned his golf prowess—that he was in the hunt for the state golf championship during high school, or that he'd had a legitimate shot at playing professionally. It was like Siegfried and Roy asking a friend—one who'd never heard of their Las Vegas stage act—to feed the cats while they were away on vacation. Chapman showed up with a bag of kitty litter, but had no clue he was about to meet the white Bengal tiger.

Chapman teed off and hit a low screamer that sliced badly to the right and bounded out of sight. He was fairly pleased with the effort, which had at least been airborne and more or less in the general direction of the eventual target. He didn't voice his smugness.

Let's see you top that one, Schechter Shorts.

Meanwhile, Schechterle was thinking: *This guy plays golf about as well as he shoots a gun.*

"That giant head of yours throws off all your mechanics," Schechterle said as he pushed the tee into the soft grass.

"You may have a point there," Chapman conceded.

Schechterle went through his normal pre-shot routine. Then he drew back his driver, released his fast, fluid swing, and launched a dead-center shot, with the ball disappearing into the high-altitude ether of sweet perfection.

"Holy shit," Chapman said. Then he just shook his head and laughed. "Hey, dickhead: You could have told me what I'm getting into here."

"What?" Schechterle said, pulling out a Marlboro and lighting it as he grabbed his clubs.

"You are an enigma wrapped in a riddle."

"Yeah, and you're a Lousy Shot."

"Sprinkles."

"Pumpkin Head."

"My head is not that big."

"Not compared to the planet Jupiter."

The constant banter and sparring concealed the mutual respect and growing admiration the two had for each other. Schechterle respected that Chapman had worn the badge, and he wanted to learn everything he could from him. Chapman admired Schechterle's unrelenting drive, perfectionism, and determination in pursuing his goals. At some point during the academy the two Phoenix PD recruits were already talking about trying to get in the same precinct and same shift so they could be patrol partners.

Like Chapman and Schechterle, Tuchfarber also wanted to work in the grittier precincts, 400 (South Mountain), 500 (Central City), or 800 (Maryvale), where the real-life version of his cops-and-robbers game would play out daily.

"I wanted to go where the action was," he said.

But getting through the academy to graduation day was anything but a given. More tough hurdles loomed: being blasted with pepper spray, learning to grapple and fight, a 400-plus-question final exam, and shooting qualification. The class began with forty-four recruits; by late December thirty-eight remained, which included the fast five of Chapman, Schechterle, Tuchfarber, Bill Evans, and Mark Roach.

Bill Evans turned 21 during the academy and was immediately dubbed "Golden Boy" by his classmates because he had a beautiful wife, a beautiful young child, and was himself young and good-looking.

"How are things in the perfect world?" Schechterle would ask.

"Perfect," Evans said, smiling.

Even the tough Sergeant Williams seemed drawn in by the charm and allure of Golden Boy. She'd walk past him and say, "Good morning, Mr. Evans." Everyone else was "Recruit so-and-so," but not Golden Boy, who was also called Mayor of Pleasantville, after the film depicting a perfect world devoid of anxiety, strife, or problems.

Mark Roach, whom everyone just called Roach, was six foot seven inches and 225 pounds. An ex-Marine with the jarhead haircut, he was talkative and squared away, which was military parlance for doing things right the first time. He was funny as hell, with a southern drawl, and everyone in class knew he had their back.

As a final test of conditioning, the recruits had to complete a grueling ten-mile run up South Mountain two days before graduation. The directive from Sergeant Williams was clear: *Finish the run, or you do not graduate.* Everyone in the class made it to the top of the mountain that day.

"You know about the final run the first week of the academy," Schechterle said. Every day for four months, they could see the towers looming at the top of the mountain. "To run up there with your fellow recruits was a very satisfying experience." Grinding up the steep road took some grit and determination, but once at the top it was nothing but hugs and high-fives. Summiting the mountain was a metaphor for surviving the academy. Schechterle never liked running, and has not officially run since (other than the times he had to run on patrol chasing a suspect).

On Friday, January 7, 2000, each recruit was authorized to slide a full magazine into his or her .40-caliber Glock sidearm: They'd made the cut and would be sworn officers. By tradition, earlier in the day Schechterle's family was allowed onto the grounds of the academy to see where he'd been toiling for four months. Jason's wife Suzie came, along with Kiley and Zane and Jason's parents. The class demonstrated a run-up-and-fall-into-place maneuver as Sergeant Williams did a ceremonial inspection. Once dismissed, the recruits led their family members on a tour.

"I can't even describe the feeling and anticipation," Schechterle said.

Bryan Chapman's twin brother had flown in from Ohio—the one who'd made the grade for the highway patrol when Chapman had not. Chapman's brother was in uniform later that night to pin Chapman's Phoenix PD badge. The ceremony was at Seventh Street and Fillmore, in downtown Phoenix, in a high school auditorium packed with eight hundred people. A variety of awards were handed out, including "exemplary recruit" as voted by his peers, which went to Bryan Chapman. Chapman was surprised and shocked. He'd been solely focused on Schechterle receiving "best marksman," which he just barely missed.

The crowning moment of the ceremony—capping twelve years of planning, dreaming, failing twice, and never quitting for Schechterle—was taking the official oath and getting pinned with a shiny new Phoenix police officer badge. Schechterle's brother Michael, who had set the dream in motion in 1988, pinned his younger brother's badge. Tuchfarber asked his mother to pin his.

The trio, who'd never met prior to the academy in September 1999, were now forever bonded in a way that went deeper than even family. They'd each toiled separately for years and years—yet on the same meandering path—to earn a spot in class 333. There they stood shoulder to shoulder and suffered, laughed, and dug deep to earn a badge number that was sacred in the chronology and history of the Phoenix Police Department. Thousands had come before them, and thousands would follow, but their exact spot in the lineage of the fraternal order was forever stamped and solidified. The public they served saw and asked for badge numbers, not names. The badge number was forever theirs and theirs alone, a hard-earned marker that followed them through a career. And, of course, as the most senior of the trio (lowest number wins), Schechterle could forever dangle that trump card over his two friends and order them around like rented mules. Eventually, the badge number, too, would retire with each officer:

Schechterle 7110

Chapman 7114

Tuchfarber 7122

The numbering, which matched the exact order they'd been accepted into their academy class, also oddly paralleled their own bonding: the ever-anal Schechterle, of course, had to be first. Chapman had to be in the middle so his pals could help support his giant head on either side. And Fatty was always dragging ass at the back, winded, and looking for something chocolate. All was right that night, in every way.

Then it was Sergeant Lauri Williams' turn, with one last duty call. "On your feet," she yelled just as she had on Day One at the academy. "For the last time, class 333, you're dismissed!"

Then former U.S. Marine and now Phoenix police officer Mark Roach screamed his familiar "Class!" that he stretched out to fifteen seconds. Then the thirty-eight new officers yelled in unison: "First to fight, never flee, Williams Wolfpack 333."

With that, yelling and screaming commenced among the ranks and from the assembled crowd. They'd all made it, but truthfully had barely begun their policing career. The next hurdle, a critical one to clear before being officially put on duty as full-authority police officers, already loomed large: field training. But for one night, no one was thinking about that. Everyone was swept away by the emotion and moment of graduation day, and the satisfaction of completing a rite of passage that few can.

The next morning, a Saturday, Schechterle woke up in a jolt of panic. He felt nervous and apprehensive. The excitement and elation of achievement had already worn off, only to be replaced by a gnawing anxiety. Twelve years of starts and stops to get to this point still had Schechterle on edge: A single major misstep during field training could end his career before it began. The twelve-week field officer training program now loomed as another especially high wall to climb. Even after that, he'd be on probation for one full year, which meant any single major screw-up and he was gone. It seemed the tests would never end. After pacing and burning through half a pack of Marlboros, Schechterle called Chapman.

"Starting Monday, there's no more instructors blowing a whistle if I screw up," Schechterle said. "I have a badge and a loaded gun. And a lot of responsibility."

"It surprised me to get that call," Chapman said, recalling the January 8, 2000, conversation. For all their "Schechter Shorts" and "Big Head" banter and merciless teasing, the two had become best friends during academy, and the tone of the conversation was real and serious. "That's Jason's level of focus, dedication, caring, and striving for perfection."

"Seriously," Schechterle said. "Can I do this job?"

Chapman likened it to skydiving: No matter how well-trained one is, the moment of truth arrives when all that's left is to jump. Rolling out on patrol for the first time, with loaded weaponry and the ultimate duty and obligation, invoked a similar rush of adrenaline and the weight of life-and-death responsibility.

One of the first things new police officers learn is that the language of law enforcement is spoken in numbered codes. Every command, statute, order, and request is communicated by a number, which differs by municipality but shares a common goal: to keep radio communications crisp, clear, confidential, and minimal. If a person about to be arrested hears a numbered code crackle over the officer's radio, rather than "Outstanding felony warrants, arrest immediately," the police maintain a position of advantage.

In Phoenix, when an officer was ready for service and available for dispatch calls, he or she radioed in the appropriate code, which was exactly what Chapman told his friend on the phone that day to ease his fears: "Jason, you are 10-8."

To a civilian, "10-8" was nonsensical. To a fully trained new police recruit, it was the most positive affirmation and comforting encouragement Schechterle could ever hope to hear, especially from someone who had already served for six years. The code simply meant Jason Schehterle was ready for duty. Although the phone call didn't completely dispel Schechterle's nervous anticipation, he felt ready again. He thanked Chapman, hung up, and took a few deep breaths.

All right. Relax. You can do this.

Indeed, he was ready. And that meant it was time to hit the mean, sun-baked streets of metropolitan Phoenix.

CHAPTER 9

Field Training Officer

THE CITY OF PHOENIX sits in a flat valley bounded by craggy desert outcroppings in Maricopa County, which sprawls across some nine thousand square miles. Throughout the 1980s and 1990s, Phoenix residents enjoyed its big-city amenities—professional sports franchises, a vibrant nightlife, abundant restaurant choices, a large state university, an international airport, and a broad-based economy—minus the gritty problems that afflicted most major cities. Oddly, Phoenix still had the feel of an overgrown small town, a 1960s throwback with nonstop sunshine and a ubiquitous blue swath overhead that fueled the spirit and optimism of the West.

Phoenix was a land of beautiful people, drawn by the lifestyle, having fun and making money. Their playground was a crisscross grid of six-lane boulevards lined with stucco block walls, apartment complexes, Circle K convenience stores, fast-food franchises, corner strip malls, and big-box superstores, all repeating endlessly in all directions. Aside from pockets here and there—the Arizona State University campus, downtown Scottsdale, a smattering of historic neighborhoods—little distinguished one part of the city from another. Pick a suburban street anywhere in Phoenix, and it looked like every other suburban street. Architectural character aside, life was good in the Valley of the Sun.

By the turn of the twenty-first century, however, a hot job market and affordable housing had attracted the multitudes to Phoenix, including droves of besieged Californians beaten down by the sky-high cost of living, mudslides, wildfires, riots, earthquakes, and—perhaps most insidious—demon-grade traffic. The Phoenix metropolitan population surged, and almost overnight, Maricopa County became America's fourth most populous county. Phoenix was in the big leagues; the affable small-town feel gave way to urban reality.

Converging factors coalesced—cheap housing, supersonic and multidirectional development, residents forced into their vehicles by great commuting distances—and finally brought the attendant big-city problems Phoenicians had never fully experienced: choking smog, crushing rush-hour traffic, gangs, graffiti, and big-city crime. By 2000, the protective fantasy bubble had popped and a more urban vibe pulsed. It was that very energy that had drawn Bryan Chapman west to do big-city police work and had excited Jason Schechterle when he first saw his older brother in uniform. Tuchfarber, too, wanted in on the action. After all their respective anticipation, attempts and failures, planning and retrying, and long, arduous months at the academy, it was finally time to roll out on those very streets they had taken a sworn oath to protect.

ON Day One of field officer training, the first thing Schechterle did was trade one admittedly bad habit for a different bad habit. After burning Marlboro Reds for twelve years—a guilty and unhealthy pleasure he'd first discovered at Sheldon's house in the early mornings before school and continued around the world with the Air Force—Schechterle had decided that a police officer in uniform smoking cigarettes just didn't look right. He'd applied that same logic to being Airman Schechterle, but just hadn't been able to quit. As proud as he was to have served in the U.S. Air Force, finally being a police officer carried an even higher standard and call of duty in his mind. It had certainly been a hell of a lot tougher to become a cop than it had been to join the military.

Schechterle took seriously the oath of honor and integrity, and the image of his crisp new Phoenix Police Department uniform clouded by nasty cigarette smoke just didn't fly. So on January 10, 2000, he put down the Marlboro Reds for good and picked up a can of Skoal Wintergreen long-cut, a nicotine habit that he could drip-feed covertly, minus any annoying smoke or burned butts and away from the eyes of the public and his uniformed peers.

Officially, the field training officer (FTO) program was twelve weeks of on-the-job training and evaluation by a more experienced officer. Fresh-scrubbed academy graduates climbed into real patrol cars for the first time and began seeing and experiencing all the sights, sounds, smells, and rigors of the job they'd been trained to do. Unofficially, the FTO program was low-grade psychological torture, to demean and beat down with the sole purpose of reminding a new recruit that he or she knew shit about real police work, knew shit about life on the streets, and that 90 percent of the classroom BS from the academy could be tossed out the window. When the first unruly citizen spat a meaty loogie in an officer's face, followed by a head-butt that opened a nasty, bloody gash on the stunned rookie's forehead, getting a 100 percent on the constitutional law examination at the academy counted for absolutely nothing. The words scribbled on the grease board at the academy were equally valid during FTO:

Sit down.
Don't touch anything.
Be quiet.

No one out on patrol cared that Bryan Chapman had gone through two police academies and already had six years on the streets back in Ohio. The fact that he'd been named "exemplary recruit" by his academy classmates carried the same weight with seasoned officers as if he'd won a sixth-grade bake-off for best brownies.

No one cared that Tuchfarber had scrubbed laundromats in the middle of the night just to survive as he weathered one rejection after another to become an officer.

No one cared that Schechterle had persisted through two failures and taken a deep pay cut to follow his dream through twelve long years. What they each got on Day One of FTO was a similar unspoken directive:

Shut up.

Watch, listen, and learn.

Shut up some more.

For the first five weeks new recruits were paired with a senior officer and then, for the next five weeks, a different officer. After that, Schechterle would be alone in a patrol car with a very short leash—that is, close and careful monitoring. To determine where they'd do their field training, each recruit had submitted his or her top three precinct choices, which had to be approved by the academy sergeant. At the time the City of Phoenix comprised six different precincts (today there are eight): 400 (South Mountain), 500 (Central City), 600 (Desert Horizon), 700 (Mountain View), 800 (Maryvale), and 900 (Cactus Park).

Schechterle's first choice had always been 800 (Maryvale). Although this west side of the city had a reputation for more violent crime and action, it was also where he'd grown up. His second choice was Central City (500), the heart of Phoenix near the airport and amid the city skyline and lights of downtown. Chapman chose Central City, too, because it would provide the sort of high-octane police work that Bowling Green had not: felony stops, street scuffles, bagging drug dealers, wrangling prostitutes, and snaring johns.

Each precinct was further divided into patrol areas. The 500 had 51, 52, and 53. Those patrol areas were further subdivided into five beats: the 51 area where Chapman was assigned included 511, 512, 513, 514, and 515. Schechterle was assigned to the 53 area, which included 531, 532, 533, 534, and 535. The final delineation was a one-word shift designator to differentiate between the midnight, afternoon, and day shifts. The afternoon shifts (3 p.m. to 1 a.m.) were Frank, George, and Henry; the day shifts (6 a.m. to 4 p.m.) were Adam or Bravo. Rookies always got handed the worst shift, midnight (9 p.m. to 7 a.m.), which was either John or King. Each patrol area always had at least one unit (patrol car) per beat plus one additional rover unit, for a total of six units per area on each shift. Multiplied by the three patrol areas, there were eighteen units patrolling Central City on any given shift at any given time of the day (and more at certain hours since shift start and stop times overlapped).

FTO assignments came down during the last week at the academy. Schechterle was working afternoons in the 500 Precinct on the 52 Frank shift. Chapman was 53 Frank: same shift time in an adjacent patrol area. Being in the same precinct put the two rookies on a more likely path to eventually patrol as partners. Tuchfarber went to FTO right in the thick of things: South Mountain (400). They'd all be working the afternoon shift for training, but would go on the midnight shift, King, once they were ready to roll solo. Schechterle's first assignment after FTO was 53 King and Chapman's 51 King. Tuchfarber, meanwhile, was banished to 44 George in the far south section of 400 Precinct, a sprawling residential area of Phoenix called Ahwatukee with little if any high-wire police work. To his academy classmates patrolling grittier sections of Phoenix, Tuchfarber was Barney Fife looking for Mayberry litterbugs.

For the first six weeks of field training Schechterle's mentor was a male officer, who immediately put Schechterle at ease with his overall positive and reassuring approach. Even so, on Day One Schechterle was a jumble of nerves.

"This was no joke," he said. "This was the real deal."

Schechterle's academy experience had been stellar, and he felt ready for whatever might arise. At the same time, he was eager to experience every type of call he'd ever get on duty, and he wanted to experience all of them on the first day.

One of the most confounding aspects was learning the streets on his new beat, and the addresses the way the dispatcher called them out over the radio, which was an altogether new language. The radio would crack, the dispatcher would speak, the senior officer would answer up the call, and Schechterle would stare at his mentor as though everything had just been communicated in Mandarin Chinese.

"What did she say? Where are we going?" Schechterle asked each time, feeling like a wide-eyed civilian out on his first ride-along. This painful learning curve took days to overcome—*What did she say? Where are we going?*—until Schechterle's ears started becoming attuned to the new language of police work:

the various numbered codes, the verbal shorthand, the odd "400 block of such and such street" vernacular. Slowly, he started to get a feel for the rhythm of it all.

During these first days and weeks the duo specifically took low-priority calls to break in the new recruit slowly. They weren't answering any hot calls; instead, they'd go 10-8 as they left the Central City Precinct headquarters and choose from the long list of paper calls stacked up from the day shift. Schechterle's first official call in uniform was a break-in. Of course any suspects were long gone, and likely whatever they'd stolen had already been converted to cash at a pawn shop and then converted again to the drug of choice and swallowed, smoked, or injected. But Schechterle took some fingerprints, interviewed the homeowner, and filled out all the requisite forms. Based on his excitement, he might as well have been single-handedly solving a high-profile triple homicide.

When he wasn't working, Schechterle sat listening to the police radio to accelerate his indoctrination. After riding patrol for a week or so, the staccato blurts of information were becoming decipherable, and he was able to at least understand what was happening. In between calls the partners talked about family, football, and life.

ON January 30, 2000, Officer Alan Neel barely escaped from his burning Ford Crown Victoria Police Interceptor after it was rear-ended and exploded in Taylor, Texas. Neel later joined a class-action suit filed by David Perry on behalf of all Texas counties and cities. News of that crash never reached Schechterle.

Nineteen days later, Arizona Department of Public Safety Trooper Skip Fink, 53, stopped an eastbound motorist on U.S. Highway 60 near McClintock Drive in the Phoenix suburb of Tempe. Known locally as the Superstition Freeway, after the desert mountain range of the same name to the east, the roadway cuts east–west through the suburbs east of Phoenix, including Tempe, Mesa, and Gilbert.

Coincidentally, Fink and the lawyer Pat McGroder were old friends going back to the late 1970s. The attorney had met the state trooper as their law-and-order professions overlapped; they bonded immediately and became lifelong friends. Sadly, that friendship was about to be cut short in another violent Crown Victoria ending.

Fink, badge 940, had joined the department in 1972 and was just two weeks short of his twenty-eight-year service anniversary. In that span, he'd performed tens of thousands of similar traffic stops, so there was nothing especially eventful about this one. But before Fink could unfasten his seatbelt or get out of his car, a Honda Prelude slammed into his 1999 Crown Victoria Police Interceptor, which burst into flames. The driver, 22-year-old Robert Stavers, likely hopped up on dope, panicked and sped away from the scene. Fink screamed for help to no avail. Schechterle woke up and saw the news the next morning.

God, it happened again? His first thought was of Juan Cruz, the 48-year-old Department of Public Safety officer who'd been similarly killed in 1998. Now Skip Fink. Two officers in uniform and working in Arizona within one hundred miles of each other and within the same radius where Schechterle was now rolling out on patrol in a Ford Crown Victoria Police Interceptor. Schechterle's second thought was that he was grateful to be a city cop, not a highway patrol officer routinely sitting in his cruiser on the side of freeways. Comparatively, *that* job seemed really dangerous, as evidenced by these recurring crashes. Schechterle, however, didn't make the connection that both deceased officers were driving Crown Victoria Police Interceptors, manufactured by Ford Motor Company—the same car he drove every shift on Phoenix streets.

The Ford Motor Company engineers had designed a vehicle that was nothing if not consistent: Fink's cruiser exploded upon impact, the suffocating flames quickly consuming metal, plastic, and human life. Though several motorists stopped and tried to help Fink, they could do little as they heard him screaming and trying to speak as he attempted escape. One or more civilians produced small fire extinguishers that helped douse the flames somewhat and extended Fink's life a few more horrible minutes.

Fire rescue crews arrived and were able to pull Fink from the smoldering wreckage, but he died en route to Maricopa County Medical Center in Phoenix, which has the Arizona Burn Center, one of the best such facilities in the entire southwestern United States. The hospital was in neighboring Phoenix and only seven miles from the crash scene. Doctors pronounced Fink dead about an hour later.

The autopsy results: Fink died of burns and smoke inhalation, not the crash impact. End of watch: February 18, 2000. Officials later caught up with Stavers, who was charged with second-degree murder, endangerment, possession and use of dangerous drugs, possession of marijuana, and leaving the scene of a fatal crash. None of that did Fink any good. Officer Fink had the most years of service among DPS officers killed in the line of duty. In December 2000, Stavers pleaded guilty to a manslaughter charge and got the maximum allowable under the plea deal reached with Maricopa County prosecutors: eighteen years.

SHORTLY after Fink's horrific death, Schechterle was in phase two of field training, which meant being paired with a new FTO for the second six weeks: Melissa Keltgen. This phase upped the ante, with Schechterle now driving the car and taking the lead on calls. Keltgen and Schechterle had good chemistry, although her style was a little more hard-line and rigid than his first FTO had been. When Schechterle screwed up, he got an earful from Keltgen: "When I tell you to do this, you do it. You got it?"

Schechterle got it. Her tough love was invaluable and helped boost his confidence. Six weeks into his new career, he'd been on hundreds of calls. By now, the police radio was music to his ears, and deciphering the chatter was no longer an issue. By phase two, the two-officer unit was answering whatever call came from dispatch: domestic, felony stop, and even homicide. Of course there was always a long list of paper calls and traffic-related calls in a career defined by paper calls and traffic-related calls. It was boring work, but it was a big part of the job.

Sometimes Schechterle and his partner were the "wagon," which meant taxi service for motos—cop-speak for officers on motorcycles—or other regular units, to transport a suspect to Madison, the jail at Madison and Second Street where every person arrested in sprawling Maricopa County got processed and put into the system. ("Madison" has since been replaced by the Fourth Avenue Jail, a few blocks west, which can house more than 2,000 inmates.)

Pulling into the sally port—the secured, enclosed intake area where all the cops parked—Schechterle would walk inside and chain the handcuffed suspect to the bench. He couldn't transfer custody to the jail staff until he'd completed the booking paperwork, made sure they had a mug shot, and took fingerprints. At the jail, Schechterle rubbed shoulders with cops in different uniforms from all over Maricopa County and various jurisdictions: Avondale, Chandler, Glendale, Mesa, Peoria, Scottsdale, Tempe, and more. On busy nights the room was packed, and invariably one irate asshole, either drunk, stoned, or both, would not shut up. Once all the administrative details were complete, Schechterle handed over the entire booking package to Maricopa County Sheriff's Office guards and went back out on patrol.

As amazing as it was to finally be out on patrol doing real police work, Schechterle's new career and higher calling was presenting real-world financial problems. Quitting his apprentice lineman position with the power company to become a cop had meant a drastic pay cut. Schechterle went from making $60,000 with overtime to less than $30,000. Subsequently, with two kids and a mortgage, things immediately slipped financially. The intangible forces that had led Schechterle back to his calling had not concurrently produced some magical financial wizardry to appease bean counters at the mortgage company. Even with Suzie working as a dental assistant at an orthodontist's office, the couple fell behind on their mortgage payments and soon went into foreclosure. Schechterle's vision to wear blue had quickly cost the couple their first home, in Goodyear.

But the drastic financial hit—and the reality of having to move into a small two-bedroom apartment with Kiley, 6, and Zane, 1, sharing a room—didn't quell the overarching mantra: *I'm meant to do this; it will all work out.* Suzie was 100 percent supportive and told her husband not to worry; it would all work out.

"I laugh and say it's the mortician, my father, in me," she said. "In other words, if you don't laugh, you'll cry. I was just so proud of Jason, and being a cop is a true piece of him."

So with a new apartment address in Arrowhead, near Seventy-Fifth Avenue and the 101 Freeway, and no discretionary income, the extra pressure squeezed Schechterle to get through his FTO program and the probationary period (one year) and succeed in law enforcement.

For the final two weeks with an FTO, officers were put in a car solo. That amped up Schechterle's nervousness again.

It's just me out here. Please give me something simple.

After breaking briefing, filling his car with gas, and driving away from the precinct gate, Schechterle grabbed the microphone and said the magic words on his own for the first time: "522 Tom. I'm 10-8."

10-8: In service and available. The "T" in Tom denoted his status as an officer in training. Almost immediately, dispatch sent out a call: "There's a 961 at Sixteenth Street and Van Buren." Schechterle's wish had come true: a minor traffic accident, which would take a good one to two hours to handle and process. He couldn't grab the mic fast enough: "I'll take it."

It was a perfect call to start his shift and break into riding solo, which really wasn't solo at all because every other officer knew Schechterle was in his final FTO phase and was paralleling his calls. At every call he took those last two weeks of training, one or two other units always rolled by just in case he needed help.

For his first official arrest, Schechterle got so excited he almost bungled it. He'd run a license plate and got a hit, which usually meant an outstanding warrant and felony stop with all the bells and whistles of big-city police work: lights and siren, multiple units, helicopter swirling overhead, guns drawn, and a K-9 poised to attack. Except Schechterle was new, and driving and trying to read the MDT screen simultaneously was an art he'd not yet perfected. This particular hit was actually a 10-52, misdemeanor warrant, which meant Schechterle could just pull the driver over and handle it himself. But he was jacked up and ready to do a felony stop, so he waited for backup, a helicopter, and a K-9 unit that weren't coming for a misdemeanor stop. Once he realized his rookie gaffe, Schechterle lit up the driver and handled the arrest without incident.

Once his fourteen weeks of field training were complete, in April 2000, Schechterle got his needed sign-off by both FTOs and his sergeant. Bryan Chapman and Shayne Tuchfarber both cleared FTO as well. Chapman would stay in Central City; Tuchfarber was in South Mountain Precinct.

Schechterle's official assignment: 53 King. Every rookie went on midnights, so Schechterle wasn't surprised. That allowed cops with more seniority to move off nights to days or afternoons. The rookies worked from nine o'clock at night until seven o'clock in the morning. Shift briefing started at 9 p.m.; they'd break briefing at 9:30, load their cars, gas up and roll at 9:35 or 9:40. Until midnight, King overlapped with the swing shift guys, to give both squads extra coverage and time to catch up on paperwork.

Suddenly, after a dozen years of applications, failures, second and third attempts, tests, interviews, polygraphs, oral board and medical examinations, background interviews and investigations, fingerprinting, physical agility testing, drug screenings, the academy, and field officer training, Schechterle had no more hurdles to clear. Now he was really nervous.

He didn't know a single person who worked 53 King. He'd never worked overnights. If the freaks came out at night, they'd be cutting a wide swath straight through his beat through the heart of Phoenix. The full force of it all really sank in as Schechterle anticipated his first official shift in uniform, riding solo, gun on hip and hands on the wheel of a police car. It was hard to believe, but the next time he hit the street on patrol, he'd finally be on his own as a full-authority Phoenix police officer. And with the reality came the ultimate responsibility: Every decision, from the most inconsequential to potentially choosing lethal force, was now his to make.

CHAPTER 10

531 King is 10-8

"I LOVED ALL COPS until I became a cop," Schechterle said.

After the long journey to finally arrive, potentialities he'd never considered were now very real. Even if only 5 percent of cops on the Phoenix force were unpleasant, maladjusted people, that meant 150 rogues out there perpetuating the bad stereotypes: Cops are jaded, cynical and condescending, badge-heavy, brutish, and misuse their position of authority to bend people to their will. They're uncaring and unfeeling drones with no heart or human soul. Divided by six precincts, that meant a couple dozen officers Schechterle didn't want to be around, much less side by side with, on calls.

"Having a badge and gun isn't a license to be disrespectful," said Schechterle.

If anything, the reality made Schechterle want to be one of the good ones who rebuilt public trust. Find ways to impart soft contacts—helping a stranded motorist push her car into a gas station—along with the requisite hard contacts, those that included handcuffs, arrests, and booking.

Another reality was that police work was not all foot pursuits of suspects through dark alleys, cuffing rapists at every turn, and engaging in high-speed pursuits of dangerous criminals. About half of all the dispatches each shift were paper calls: a burglary, vandalism, or other relatively lesser crime had been committed. A police officer needed to make an official report, but with little, if any, chance that the crime would be solved or the perpetrator ever caught. Paper calls were the bane of every cop, so seniority meant moving into beats with fewer paper calls. As the rookie, Schechterle got the paper-call-hell beat known as 531 King: an urban cluster packed to the gills with lower-tier single-family houses, dense apartment complexes and the 24/7 Walmart on Thomas Road that generated its own volume of paper calls every shift. Schechterle rolled into the Walmart parking lot almost every shift for a shoplifting call, and often two or more times during the same shift. Another 20 percent of the job was handling traffic violations and collisions, and another 20 percent answering domestic violence calls. The remaining 10 percent, the smallest bucket, included everything else: serious felony crimes and the other high action that, in movies and TV shows depicting working cops and detectives, gets 95 percent of the airplay. In reality, it was by far the smallest slice of what Schechterle did each ten-hour block of riding 53 King.

"It's a pretty safe, boring job for the most part," Schechterle said. "I loved every minute of the time I was on patrol. And 'boring' is OK: It means everybody's safe, you did your job, and you're going home."

Working the Central City Precinct, Schechterle might as well have been on a different planet from the department brass at 620 West Washington. He saw his immediate supervising sergeant regularly and, once in a while, the lieutenant. But Schechterle's world and focus was patrol area 53, one of three in his assigned precinct and, specifically, his even-narrower beat. Each shift revolved around patrolling the beat and answering up calls from the dispatcher. When the radio was quiet, Schechterle looked for OV work: find lawbreakers in action—on-view—whether a traffic misstep, prostitution, drug exchanges, or a rolling stolen. And if the overarching goal of police work was to change people's behavior—*Hey, don't do this again or you're going to get popped*—then 53 King was rife with opportunities to counsel the masses.

"I wanted to take bad guys to jail," said Schechterle. "But in between that you do a lot of other equally important stuff."

His plan and vision was to work as a patrol officer, be promoted to field training officer to mentor new recruits, and then eventually become a detective. Schechterle had no interest in moving up the promotion chain from there to supervisor. He simply wanted to be a cop, on the street and solving crimes hands-on.

Becoming a cop, through academy training and then his short time on the streets, had already changed Schechterle. It was inevitable. When cops go to restaurants, on or off duty, solo or with family, they seek out a table toward the back, facing the door. They mentally run through escape and shooting scenarios—three to five seconds—and only then enjoy the meal. The odds are low that anything will transpire, but if the possibility exists the police officer must be ready. That is drilled into police recruits from Day One at the academy: *Attention to detail is critical, because one day it might just save your life.* Civilians might tell their cop friends they're paranoid.

"We're not overly paranoid, just prepared," said Schechterle. "Having said that, the street was a lot of fun. Having people look at you and know, 'Help is here' was the best feeling in the world."

Every cop who patrols a beat is a human being with his or her own history, biases, experiences, personality, and style. One of the style points Schechterle adopted early was an inflexible code: If he stopped a good-looking woman for any infraction—or if she cried—she was getting a ticket. Why should attractive women get off easy just because of their looks? Or by feigning helplessness?

One night Schechterle stopped a stripper for speeding on her way home from work at 3 a.m. As he walked to the car and the driver's window went down, the overall effect was powerful: sticky-sweet wafting perfume, techno pulse from the radio with a heavy bass thump, and a sparkling silvery dress that had likely been her get-of-out-jail-free card more than once on this same route. The hemline was more like a belt that rode just above her neon green G-string, revealing thin, tan legs that disappeared into darkness below the dash, and the plunging V-cut at her chest exposed a sumptuous cleft of glittered, after-market cleavage. Lesser men would've already been taken down by the heady siren call, but Schechterle lashed himself to the mast and sent her home with a speeding ticket and a pissy frown on her face.

Another call, 2 a.m., put Schechterle in the thick of a high school party along Fifty-Second Street. Out of the car and into the melee, Schechterle caught and detained three of the teenagers, who were terrified. But instead of calling it in and putting the obviously stunned kids into the system, Schechterle told them to clean up the empties and scattered cups on the street as he stood watch. Once done, he reminded them of the gift they'd received: "OK, you're not in the system, and I'm not going to call your parents. So ten years from now you're not going to have to explain to a prospective employer why you were arrested. Now go home and don't do it again."

Again, the goal was to change behavior, not clog the courts and jails with petty offenses and misdemeanors. On another call, when a woman had been raped, Schechterle heard an officer already on scene tell the victim he didn't believe her story. Schechterle immediately got the vibe that his fellow officer was one of the five-percenters who shouldn't be wearing the uniform.

"I got this one," Schechterle said, inserting himself between the cop and the victim. "Get out of here." Schechterle provided the woman the empathy, understanding, and calm she'd deserved from the outset and listened carefully as she told him exactly what had happened.

On a 10-52 call, misdemeanor warrant, Schechterle and two other cops got into it with a suspect who decided he didn't want to go to jail that night. The outstanding warrant could've been cleared by paying a $200 fine; the suspect had $800 cash on his person.

"What is your problem?" Schechterle asked after the scuffle ended and he'd cuffed his suspect. Welcome to police work: Human behavior leaves cops everywhere bewildered by what they see every shift.

Another time on a domestic call, a 19-year-old kid was being cocky, disregarding Schechterle's instructions and continuing to talk on his cellphone.

"Put down your phone and get on your knees," Schechterle said. The kid ignored the command, so Schechterle took him down and cuffed his hands behind his back. Then the kid started spitting, so he got "bagged": Cops carry mesh nets to put on suspects who spit. But the wiry kid was not done: In the back of Schechterle's cruiser he slipped his legs through and got his cuffed hands in front and removed the net. Schechterle had to uncuff him, cuff him again behind his back, and put the net back on. Then he upped the verbal force: "If you do anything inappropriate I'm going to fuck you up." The f-bomb was the level of force required to get the young man's attention; he complied thereafter.

One night Schechterle answered a hot call, burglary in progress. When he rolled up to the address, unbelievably, there was the suspect in the act: Schechterle shined his light on a guy trying to break into the house. Criminals are like cockroaches: Hit them with light, and they scatter. The guy took off around the back of the house. Schechterle parked, chased, and radioed: *Foot pursuit eastbound through the park.* The park was large. Schechterle still had a visual and saw his suspect hop another fence into a backyard. Schechterle followed, up and over fences, running through dark backyards as the house occupants slept unaware.

Then Schechterle saw a Phoenix PD car parked on the street with the driver's door open. The officer was a short, squat cop, standing with one arm on the open door and one arm on the roof, with a big cigar in his mouth.

"You looking for this guy?" he said, smiling. As Schechterle stopped and leaned forward with his hands on his knees to catch his breath, he could see the skell he'd been chasing, handcuffed and face-planted on asphalt.

"You're my hero," Schechterle said, laughing.

Shift by shift and month by month, Schechterle gained confidence and found his rhythm as a cop patrolling his domain: For forty hours each week, 53 King was his entire universe and garnered 100 percent of his focus, concentration, commitment, duty, hypervigilance, and effort. Through it all, even as the balmy desert spring gave way to the brutal summer heat, Schechterle rolled through his beat with his driver's-side window down. Rain or shine, searing 115-degree heat or 40-degree cold, Schechterle could get a better pulse on things with the window open. Other cops said he was crazy, but Schechterle didn't care: He loved nothing more than being in his patrol car, alone and working his beat.

SIX states to the east and more than 1,500 miles from Schechterle's narrow patrol zone, on July 26, 2000, trucker Clifford Engum fell asleep at the wheel of the big rig he was driving through Tennessee. That same morning two Tennessee state troopers were using their respective patrol cars to block the right lane of eastbound I-40 and protect a construction crew installing rumble strips on the highway shoulder. One of those officers was Trooper Lynn Ross, a 40-year-old father of three with five years at the agency.

Engum's truck and trailer careened into Trooper Ross's Ford Crown Victoria Police Interceptor, which exploded into flames. The patrol car slid approximately 192 feet before coming to rest on the median. The truck rolled through the median and into westbound lanes, where it collided with another vehicle. Inside the Crown Victoria and unable to escape the searing flames, Ross burned to death in his cruiser.

BACK across the country in the lower desert, on August 31, 2000, lawyer Pat McGroder aimed his car south from the Gallagher & Kennedy offices in Phoenix and made the hundred-mile drive to meet with the family of deceased officer Juan Cruz. At three o'clock that afternoon, McGroder was seated with the Cruz family.

"The children were very close to their father," McGroder said. "The family wanted answers."

The deceased officer left behind four sons and a daughter, as well as eight siblings who'd all grown up with Juan Cruz in Douglas, Arizona. His parents were originally from Mexico, but came to Arizona in 1955. McGroder used the time with the family to outline the legal plan. He shared news of Trooper Ross's Crown Victoria Police Interceptor crash the previous month and, sadly, the repeated tale for Lynn Ross: impact, fire, and death of another officer. The family approved McGroder's inclusion of Texas lawyer David Perry in their case. When the meeting ended, Mrs. Cruz hugged McGroder and held him in her arms for an extended time. When she finally released her grip she said, in Spanish, "I feel good things about this man."

Later that night McGroder jotted notes about the day on a legal pad, a pattern he'd begun to track his efforts against Ford Motor Company. McGroder ended that day's entry with: *My commitment to this case has never been stronger.*

The next day, McGroder watched Ford's president and CEO make the claim in paid advertisements that, throughout the Firestone tire recall effort going on at the time, public and customer safety was the number-one priority at the company. The same executive had also just announced that he'd make public all Ford internal documents showing when Ford engineers and executives knew there was a problem with Firestone tires.

Who do they think they're kidding? McGroder said aloud to himself: It had only taken lawsuit after lawsuit to bring the defective tire problem to the attention of the U.S. government and public. The hide-and-seek played by Ford lawyers in the Firestone case illustrated for McGroder where he stood. Obviously, no one at Ford was going to willingly acquiesce to the demands of some ambulance-chaser from a cow town in Arizona.

McGroder spent a lot of time reading transcripts of communications between the criminal defense lawyer representing the drunk driver who struck Juan Cruz's cruiser and Pima County Sheriff's Office investigators. McGroder started to see a pattern: Investigators suspected, but never followed up on, the gas-tank location issue in the Crown Victoria. That, McGroder believed, was the clear cause of Cruz's death. On September 9, 2000, McGroder noted his developing theory on the legal pad: *The more I reflect on the case and the most recent death of trooper Lynn Ross in Tennessee, the more convinced I am that Ford should bear criminal as well as civil responsibility for the deaths of Cruz and Ross. I will call the county attorney next week.*

The problem is that the fire caused the deaths of these officers, not the collision. I'm not sure how that plays criminally, but if I were defending this case criminally, I'd sure raise the fire issue all over the place.

Soon McGroder and Perry were ensconced in Dearborn, Michigan, for a week at a time, deposing Ford executives for the Cruz case. William Clay Ford, who was chairman of the board at the time, endured a two-day deposition under the careful questioning and glare of the two attorneys. Depositions are the legal equivalent of a root canal: drilling down without mercy in search of the truth— who knew what, and when? Then the two lawyers, along with their respective teams of peers, paralegals, and administrative support personnel, hunkered down together in Durango, Colorado, in a hotel conference room. During those around-the-clock sessions, for days on end, they reviewed hundreds and hundreds of case documents and discussed case strategies.

As McGroder and Perry methodically worked the case, the official company stance from Ford spokespeople was that the Crown Victoria Police Interceptor was rugged, reliable, and statistically safer than ever. Police vehicles endured especially arduous conditions, running all day, every day of the year, year after year after year. However, McGroder guessed that, at least privately, executives and lawyers at Ford had to be concerned. The July 2000 death of Trooper Ross in Tennessee, the second fatality in just five months, brought the total to nine officers who had been burned alive in Crown Victoria Police Interceptors after a rear collision.

Another six officers had suffered similar events—crash, explosion, fire—but had escaped the flaming wreckage and survived with various degrees of burn injuries. In one other instance, Officer Melanie Funk's Ford CVPI patrol car was rear-ended in August 1997 in Florida. The collision punctured the fuel tank, but with no resulting fire.

By the lawyers' calculations, that meant sixteen incidents since 1981, with nine deaths by fire and six more officers seriously burned. Neither of the plaintiffs' lawyers in the Cruz case—Pat McGroder and David Perry—was intimidated by Ford's immense resources and stonewalling behind corporate walls. The two lawyers, raconteurs both, were determined to play out the drama in court, with the ultimate goal of getting Ford engineers to reconfigure the fuel tank design and position on the Crown Victoria Police Interceptor.

To the lawyers, even one more horribly burned or dead police officer was unacceptable. McGroder and Perry were determined to stop the insanity through the powerful weapon they wielded: civil action. Someone at Ford Motor Company was going to have to start answering questions about why their police cars continued to catch fire and kill upon impact.

MEANWHILE, outside the purview of civil actions, court rooms, corporate litigation, and motions by plaintiffs' and defense attorneys, Jason Schechterle was loving every minute of being a cop. He was also quickly racking up the street experience he'd one day need to be promoted to detective. Through the remaining months of 2000 and into 2001, Schechterle encountered the full range of police calls and situations. He'd been involved in about thirty felony stops. He'd watched johns pick up prostitutes on Van Buren Street—a notorious strip just east of downtown Phoenix rife with colorful characters and lined with motels that rented rooms by the hour—and pulled the johns over after some minor traffic violation to make an arrest.

As he approached his one-year anniversary, he'd been on more paper calls than he could count, a boatload of lesser crimes neatly organized into dossiers and cooling in some detective's filing cabinet. He'd never been first on scene for a murder, nor had he arrested a homicide suspect. He'd regularly drawn his weapon but never fired it while on duty.

"There are a lot of times you have your gun out," he said. "But I was never close to firing it."

In February 2001, Schechterle and his wife moved from the apartment to a rented house in Avondale. Of course, Bryan Chapman and Shayne Tuchfarber were recruited as free labor to heft furniture and boxes. It was the first time the two academy pals saw the new place. For Chapman, the second time he would come to Schechterle's house, the following month, would be the worst night of his life. But for now, Schechterle was settled into his shift and routine, 53 King, and making a little more money. He was also taking as much off-duty work as he could handle.

With Monday, Tuesday, and Wednesday as off days, Schechterle could sign up to stand watch while crews paved roads or worked on other projects that required a police officer presence, at $35 per hour, slightly more than double his normal pay rate. While good pay, the off-duty gigs did have a downside, especially during the summer: Standing next to hot asphalt for ten hours when it was 112 degrees was particularly brutal. And as new cops, the more plum security details were not available to Chapman, Tuchfarber, or Schechterle.

Then, just fourteen months into their respective nascent careers with the Phoenix Police Department, in March 2001, Jason Schechterle and Bryan Chapman orchestrated the culmination of their master plan of epic proportions. Their careers had begun on the same shift—the overnight—in the same Central City Precinct. From Day One the plan was to move to afternoons, 3 p.m. to 1 a.m., and patrol as partners. Such a maneuver, however, was tricky because there usually weren't two openings on the same shift at the same time. The two newbies, however, had somehow pulled it off, and were reassigned together to 51 George. They'd work four ten-hour days, Saturday, Sunday, Monday, and Tuesday, with a three-day break Wednesday through Friday.

On the first day as they walked toward their car, Schechterle called it: "I'm driving. You can drive tomorrow."

Of course Chapman wanted to drive, too (every cop wanted to drive), but he let it go: He knew his obsessive-compulsive partner would hate *not* driving enough that the next ten hours would be unbearable. As they rolled out of the Central City Precinct headquarters and turned north on Sixteenth Street, just north of I-17, the two cops looked at each other, smiled, and laughed.

"Can you believe it?" Schechterle said.

"No, I really can't," Chapman said, laughing.

Indeed, it was daylight instead of pitch black, and they were partners. The moment and the feeling it engendered was beyond what either could articulate. Chapman had a brief flash of being socked in back in Bowling Green, ass-deep in snow, fingers frozen, shouldering the back of a rusted Datsun B-210. Schechterle, too, had a similar epiphany of how far he'd come when he remembered the sickening crunch of his collarbone snapping on hardened North Dakota ice. To be here, now, patrolling together, was the tandem dream finally put into action. Chapman was 513 George; Schechterle was 513 Henry. That was the same precinct (500), patrol area (51) and beat (3) with a different designator for each cop. And if it was action they both sought, 513 offered all they could handle.

On one domestic call, as the duo went through the front door, Chapman immediately broke leather when he saw a shirtless male—apparently spun out on coke—who was irate and waving a weapon that flashed silver in the dimly lit house. His wife or girlfriend wanted to defuse things, but was actually screaming hysterically and only fueling the intensity of what might happen next. In seconds the stress escalated as the man ignored every verbal command yelled by Chapman, who'd taken the lead position, his Glock leveled on the suspect, index finger on the trigger frame. In a split second, Chapman could squeeze off two shots center-mass and end a life. The adrenaline dump was hitting both Chapman and Schechterle full tilt, although it wouldn't fully register until the event was over.

"Your mouth is your best weapon," Chapman had often reminded his new partner. That is, suspects just need guidance: Or as ranchers will tell you, no matter how big the bull, if you put a ring in his nose he'll follow you anywhere.

Except in this case, the mouth was 100 percent ineffective against the white-hot buzz of Colombia's most notorious export. "I thought I was going to shoot that guy," Chapman said. "I thought it was the end of the line."

With the stress-blast and intensity redlining for both Chapman and Schechterle, the crazed man continued to wave his weapon. Both partners were also thinking that Schechterle should be on point, as the better shooter of the two: Even at this range Chapman might miss and take down the TV instead. With his index finger ready to squeeze two, everything suddenly de-escalated: The man was holding a spatula. Chapman holstered the Glock he had nearly fired, they took the man down easily and cuffed him, and it was all over in seconds.

Death, spatula. Death, spatula. Death, spatula. It was an insane teeter-totter cops had to ride and then process afterward.

On another call near Eleventh Street and Pierce, the partners had guns drawn on four suspects. Once the situation went code 4—everyone cuffed and contained—the two cops heard a shot buzz over their heads. They looked at each other in silence, wondering, *What the f—?* (Officially, cops are drilled not to use profanity within earshot of the public they serve. Unofficially, f-bombs are the only way to motivate certain segments of the population.) They'd never find out who fired on them; apparently some low-level split-tooth had taken a free potshot at two police officers just for the hell of it.

Another time Chapman's brother—the proud member of the Ohio State Highway Patrol who'd made the cut—was in town for a visit and ride-along. After a lunch break, Chapman issued the challenge to Schechterle: "We'll find a stolen before you."

"I'll take that bet," Schechterle said. With that, the two brothers went off in one unit and Schechterle went solo in another. While running plates through the MDT, no one could see what was happening except the dispatcher. Only when a plate came back hot would the losing side in this game hear the bad news. It couldn't have been more than fifteen minutes before Schechterle heard the radio crack: "513 George, is that your vehicle."

"You have got to be kidding me," Schechterle mumbled aloud. *Already?* He typed the same into the MDT: *Are you kidding???*

Indeed, Chapman had run a late-model blue Honda Accord that came back hot. He and his brother were near Seventh Street and Roosevelt, near downtown Phoenix.

"10-4," Chapman said. "It's my vehicle. Eastbound Roosevelt approaching Eleventh Street. Occupied two times. Light traffic, no pedestrians."

"Copy," the dispatcher said. "Blind call for an aircraft."

Within thirty seconds, another Phoenix police car dropped in behind Chapman, OW—out with—513 George. Seconds later a third unit appeared. Chapman also knew other units were bull's-eye, which meant running parallels on adjacent streets to create a rolling perimeter. However, no units were ever down range, so that if gunfire ensued, sight lines were clean.

"K-9 pushed the neighborhood," the dispatcher relayed. Having ferocious barking dogs on scene was always a nice deterrent for suspects considering stupidity such as fleeing. Then Chapman and his brother could hear the helicopter blades chopping black air right above their position, and the pilot gave the go-signal: "Light 'em up."

Chapman did just that, flashing red and blue lights along with the helicopter search beam pinned on the suspect vehicle. Schechterle raced to the left of Chapman's position while the third unit took the right, creating a fan of three behind the suspect vehicle. In the twisted vernacular of being a cop, felony stops were a lot of fun.

This kind of heart-thumping tactical maneuver was just what they'd trained so hard for during the academy. To pull it all off smoothly, with the helo turning night into day, an equally well-trained K-9 ready to chomp flesh, and without incident, was pure magic. If the suspects were dumb enough to run into the night, the dogs and/or FLIR infrared on the helo would track them quickly. The sticky web rarely failed to snare its prey.

"Code 4," Chapman said once the suspects were face-down and cuffed. "Two in custody."

When the scene was secured, Chapman had to gloat a bit. Just before he and his brother climbed back in the patrol car to leave, Chapman turned to his partner and said, "Someday you'll learn how to do real police work."

BY then, in the waning days of March 2001, all the players were in place for a collision twenty-three years in the making. In 1978, when Schechterle was just 6 years old, prowling the dusty nirvana encircling the house on Hidalgo, Ford Motor Company had introduced the Crown Victoria Police Interceptor for model year 1979.

Now the clock was ticking. Exactly eight months to the day after the burning death of Officer Lynn Ross in Tennessee in 2000, the next fire would ignite inside a Crown Victoria—on March 26, 2001.

Part II

Burn Odyssey

CHAPTER 11

Central City Precinct, patrol unit 513 Henry

March 26, 2001, 11:21 p.m.

IT ALL HAPPENED in such rapid succession that it was hard for any of the four firefighters rolling northbound near the same intersection to immediately comprehend and process: a crash explosion to their left, followed by a massive fireball flaring upward twenty feet and curling above the freeway overpass.

None of the four saw the impact; Darren Boyce opened his eyes and saw the fireball and police car being projected forward straight toward the moving fire truck. With the flaming wreckage beneath the overpass and hurtling eastbound, the sound of metal scraping asphalt was especially amplified.

"We were en route to another non-emergency call that might require medical treatment, so we were at the bottom end of the preparation scale to fight a fire when all this happened," Boyce said.

"To suddenly be facing a car fire skidding toward us was the last thing we expected," Rebecca Joy said. As the fire truck approached Thomas Road, never stopping, the flaming police cruiser was on a direct line to it.

"I turned toward this exploding fireball coming toward us," Boyce said. "It was really loud." Immediately, Boyce instinctively reached for his turnouts, kicked off his shoes, put his feet into his boots, and pulled up his bunker pants while stooped over in the tight cab.

Driving in the far right lane of the access road, Joy was already committed to the originally planned turn, so she steered the massive truck through the gentle right-hand sweeper merging onto Thomas Road eastbound. She heard the explosion and saw the fire lick up and above the overpass. With the flaming wreckage not even at a full stop yet, Captain Michael Ore was grabbing the radio mic to call the Alarm Room.

Without ever slowing, Joy immediately made a left-hand turn, steered the massive truck back westbound on Thomas Road, and nosed the truck 40 feet from the devastating crumple of fire and metal. Her quick thinking saved more precious seconds: If she had made the right-hand turn eastbound, she would have had to navigate the lumbering truck over the concrete median to make the U-turn back westbound to the scene. There was a yellow taxi and a flaming police cruiser with the red and blue lights atop the car still silently flashing.

"Engine 5 to Alarm, we're on the scene of a 962 with a police officer trapped," Ore told the dispatcher. "Give me the balance of a first alarm medical, and Engine 5 will be Thomas Road command. We're at Twentieth Street and Thomas." Ore's rapid radio response would turn out to be one of the key elements in the life-saving formula.

"Michael Ore did exactly what he was supposed to do," Boyce said. "He had the frame of mind to call in the incident immediately as it was happening."

In fact, every task by each firefighter was already being measured in seconds and fractions of seconds, and so far all their movements had been textbook: Joy instinctively positioning the truck perfectly—within reach of the wreckage for the shorter jump lines in the fire truck's front bumper—without ever stopping; Boyce gearing out even as the truck was still moving; and Ore calling it in immediately without delay, which set the Rescue 11 ambulance in motion, rather than first jumping out to assist as would be the normal default reaction at such an intense scene. And although a gaffe by any measure, Narvaez's oversleep and the subsequent delay of thirty seconds had put the fire truck at the precise point for the fastest possible response. In other words, minus those thirty seconds, Engine 5 would have already been eastbound and well down Thomas Road at the moment of impact. And in that scenario, Jason Schechterle would be dead on scene.

"The hot call went out for a traffic accident involving the police department," said Phoenix Police Officer Bryan Brooks, who was driving westbound on Thomas Road toward the fire and would be the first officer on scene. "Basically I looked down the street, and I could see an enormous fireball. From that point it looked like it was at least twenty or thirty feet high, as high as the freeway overpass."

"When I first got there the fire was super-intense," said Officer Brooks, badge 6635. He had been around a handful of raging automobile and house fires during his four years on the force, but nothing with the searing intensity of what he was seeing, feeling, and smelling just a few feet away. That one of his own was trapped inside in uniform made it especially sickening and wrenching.

"I looked in the sky toward that direction… I could see a light in the sky, basically," said Kevin Chadwick, the second officer from the Phoenix Police Department on scene. He and Brooks were partners, but had rolled out separately for the night.

"Bryan Brooks is one of the best decision-making cops I've ever met," said Chadwick. "I heard a slight quiver in his voice, which was not like him, which meant this was far more serious than anything I could have imagined."

"The incident looked like something from a movie, with a wake of flames trailing a huge fireball attached to a police car with its light bar still flashing," said Joy. When the flaming wreckage of police car and taxi finally stopped, the smoke and fire swept forward and up like a dust cloud after a stop on a dirt road. Joy stopped the truck and yelled, "Let's go!"

Boyce jumped out of the truck, grabbed his air bottle, and strapped it on his back; he left the respirator mask dangling by its hose. When he turned toward the fire, he saw Joy already pulling the front jump line from the thick front bumper.

This specific line connected to a foam-and-water solution with the capability to snuff out fires more effectively than just using plain water.

Also called "trash lines" because they're often used to douse Dumpster fires and debris, the two seventy-five-foot lines were smaller and shorter hoses, which offer less water capacity than the main lines, but more maneuverability. At less than half the length of the two-hundred-foot main lines, Joy and Boyce could deploy them much more quickly. The entire length of hose had to be pulled from the basket before charging it with water, or the hose would kink, tangle, and become very ineffective for fighting fire.

"At that point, my job was to put the truck in pump gear and get water down the line as fast as possible," Joy said. "I knew the front left jump line was our go-to line." The typical operating protocol on any fire was for the firefighters to pull the line while the engineer focused on charging it with water. But in this scenario each crew member was doing everything possible to reduce response time, which is why Joy started pulling the line.

Boyce slipped on his helmet, broke into a dead run toward the flaming vehicles, and grabbed the hose nozzle on the line Joy was already pulling. Before reaching the flaming cars Boyce saw a body lying motionless in the street, which he assumed was the dead taxi driver. Then he saw a person in plainclothes running toward the fire.

A civilian named Ralph Koepke, on his way home from his normal 3 p.m.-to-11 p.m. second shift, had also been stopped at the red light, watched the horrible collision and fireball, and leaped from his truck to help. Without thinking he ran to the burning cruiser, but the intense heat drove him back before he could do anything.

With the truck already in pump gear, Joy ran back to the truck's pump panel and charged the front left jump line, by pulling down a lever, assuring Boyce would have water just as he opened the nozzle. She had already cleared the remaining hose from the hose bed on the bumper.

Boyce could feel the hose charging as he reached the vehicles; then he heard and felt a blast of heat, smoke, and flames pop from the rear of the police car. Fire was pouring out from under the driver's side of the vehicle, with thick black smoke and fire filling the passenger compartment. There were also flames shooting straight up the back of the vehicle, and Boyce could see fuel dripping everywhere that was also on fire.

All the windows on the police car were up and intact except the small wing window on the rear passenger side, which was broken. While Schechterle always patrolled windows down, once on the way to a call he put them up for less noise. Boyce stuck the nozzle through the broken opening and blasted the flames for a couple seconds. As he did so, the pressure of the air and water from the hose pushed the flames and smoke outward from underneath the car.

"I could feel the intense heat go up my legs even with my turnouts on," Boyce said.

Boyce pulled the hose from the window and sprayed downward to the street with the nozzle in a wide-open fog pattern, which was sending atomized air and water in a large cone pattern. Boyce quickly worked back and forth, from inside to outside, numerous times. Officer Brooks was already calling off intersection blockages.

To anyone watching Boyce, they might have wondered why the other firefighters weren't all equipped with hoses and dousing the blaze from every angle. But the trained firefighters knew that each hose blast pushed flames, smoke and debris the opposite direction, which meant anyone on the other side—with an opposing hose line—would be in the crossfire.

Knowing this, Joy ran back and grabbed the red line, which was also at the front bumper on a reel and pumped about thirty gallons a minute. While the line Boyce was using had an output of 175 gallons a minute, the red line was a quick and efficient solution to help douse the taxi on the far side away from the cop car.

"My intention was to help contain the taxi fire and the burning fuel heading down the street," Joy said.

Meanwhile, Boyce saw his crewmate Narvaez and yelled, "Break the window!"

The booter took his axe and smashed the driver's-side window, which fell out in one big clump of shattered glass attached to window tint. Thick black smoke poured out.

"I needed to get the nozzle fog pattern right by Jason's face to push in fresh air and water," Boyce said. But as Boyce blasted inside the compartment, flames and smoke flared from under the car again. Boyce knew through his training that from the time of impact to this exact moment was the most critical period to give the officer a chance to survive. Unconsciously, during intense fires the human body's natural response is to shut down the airway for protection; the victim literally stops breathing. But at some point, the body has to have oxygen, releasing the airway safety shutdown mechanism and taking in a huge gasping breath. If done when surrounded by flames and smoke, this single inhalation can sear and ravage the esophagus, and the victim can bleed out internally. Now, however, with Boyce clearing the area around Schechterle's face, that necessary gasp might not prove fatal.

"Another ten or fifteen seconds, and it would have been a fatal accident," Boyce said. "All it would have taken was one deep breath, and he would have died. He was already pure black."

Each member of the Engine 5 crew was well aware of the running clock: From impact to now, with the foam just starting to cool the blaze, it had been less than a minute. But that was an eternity in flames of this intensity: Holding a hand over hot grill coals for ten *seconds* will produce third-degree burns. The officer still trapped was grotesque, now splitting open like a hot dog left on the rotisserie too long.

The rear half of the police cruiser looked as though it had been hit by an FIM-92 Stinger missile, and was just completely destroyed; the front half of the car was relatively intact. From where the firefighters and police officers stood and what they could see through the driver's side window, whoever was in the car was likely dead already. This was no longer a rescue but rather a body recovery.

"Get him out!" Boyce yelled to the booter as he worked the nozzle back and forth. Boyce would pause and step to his right to allow Narvaez the space to lean in and try to pull out the officer, then Boyce would slide back over and spray again.

Narvaez leaned into the police cruiser to try to unlatch the damaged seatbelt mechanism. He frantically tried the door, too, which was crumpled shut. Even this close, he still could not tell if the officer was alive or dead, or if it was a man or a woman. Schechterle's skin was already charred black, and the smell of it bubbling away was horrific. With each attempt, Narvaez could not unlatch the clasp. He tried frantically tugging on the officer's shirt, but the body was immovable inside the burning wreckage. An intense aggravation swept through Narvaez as he repeatedly tried to extricate the trapped officer from the cruiser.

Boyce blasted another heavy mist near the driver's seat, hoping the burning officer would take a breath from the atomized and oxygenated water being pumped through the fog nozzle. But working the nozzle around the interior sent massive flare-ups in every other direction. Boyce could see the officer sitting motionless, upright with hands on thighs like some sort of horror image from a Stephen King novel—a stoic, black-charcoaled mannequin among swirling flames. *OK, if you're dead, please be dead. You don't want to live through this.*

Officer Brooks felt frustrated beyond words. "For a moment I was helpless, so the training kicks in and you try to find something to do," he said. That something was trying to figure out who was trapped in the patrol car. The unit number on the car's back end had already been obliterated by collision and flames.

"I thought it was a black officer, but I knew we didn't have any black officers on shift on our squad," said Brooks, who was patrolling 52 King. He also knew Thomas Road was the north-south border between precincts 500 (Central City) and 700 (Squaw Peak), so it would not be uncommon for an officer from the other precinct to respond. He radioed his observation and listened as the dispatcher did an all-call for every officer working in 700. Although it was incorrect, all the first responders could see a black officer still trapped in the car. As the dispatcher tried to identify the trapped cop—which would have been verified with a moment of eerie radio silence after one of the names—no one knew they were roll-calling the wrong precinct. Schechterle worked the 500 precinct, and he was not African American. As Brooks listened to the all-call, Chadwick rolled up and parked.

"My first thought was, guys, it's just a car: You can relax," he said. "From what I could see, there was no way there was someone in that car. The fire department crew was working as feverishly as I've ever seen them work, as efficiently as I've ever seen them work. And then I saw what I thought was a silhouette, and I couldn't believe there was still an officer inside the car. At that point the fire was too strong, and the smoke was too thick."

For Chadwick, one of the oddest and eeriest sights was the red and blue lights, still silently flashing atop the light bar, and engulfed in flames.

"I can't get the seat belt," Narvaez yelled.

Amid the chaos and intense heat and smoke Boyce only heard "seat belt" and yelled, "Cut it!" Neither Boyce nor Narvaez had taken the time to affix a respirator mask, and the fire was still lashing out from under the car and climbing up the back, with smoke pouring from the passenger compartment.

Narvaez yelled back toward the truck, "Skip, bring a fixed blade. We'll cut him out." Narvaez had his own knife, but it was buried underneath his heavy bunker pants, and there was no way he could remove his fire-retardant gloves this close to the heat. A thick thundercloud of acrid black smoke was pouring upward, swirling around the underpass and then melding into what had been a balmy, sparkling city night. As Narvaez yelled for the knife, Officer Chadwick stood five feet away.

As the flames ebbed slightly under Boyce's careful dousing, the firefighters and two cops could all see that the entire mobile data terminal attached to the dashboard was melted into a massive glob of black. Then, without warning, the blackened body inside the cruiser gasped with a guttural roar, arms reaching toward the window as if he were trying to escape the flames. Schechterle was unconscious, but some primal and pulsing genetic glow to live was fully awake and cognizant of imminent death.

"That was freaky," Chadwick said. "It scared the living crap out of all of us."

The firefighters and cops, all normally inured to such scenes, were at first shocked for a brief second. Then they were all infused with a massive adrenaline dump: *Holy shit… how is he still alive? Get him out, get him out, get him out!*

Unconsciously, Officer Chadwick reached to his weak-side, non-gun hip, drew his knife with his left hand and opened it in a quick one-handed flip that he had practiced hundreds of times to perfect. He always wore the knife on his non-dominant side, away from his gun, so that if he were ever in a scuffle with someone trying to unholster his firearm, he would still be able to defend himself by opening and using the knife with only his left hand. Now it was all unconscious muscle memory doing the work. Boyce never saw Chadwick except for the fast swoop of his arm inside the passenger compartment and then an almost instant retraction.

As he reflected later, Chadwick would have no recollection of grabbing the knife or the searing heat as he leaned in to save his fellow officer. Chadwick cut the seat belt strap and yanked on Schechterle, but could not free the officer because Schechterle's right foot was entangled under the pedals. His partner Brooks reached through the driver's-side window and helped untangle Schechterle's legs. Then the two cops and rookie firefighter, all to Boyce's left, yanked Schechterle free.

"That was the last time I saw Jason until June," Boyce said.

"I can remember the swirling fire above the passenger seat," Brooks said. He would also be coughing for a couple days afterward from gulping smoke.

Meanwhile, the radio cracked, "Rescue 11 to Thomas Command; where do you want us?"

With Michael Ore preoccupied and unable to respond, Joy, juggling the redline, grabbed her portable radio from her belt and answered with, "Rescue 11, pull up alongside the cop car."

As they were pulling the charred body out—no one could identify whom they had just freed—the ambulance arrived on cue. Amid the blur of activity, Brooks pulled the burned officer's name tag to get a positive ID. As the Rescue 11 firefighters opened the back of the ambulance to wheel out the gurney, Chadwick yelled, "Leave the gurney in there!"

By now, there were others on scene helping float Schechterle along. The group only had to walk about ten steps before putting Schechterle directly onto the gurney inside the ambulance, another critical time-saving maneuver that shaved more seconds.

"By that time, we had a few more firefighters on scene helping," Joy said. "It was like Jason was as light as a feather with all those hands."

None would have any recollection of Schechterle being hot to the touch. More rescuers at the window of Schechterle's car would have been too many; any fewer would not have been enough. The paramedics tended to the severely burned officer immediately and started on-scene prep inside the ambulance, including inserting a critical breathing tube. Then Chadwick noticed Brooks staring at something in his cupped hand.

"It's Jason," Brooks said. He was holding the name tag he had removed.

"Jason who?"

"Jason Schechterle."

This revelation did not make any sense: They had both just seen a black officer, but Jason Schechterle was Caucasian, the Karate Kid from the Hidalgo House. Chadwick ran back to the ambulance and said, "I need his wallet." He saw the paramedics struggling with the tangled radio cord that ran from Schechterle's duty belt, up his back, and over his shoulder.

"Cut the cord!" Chadwick yelled, which the paramedics did, enabling them to remove the duty belt altogether and hand over everything, including the wallet. Chadwick rifled through the wallet and found the commission card that every officer carried: Indeed, it was Jason Schechterle they had just pulled from the burning car. As the two cops stood in disbelief, the number of responders at the scene increased dramatically as more fire and police personnel arrived.

Miraculously, Schechterle had "only" been trapped in the inferno for less than a minute. Had the Phoenix Fire Engine 5 crew not been at that same intersection at the time of impact, Joy would have had to pull a U-turn over the concrete median to get back to the scene. Because of the collective synchronistic timing to that point, Joy was able to maneuver the fire truck into the direction of the burning inferno immediately after impact to begin the rescue. Had the crash occurred at any of thousands of other intersections in metropolitan Phoenix, Schechterle would already be dead.

From the crash scene, the best burn doctors in the southwestern United States were only two miles away: the Arizona Burn Center at Maricopa County Medical Center. An unlikely chronology and collection of events had converged to give Schechterle the narrowest possibility of survival.

Meanwhile, Boyce still had some hot spots to extinguish. That's when he first saw the taxi driver, awake and staring straight at the firefighter, pinned behind the steering wheel of his car with both vehicles still burning. Boyce had thought the body he saw in the street was the dead taxi driver, so this didn't make any sense.

"Someone will come get you out," Boyce yelled to him, thinking, *What are you doing in there?* Eventually, Boyce's hose nozzle went dry. Engine 5 had dumped its full tank of five hundred gallons of water onto the fire, which was an enormous amount for a two-vehicle fire. With Schechterle en route to the Arizona Burn Center at County, and the fire out, the first responders turned their full attention to cutting free the pinned taxi driver and treating the ejected passenger. The fare, the man Boyce had seen lying on Thomas Road approximately 150 feet from the impact site, had just been released from jail before climbing in the taxi. He was severely cut and scraped and would spend the next two weeks in the hospital.

How in the hell were all three people, after one of the most horrific collisions the firefighters had ever seen and heard, all still alive? Indeed, thermodynamics, physics, and logic just would not allow it. It seemed some inexplicable protective force was at work.

As the ambulance raced away with Schechterle, no one on scene thought there was any way he would survive the night, much less go on living; he probably would not even make it to the emergency room.

"Damn," Brooks said after the ambulance departed. "That was intense." Chadwick nodded. Both he and Brooks immediately felt exhausted.

"Our part of the event was done," Chadwick said.

However, officers Brooks and Chadwick would be at the crash site for two hours, as it was now a crime scene. The two partners and four firefighters would gather with others for the debriefing with department brass before heading to the hospital later, where Chadwick would hand the wallet to Schechterle's wife Suzie. For the immediate debriefing police officers and firefighters stood around the hood of a police car in the Food City parking lot immediately north of the crash scene. One of the concerns that arose collectively: *Did we do this guy a favor?*

For everyone involved, there had not yet been time to contemplate the near-impossible chronology and timing of events that had kept Schechterle alive. First, Narvaez oversleeping, which delayed the response time by thirty seconds and allowed Joy to place the fire truck at the perfect location to begin a rescue and not a body recovery. Second, Joy's precise maneuvering of the truck without slowing down at the intersection, and parking as close as safely possible to the fire. Third, Ore's immediate radio call, which had the ambulance arriving exactly at the time Schechterle was ready for transport. Fourth, Boyce's and Joy's precise teamwork in getting the jump line readied and charged without even one second of delay in putting water on the fire, and carefully spraying the aerated water past Schechterle's face to displace the toxic smoke. Fifth, Narvaez breaking the window as needed, and sixth, Chadwick having the knife and cutting the seat belt. Seventh, Brooks having the wherewithal to reach in and untangle Schechterle's legs. Remove any one of those elements, thus changing timetable and trajectory, and there was no way they pulled Schechterle out alive.

THAT hot call changed everything for a long list of people that night, starting with Jason Schechterle. The impact waves would soon ripple eastward to high-ranking executives and attorneys in the Ford Motor Company who, at that moment, were prostrate on six-hundred-thread-count sheets in highbrow Detroit suburbs Ann Arbor, Gross Pointe, Harper Woods, and Lake St. Clair. Ford executives, engineers, and lawyers would have to face tough questions raised by McGroder and Perry: Was there something inherently wrong with the Ford Crown Victoria Police Interceptor? That is, why does it keep bursting into flames and burning people alive?

Back at the scene in the desert metropolis, the firefighters and cops all had other private thoughts: *Under the circumstances, God help him, there's no way our brother survives. Please let Jason go quickly so that he suffers no more.*

CHAPTER 12

Down to Bone

ABOUT 10 MINUTES before Schechterle's patrol car was blasted into a fireball, he'd finally escaped paper-call hell and had rolled by on a domestic violence call (simply a "DV call" in the police world), which Bryan Chapman had already responded to minutes earlier. As Schechterle slowed and rolled up, he could see Chapman standing in the darkened doorway with light spilling out from inside.

In police work, calm conversation on scene was always a good sign, so Schechterle was not surprised when he saw Chapman hold up four fingers, code 4: Schechterle wasn't needed. Events that happened or did not happen in the next seconds and minutes that night determined the course of everything for Schechterle from that day forward. In the end, the ticking clock and converging events put him in the intersection at Twentieth Street and the 51 Freeway, in the far left lane, at the exact moment of rear impact.

In an alternate world, Chapman might have waved Schechterle on scene, not because he needed him but rather to trade jabs and share a laugh with his best friend before the next call. They'd finally orchestrated working the same shift and becoming partners for this exact reason: the chance to work side by side and shoot the breeze when the opportunity arose. That one simple decision, to wave Schechterle to a stop, would have changed everything.

Instead, Schechterle stopped but remained in his car, letting the engine idle as he talked with the other officers on scene. One of them bummed a chew, which meant Schechterle had to dig out his can of Skoal Wintergreen long-cut and chide the fellow officer for not buying his own, all of which took a minute or two. That process, too, became a part of the ominous timetable. Minus the plea for chew, Schechterle would have been farther down the road and, in all likelihood, ahead of the speeding danger of the rocketing taxi.

Or, it would have been completely normal for Schechterle to, at that point, simply park the cruiser, climb out, and spend a few minutes talking shop to wait for Chapman to finish. Had he done that, Schechterle would've still heard the hot call but likely wouldn't have responded, since it was in the 52 area and he was patrolling 51, the 513 Henry beat. Instead, it played out the way it did: Schechterle was ablaze, unconscious, and quickly sliding into the uncharted realm of death.

AFTER wrapping up the DV call, Bryan Chapman suggested a coffee break to the other officers, who were midnight-shift guys. Chapman and Schechterle had just come off the same shift a month prior, so it was a good time to catch up with his old pals who were still riding the long sleepy grind of 51 King. Hours later, even most criminals would be in bed, leaving every Phoenix cop riding King across six precincts with little to do except patrol, shake off slumber, and try to find some wrongdoing to stay awake.

Springhill Suites, at Ninth Street and Van Buren near downtown Phoenix, was a well-lit, bright, clean hotel frequented by Central City cops for its quiet lobby (for doing paperwork), clean restrooms, and unlimited 24/7 supply of fresh, free coffee for hotel guests and law enforcement. Chapman and the two other officers stood near the coffee urn, talked, and kept ears tuned to the radio traffic. Even so, none of them heard the first emergency call that went out on the horrible collision that had just happened in the 51 area.

Then, minutes later, Chapman heard the emergency pulse beat, which always sharpened the focus to see if the call was in his precinct areas: 51, 52, or 53. Then he heard the dispatcher relay, "962, Twentieth Street and Thomas."

Chapman relaxed: A vehicle smashup that far away was no cause for alarm. Plenty of other units were closer to respond. Just as Chapman was easing back into the conversation, the hot tone went out with the dispatcher relaying more information, "Anyone responding to the 962 PD-involved vehicle on fire?"

A hot tone for a PD-involved 962 vehicle on fire was a rare call.

Full coffee cups hit the trash can as the three officers ran to their cruisers: Chapman was riding solo, and the other two were 515 Mary, a two-man unit designator. As the clock approached midnight, there was little traffic along Van Buren Street, the notorious den of prostitution, pimps, drug dealing, seedy motels renting rooms by the hour, and an abundant supply of suspects with outstanding warrants ripe for pickup. By the mid-2000s Van Buren Street would be scrubbed clean, with much of the former criminal activity migrating west to the numbered avenues in the Maryvale Precinct.

Chapman rocketed westbound on Van Buren, no lights or siren, and listened to the radio closely. He immediately typed his partner a message on the MDT: *Let's meet up and do traffic control.* He figured if there were fatalities, they would be on scene for hours. At least this way they could be in proximity to kill time through the wee hours together in their reflective orange vests. But there was no response. Chapman sent another message: *Are you en route to 962?*

The MDT spit back a message Chapman had only ever seen when an officer's MDT was turned off: *Message undeliverable.* But that didn't make any sense: Schechterle was on duty.

Unless that slacker Schechter Shorts signed off at 11:30. But that didn't make any sense either: *Super Cop Schechterle was the slacker antithesis: No way Anal Andy signs off early.*

Chapman checked the status of 513 Henry, his partner's designator: *En route to call in 52.* Now he was starting to piece it together, and he did not like that Schechterle had been en route to the call and was now not responding. Feeling more desperate, Chapman sent another MDT message and got the same response: *Message undeliverable.*

At Sixteenth Street, Chapman smoked the tires all the way through the left turn as he proceeded northbound. He was picking up more details from the dispatcher: *Other units on scene. PD involved. Need additional units. Ambulance en route with one officer to county.* As Chapman approached McDowell Road, he knew the ambulance would be heading toward him. Another dispatch: "Unit available to do follow-up at County?"

At that moment, Chapman saw the flashing lights of the ambulance heading south, but the vehicle wasn't going all that fast. Chapman breathed a bit of relief: perhaps the officer involved wasn't hurt all that bad. Maybe this was all procedural. As the ambulance passed, Chapman had a clear view into the well-lit interior, where he could see paramedics attending to someone.

"513 George," Chapman said. "Will follow up at County."

The ambulance rolled into the County parking lot—Maricopa Medical Center—with Chapman's patrol car tailing. Both vehicles parked, and Chapman climbed out and watched the paramedics pull the gurney. Chapman could see now that the officer was in really bad shape.

I hope this isn't Jason. It was a disturbing thought: Every officer was part of the brotherhood and family, but Chapman still breathed a macabre and understandable sigh of relief when he realized this was not his partner Jason Schechterle. No way it could be: The officer on this gurney was African American, someone from a different precinct.

WHEN Jason Schechterle first hit the street in January 2000, the cops who worked Central City Precinct joked they should each use a black Sharpie to write on their body armor: *If found, take to County.* Maricopa Medical Center, as part of Maricopa Integrated Health System in Phoenix, was one of the fifty largest public hospitals in the country, with 449 patient beds and more than 3,400 employees. Officials designated it the Maricopa County hospital in 1883, and by 2001 the facility housed one of the best burn and trauma centers in the nation. To local cops and firefighters, Maricopa Medical Center was simply called "County." The hospital was also in the 500 Precinct.

When emergency room doctors saw the charred body being wheeled in on a gurney, gasps escaped even trained medical professionals inured to such tragedy.

On scene, paramedics had intubated Schechterle, which gave him an airway to breathe. At County, doctors replaced the temporary breathing tube with a more permanent endotracheal tube as well as inserting a second tube for feeding.

Soon they would also put Schechterle into a medically induced coma, a deeper black hole than the murky abyss in which he was already mired. If he managed to somehow survive the burn trauma itself, his odds were unbelievably long. As Schechterle had sat burning alive, he'd inhaled all manner of searing toxic fumes: melting plastics, metal, gasoline, vinyl, fabric, insulation, and carbon monoxide. His lungs were severely compromised. Secondary infections would spread quickly, without mercy, and consume his trauma-weakened body. On a scale of one to one hundred, Schechterle's life glow was "1" and fading fast.

Meanwhile, Chapman was still trying to determine the identity of his fallen comrade. Kathleen Packer, a squadmate, had arrived, as well as another officer. Amid the frenzied work of the medical team, the three cops stood watching. Just a few feet away, whoever was on the gurney was unrecognizable.

Chapman reached in to try to grab the officer's name badge, but it was gone. The medical staff began cutting away Schechterle's clothing, so when the shredded uniform pants hit the floor Chapman rifled them looking for a wallet, but found none. The pants were infused with an overpowering, toxic smell of gasoline. Although no one noticed, also missing was Schechterle's wristwatch, which had been a gift from his older brother Michael. Michael had given his younger brother the watch engraved with both their badge numbers in celebration of his own ten-year service anniversary and Schechterle's new career. The watch was a casualty of the collision and fire, never to be found. But it did leave a narrow band of intact white skin on Schechterle's arm.

The organized chaos was efficient, as the multiple doctors and nurses quickly removed Schechterle's clothes. Then Chapman saw the tattoo: a Tasmanian Devil on the victim's upper left arm.

"Holy shit, that's Jason," he said.

"Jason who?" someone asked.

"Jason Schechterle."

Packer was stunned. The medical team was unfazed by the identification, which was to them unimportant: They were all frantically absorbed in trying to save a man's life. The team was a blur of activity when Schechterle vomited a brown swill, the distilled remnants of the Taco Bell meal he'd eaten with his partner at the fire station. The medical team watched the monitors and checked for a pulse. Doctors blurted commands, which turned to a din of white noise for Chapman, who still couldn't believe it was his partner on the table, naked and charred beyond recognition. Despite the overwhelming emotional panic, Chapman's police training kicked in: *What's important now?*

He's going to die. I've got to go tell Suzie.

A soldier wrote his final letter, sealed and addressed for delivery if he ever went KIA. Many cops made similar arrangements. The deal between the two partners, which they had struck during the academy, was that each would personally take the grim task of notifying the other's wife. Another related talk they had had was in 2000, after Arizona Department of Public Safety Trooper Skip Fink, 53, was burned alive in his Ford Crown Victoria Police Interceptor in the nearby Phoenix suburb of Tempe.

"That ever happens to me, pal," Schechterle told his partner, "Promise me you'll put a bullet in me and end it quickly and mercifully."

"Consider it done," Chapman said, slapping his partner's back.

"Little too quick and eager there, right?"

"Hey," Chapman had said, smiling, "What are friends for?"

These were actually serious pledges made amid the normal lighthearted jabs of male friendship, each envisioning they would go twenty-plus on the job and pension out unharmed. But for Jason Schechterle the blow, likely fatal, had come during month fifteen of his new career, the profession he had given up everything to pursue.

Chapman stepped away from the melee and called his duty sergeant, Theresa Clark, on his cellphone: "It's Jason."

"I know," she said, having heard the news from Brooks and Chadwick on scene, who had grabbed Schechterle's name plate and wallet.

"What the hell happened?" Chapman asked.

"Looks like he was hit by a taxi. Is he going to make it?"

"No," Chapman said, grimacing. "I don't think he will."

Clark was privy to the pledge between the partners. "Then don't you have a job to do?"

"Yeah," Chapman said, nodding.

"Do you want anyone to go with you?"

"No. I'll go by myself."

Chapman stepped back toward the trauma team. His buddy was completely unrecognizable. Still alive, barely, but Chapman resigned himself to the reality.

This is the last time I'll see him alive. The only thing I can do is uphold my promise and go tell his wife.

Chapman said a silent goodbye as a hospital technician handed him a bag filled with his partner's burned uniform and black boots. The aroma of gasoline was powerful without even opening the bag. Chapman walked back into the night in a daze, opened the trunk to his cruiser, and carefully placed the bag inside. It was all too strange, because Chapman had taken dozens of similar bags from various arrests and scenes without much more thought than having another to-do on the list before shift's end: *Transport personal effects to 620.* He closed the trunk with a reverence for what it now held.

There were no tears, no sobs of agony. The shock of the entire situation was partially numbing the free flow of emotions. The bigger block was police training, laser focus amid chaos, mayhem, and tragedy, and this cop had a sacred job to do. He could not be falling apart now; that privilege was being reserved for Suzie Schechterle. Chapman had been trained how to handle this sort of situation, and he had heard and watched other officers deliver similarly grim news. But nothing had truly prepared him for this duty. This was *his* partner, and his partner's wife.

Chapman climbed into his cruiser, raced onto the westbound 202 Freeway, and then the I-10 westbound to Avondale. With no lights or siren, he was in the far left lane pushing 100 miles per hour. Then something occurred to him, and he backed off to 65.

The sooner I get there, the sooner her life will change forever. Why not give her a few more minutes of blissful peace, which she'll never again have from this point forward?

Chapman called his wife and relayed what he knew, which was that his partner would soon be dead. He called Fatso, too, Officer Shayne Tuchfarber, but they exchanged no "man boobs" or "pumpkin head" jabs on this night.

"Jason's been in an accident," Chapman said.

"What? What happened?"

"He's at County. Car rear-ended him. He's not going to make it."

There was dead silence as all the wind went out of Tuchfarber on the other end of the line. Then, "I'll be at County in fifteen minutes."

Tuchfarber, who had been off that day to dig trenches for sprinkler lines in Chapman's front yard, was shaking off sleep and trying to process what Chapman was saying: *I just saw him a few hours ago.* After the call Tuchfarber called their academy pal Mark Roach, and the ripple effect continued. Soon County would be swarming with cops.

AT County, Schechterle freefell into a painless netherworld, his body prostrate in the CT scan machine. Dr. Daniel Caruso, co-director at Arizona Burn Center, a department of Maricopa Medical Center, tapped his fingers against his patient's face, and he did not like the sound he heard. A mild sunburn was a first-degree burn; burns with blisters were second-degree; third-degree burns turned white and consumed all layers of skin down to the body's fat.

As he tapped and listened, Dr. Caruso knew he was staring at the worst of the worst: fourth-degree burns, which consumed the fat, too, and exposed tendons, blood vessels, cartilage, and bone. The sound emitted by his knuckles across the blackened face was not good, like that of tapping a coconut. Severe burns caused skin and tissue to harden in the first twenty-four to seventy-two hours; Schechterle was already in that red zone after minutes.

The gasoline inferno of Schechterle's police cruiser likely burned at seven hundred degrees. That meant instant third-degree burns, and fourth-degree in seconds. The firefighters had said Schechterle was *on* fire for at least fifteen seconds, but probably closer to a full minute. The doctors could see that close to half his body was burned; it would turn out to be 43 percent. Schechterle's face, head, and both hands were fourth-degree. The only area spared, thanks to his body armor, was his chest and torso. That protection of all his major organs might just save his life.

Severe burns are treated with one of two competing philosophies: minimize trauma by leaving the burned tissue in place, or excise all burned tissue and graft over with new skin.

Each has pros and cons, but Schechterle's burns were so deep and hardening so fast that both Dr. Caruso and Dr. Kevin Foster, co-directors of the Burn Center, agreed that excising the tissue was the only chance of saving the man's life. The officer was young and fit, bolstering his chances of survival.

As Schechterle's head continued to swell and split apart, Dr. Caruso was aghast at the level of trauma. He'd never seen anything so severe, which left only one possible course of treatment, which had to begin immediately. In layman's terms, Dr. Caruso would have to scrape off Jason's face and entire head. Medically, the doctors would be excising, which was surgically and completely removing all the layers of Jason's face, including skin, fat, some muscle, and the cartilage of his nose and ears.

AFTER midnight, Chapman parked in the dark suburb and killed the lights and engine. His partner had recently moved here, and in the days before smartphone GPS Chapman was only about 90 percent certain he even had the right house. He at least had it narrowed down to these two choices. Chapman had only been to the new place once, on that bright moving day. Now it was the dead of night, his partner was dying, and everything looked different. His partner's Anal Andy ways, however, were proving helpful to Chapman as he scanned the house. Schechterle had previously told Chapman it was thirteen miles from the freeway exit to his house; not 12.9 or 13.1. *Exactly thirteen miles*, which, in Schechterle's world of order, structure, precision, and punctuality meant thirteen miles exactly. Chapman had eyed the odometer and stopped at the precise count. He climbed out, stood at his car to give Suzie another moment or two of peace, and took a deep breath. A regular and uneventful shift had turned into the single worst hour of Chapman's life.

Give me the strength to do this.

He walked to the door and pounded three times, just as they'd learned from Day One at the academy. The nightmare for Suzie had officially started. No answer. Chapman pounded three more times with a little more force and waited. Again, no answer. He upped the volume on the third attempt, and when that didn't elicit any response he let loose with three fisted raps that shook the door. Just when he was thinking he might have to go to the backyard and knock on the bedroom window, the porch light came on and the door cracked open.

"Oh, dear God, Bryan, what happened?"

It was not Jason's wife, but rather her mother Louise—Schechterle's mother-in-law—who was living with the couple and their two children.

"Where's Suzie?"

"She's asleep. What happened? Did something happen to Jason?"

"I need to talk to Suzie."

Chapman walked past and quietly pushed open the double bedroom doors. He ghosted through the flickering room to the bedside, where he saw Suzie sleeping with her 7-year-old daughter Kiley snuggled next to her. The TV was on with no volume, throwing flashes of ambient light. He kneeled down and slowly shook Suzie's shoulder.

"Suzie… Suzie…"

Her eyes opened slowly, and she looked up and saw the uniform. But when she saw the face of her husband's partner, she started sobbing and hugged him. "No, no, no, no…" Kiley continued sleeping through the turmoil.

"Jason's been in a very bad accident," Chapman said. "He's alive. He's at County hospital. We need to get there right now. I'm going to take you in the car."

Like every cop beset by emotional duress, Chapman instinctively reverted to his hundreds of hours of training: take control, take command, project calm and confidence, work the situation to resolution. Step One…

But he's alive, Suzie thought, her worst fear at least temporarily alleviated. Chapman's uniform felt cold as he hugged her.

"Can my mom go with me?" Suzie asked, climbing from her bed.

"Yes."

"I need someone to watch Kiley and Zane."

"OK," Chapman said. "You get dressed. We'll figure that out." Chapman called his partner's brother Michael, also a Phoenix cop, and told him.

"Is he going to make it?" Michael asked.

"No," Chapman said. "Unfortunately, he's not."

"I'll go get my mom and dad and see you at the hospital," Michael said.

Within thirty minutes, Suzie's ex-husband—a cop himself, for the city of Avondale—was at the house to watch his daughter and Zane, Suzie and Jason's 2-and-a-half-year-old son.

Outside, when the three got in the cruiser, Chapman saw a long list of messages stacked up on his MDT. He turned off the radio in case the pronouncement of Jason Schechterle's death went out while they were en route.

Chapman reversed his route, heading eastbound on I-10, and this time took it back up over 100 miles per hour. Perhaps he could at least get her there to say goodbye before he passed. The ride was mostly silent. Chapman relayed what little he knew.

"I never went to the scene, but I saw him. You need to be prepared: He's in really bad shape. We'll find out more when we get there."

Chapman exited at Twenty-Fourth Street and raced south to Roosevelt. When he had followed the ambulance into the County parking lot just an hour ago, his cruiser had been the only police car. Now a sea of Phoenix police cars, together with the vans and lights of media people setting up outside the emergency room entrance, left absolutely nowhere to park. Chapman pulled up to the ER entrance and parked at the curb. He asked another officer to park the car and saw a priest standing right behind that same officer.

"What's the priest doing here?" Suzie's mother Louise asked. Suzie was crying uncontrollably.

Chapman immediately thought, *Jason has passed.* He steeled himself to be the pillar when the floodgates of grief poured out of the young wife. Chapman led the two women through the entrance and then into the waiting room, with the priest trailing behind. The waiting room was jammed with people, every single one in the same Phoenix PD uniform. The assembled officers had been talking, some sitting and some standing, but when Chapman stepped into the room with the two family members and the priest, every single officer stood. The room went silent.

Without anyone uttering a word, Chapman stepped forward, and a silent parting of the assembled masses created a pathway through the room. It was the single most solemn, respectful act Chapman had ever witnessed. The foursome walked the path through the sea of blue to the Arizona Burn Center and into a conference room.

Assembled were the two doctors, Schechterle's parents Karen and Fred, brother Michael, sister Alissa Felker with her husband Eric, and representatives from both the fire and police departments. The room was full of the soft murmur of crying, sniffles, and embraces. Chapman approached his commander, Joe Klima, a man he respected immensely but had never personally met because he was so far up the chain of command. Chapman quietly asked, "Is he dead?"

"Not yet," Klima said.

Chapman was surprised by the news, but not necessarily heartened. His partner's death was sure and imminent, and perhaps the sooner the better. Dr. Caruso sat and introduced himself to Suzie and explained the scenario. There was no time for warm and fuzzy: This was the gravest of situations.

"We need to operate," the doctor said. "Your husband has significant burn injuries. In fact, these are the worst I've ever seen. He has fourth-degree burns. We are going to do our absolute best to save him, but you should also be prepared for the worst. I don't think he will survive."

"Oh my God," Suzie said. "Please do your best to save him." Then she thought, *Holy crap, this is really serious.* However, she was not yet ready to see the extent of her husband's burn injuries. "I had papers to sign and decisions to make. I guess I never considered I would be the one who had to make all these decisions. I was very much at peace without actually seeing Jason. I knew my strength was important at that time."

Caruso, dressed in operating scrubs, was direct in explaining how the fire had consumed Jason's face, ears, nose, and hands. He detailed the plan, to excise all the burned tissue, which had continued to cook with residual heat like a pan of brownies atop the kitchen counter after being pulled from the oven.

While Suzie signed hospital forms, Klima pulled Chapman into the hall. The overlord of the entire 500 Precinct had an innate ability to lead people, which had always impressed the rookie charge Chapman. Klima was brief and direct to the young patrol officer: "Your only job going forward is taking care of this family."

That single statement and act forever changed Chapman's perspective of being a police officer. Fundamentally, what mattered most was compassion, care for one's fellow man, and taking care of family. True to Klima's directive, Chapman would not work another regular shift until July 2001. Chapman's and Schechterle's academy alum Shayne Tuchfarber would be a part of that duty, too. Said then-Chief Harold Hurtt: "I was convinced that Jason would never leave the hospital alive... I had no hopes at all."

Meanwhile, Suzie had stepped outside. And she prayed: *God, if he can't make it here on Earth, just take him. I will be OK and be able to take care of the kids. If you decide to leave him here with us, I swear I will do everything in my power to give him the best life possible.*

"When I made that pledge, I thought I was making it to someone who was going to be an invalid, a pile of mush for the rest of his life," Suzie said. "It was almost too much to comprehend."

As officers gathered on site, new alliances formed amid the darkness. Officer Bryan Brooks, who had been first on scene, met Officer Shayne Tuchfarber for the first time. Brooks had graduated the academy in 1997, two years before the Three Amigos (Chapman, Schechterle, and Tuchfarber). Brooks and Tuchfarber would soon be partners on patrol and, later, as detectives. Officer Mark Roach, another one of the 1999 academy alums, was sitting on a table, which snapped in half under his immense frame. At any other time, it would have been a moment of slapstick relief. But now it was time to save Schechterle's life.

Caruso and Foster would lead the surgery; Dr. Clifford Smith, chief resident, would also scrub in on this case of a lifetime. Collectively, the three doctors were stunned by Schechterle's condition. It was already somewhat miraculous that he had survived to this point. The doctors also knew if they didn't move swiftly and operate immediately, he would soon be dead.

At 2 a.m., in a brightly lit operating room, Caruso began at the top of Schechterle's head. Foster and Smith each took a side of Jason's face. Using special blades similar to cheese graters, the doctors started carving away the layers of scorched, blackened skin. Healthy tissue bled when cut; with each swipe of the blade, there was no blood. It was like honing a 20-year-old leather jacket rather than human skin.

Caruso switched out the blade for an instrument that cut deeper, an electronic, pen-sized unit that sliced through skin. But still, as he cut and cut at Jason's head, not a drop of blood. Caruso stopped.

"Just what the hell are we doing here?" he wondered aloud. "We're about to take off this man's entire face."

Though none voiced the thought, each doctor would have chosen death over what they were attempting. At one of the country's premier burn centers, none of them had ever attempted to excise such burns from a head and face. But still, under the hot glare of the OR lamps, hours ticked by as Schechterle's skin came off. There was little, if any, blood. Then there was nothing left to scrape, just muscle.

And then: down to bone.

AFTER the seven-hour surgery, Caruso was direct with Schechterle's wife and the others still assembled, including Chapman: "We don't expect him to make it through the night."

Caruso explained that most burn victims die from infection, not from the burns themselves. Schechterle's risk of infection was off the charts due to the horrific skin damage. And even if he did survive, at that moment Caruso couldn't accurately relay any prognosis about Schechterle's long-term quality of life.

Chapman didn't know what to do or think. He knew his partner wouldn't want to survive in some lesser state of functionality. Chapman was not an overtly religious person, the flashy and righteous holy-roller type, but privately he was certainly a believer in God and the power of faith. Chapman's main prayer was one of general surrender: *Thy will be done.*

The mood in the waiting room over the next hours was dim and grim. Outside, the first purple light of dawn started to illuminate the sprawling desert metropolis. Normally, after the afternoon shift the two partners had just started a few weeks prior, by now they would each be sleeping peacefully, grateful to be off the grind of riding King, midnights.

Inside the hospital, those assembled were mostly quiet except for the intermittent soft sobs—family, friends, and fellow officers lost in their own thoughts and praying for strength, guidance, and some sort of workable resolution. No one spoke it, but a swift death for the fallen officer seemed the only humane outcome. Because the doctors had Schechterle in a medically induced coma to keep him from moving at all, he would feel no pain as he slipped away.

Please let it be fast, his wife repeated in her mind.

Just as he had with his partner, Schechterle had discussed his fear of fire with his mother Karen Schechterle. They had talked about how being trapped in a burning car would be the worst horror. Some time after the surgery in the darkness, Jason's mother was adamant about wanting to see her son's destroyed police car. Reluctantly, a sergeant drove Karen, her daughter Alissa, and son-in-law Eric to the gruesome crash scene. When Karen saw the wreckage, her reaction was swift.

"I knew without a doubt that Jason would live," she said. "When I saw the car I got an instant sense of calm." She was the first and only person holding that particular opinion, but as the mother of the victim it was her duty and right. Her intuition, in fact, would be prophetic: "If he could get out of that car, he was not going to die."

AROUND 9 a.m. on March 27, Chapman's wife Dawn, who had driven herself to the hospital as soon as she heard, reminded her husband they should go home to get some well-needed rest to be prepared for what would come next. Chapman agreed. But once home, Chapman tossed and turned, unable to sleep, and returned to the hospital a couple hours later in a fog of adrenaline and exhaustion. By the time they returned, the police had set up a Mobile Assistance Command (MAC) van, a large recreational vehicle used at critical events and crime scenes where the police needed to stay on site. The van would serve as a communications hub and sacred space to escape the media. An onboard restroom and phone made the MAC van a self-contained central post from which to conduct the lengthy investigation. Cops and detectives would go to the MAC van for updates rather than streaming in and out of the Arizona Burn Center.

Prepared for the worst as he walked in, Chapman was surprised to hear his partner was still alive and hanging in there. The doctors had even revised their prognosis: Although Schechterle had somehow survived the surgery—a miracle unto itself—they didn't expect him to make it to the twenty-four-hour mark. With the vigil extended, the clock continued to tick.

Shayne Tuchfarber was at County, and for the next full week would only go home to take a shower and change clothes. Commander Klima was already pulling bureaucratic strings to get Tuchfarber temporarily transferred from the 400 Precinct into Central City to be assigned alongside Chapman for the special duty to help the Schechterle family. Soon the two academy classmates had their new assignment, stamped "Until further notice." No one said it, but "further notice" meant after Schechterle's imminent death and funeral, when things had more or less stabilized. Then it would be time for the department to move forward and for Chapman and Tuchfarber to return to street patrol.

"Emotionally, I was trying to be strong on the outside," Tuchfarber said. "But when I was alone I would sit on the edge of the bed and cry my eyes out. I didn't want him to be in pain. What are you supposed to do?"

Chapman, too, struggled with the onslaught of emotions. At one moment he was afforded some alone time with his partner. He sat staring and praying as the monitors beeped. The "Mercy Bullet" promise came into Chapman's mind—*What are friends for, right?*—and he shook his head, smiling. Chapman's .40-caliber Glock was holstered on his right hip as he sat in his dark blue uniform.

"Sorry, pal," he said aloud with his hand on Schechterle's chest. "You made it this far; I just can't do it."

One day this would become another point of delight, folly, and banter. Jason Schechterle was going to live, and as he would regularly remind people, the only reason he survived was that his best friend could not keep a promise.

Unless otherwise noted, all photographs courtesy of Jason Schechterle family archives.

The original *The Karate Kid* film came out in 1984, when I turned 12, timing that earned me the same nickname.

I enjoyed playing basketball as a kid, but my true sporting passion has always been golf.

Even as a wide-eyed United States Air Force recruit I knew my ultimate goal: to be a Phoenix police officer.

Suzie and I married April 26, 1997, before I was a cop, and less than four years before everything changed forever on March 26, 2001.

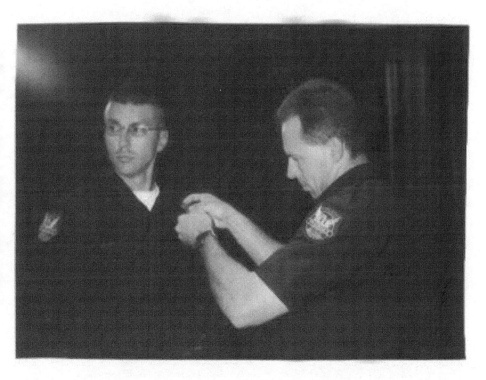

January 7, 2000: There was no greater feeling than the night I officially became a police officer. That's my brother Michael pinning my badge at academy graduation.

After all the years pursuing my goal, the dream was officially mine in 2000. Unfortunately, I would only be in uniform fifteen months.

Happy times with my wife Suzie before our lives went on an entirely new trajectory.

What's left of my patrol car after the crash March 26, 2001. With me inside, the wreckage traveled 271 feet before stopping.

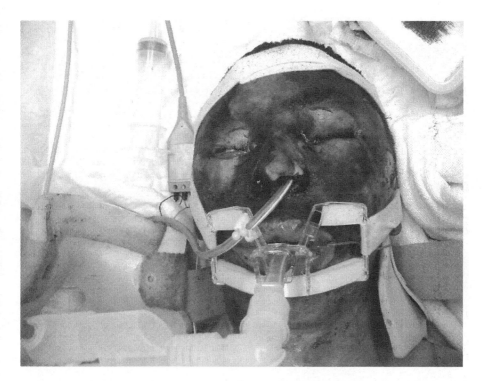

It's easy to see why first responders had no idea who they had just pulled from the burning police cruiser.

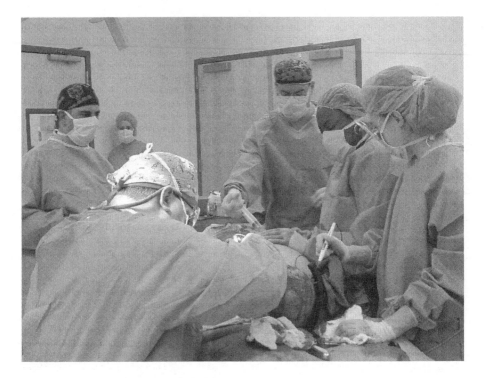

The medical team at Arizona Burn Center, at Maricopa Medical Center in Phoenix, performing another surgery on day three after the crash.

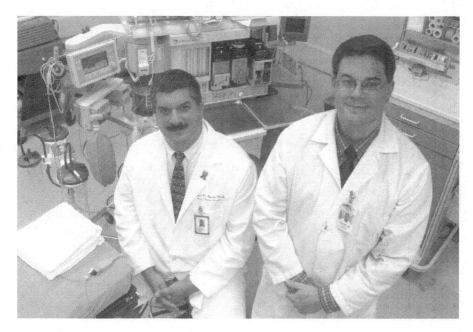

Dr. Daniel Caruso and Dr. Kevin Foster, co-directors of Arizona Burn Center, agreed that excising my tissue was the only chance to save my life after the crash.

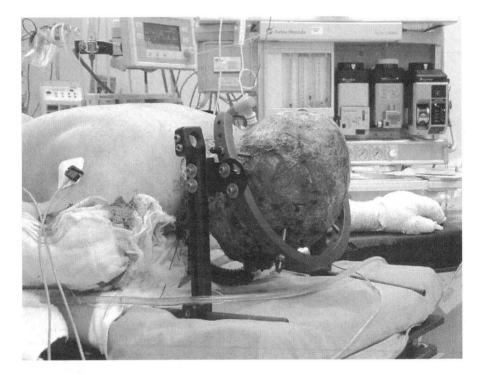

Fourth-degree burns: My head and face were gone. Note how the flames never reached my back (or torso) thanks to my bulletproof vest.

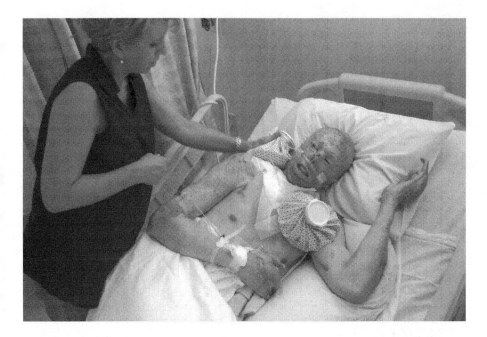

Photograph by Michael Chow, The Arizona Republic. Reprinted with permission by Gannett Company.

It was a long road back that was only made possible by my wife Suzie.

Photograph by Michael Chow, The Arizona Republic. Reprinted with permission by Gannett Company.

Another day, another doctor visit. Here I am at Dr. Craig Dufresne's office in Fairfax, Virginia, doing some light reading with Bryan Chapman (left) and my dad looking over my shoulder.

Above it's The Three Amigos Bryan Chapman (Bighead) on my right and Shayne Tuchfarber (Fatty) on my left. Below, that's me reuniting with my Phoenix police buddies in an emotional moment. Brian Brooks, on my right, was first on scene March 26, 2001, and Kevin Chadwick—whom I'm hugging—cut my seatbelt so they could both help pull me out of the inferno.

Photograph by Michael Chow, The Arizona Republic. Reprinted with permission by Gannett Company.

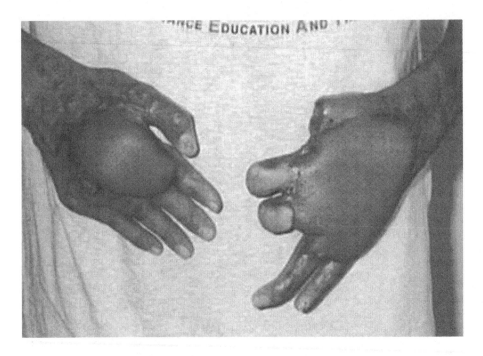

Although doctors seriously discussed the possibility of amputating both my hands to limit infection, I'm obviously grateful they were able to save them. The bulbous tissue is from my hands being sewn inside my abdomen wall. This photograph is from August 2001, when I had all four fingers on my right hand, but no thumb on my left.

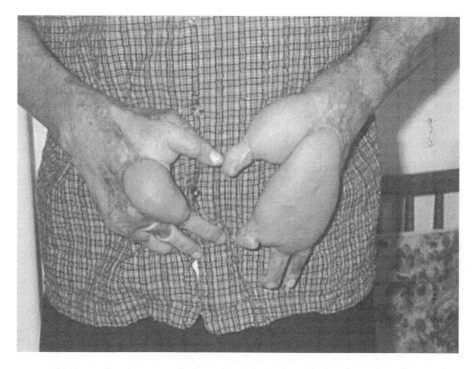

One year later, by August 2002, my doctors had to amputate the right index finger, but I also gained a new left thumb that has given me usable functionality in both hands.

My favorite place on the planet: the third hole at Torrey Pines South course in San Diego, California. That I have been able to relearn to play golf with my new hands is a true gift; that I can still beat friends and family members is a kick!

Happier times as I continue to recover. From the left: my brother-in-law Eric Felker and my sister Alissa Felker, my wife Suzie, our daughter Kiley, and my parents Karen and Fred Schechterle.

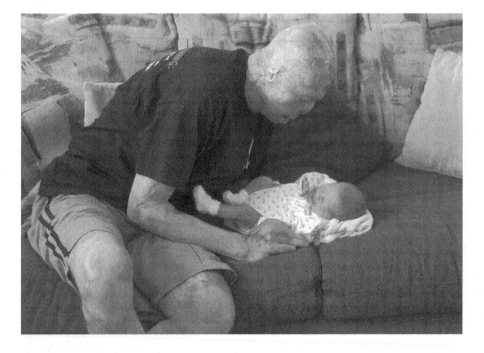

The miracle baby, my son Masen, who was conceived and born after my crash.

Just one month after having my right index finger amputated, I was throwing out the first pitch at an Arizona Diamondbacks Major League Baseball game. Thank, God, I didn't short hop it, because Curt Schilling told me he wasn't wearing a cup.

Photograph by Peter Scanlon, New Times.

The Greatest Job in the World: The C-32 homicide squad made me feel like one of the guys again. From left: Detectives Tom D'Aguanno, Barry Giesemann, me, Carl Caruso, Sergeant Patrick Kotecki, Alex Femenia, our Crime Scene Specialist Elaine Finlay, and Detectives Jack Ballentine and Steve Orona.

Photograph by Peter Scanlon, New Times.

My mentor Jack Ballentine, who helped get me transferred to the C-32 homicide squad. We are standing near the crime scene at the beginning of the Valentin Cruz-Gabriel murder investigation that took us on a wild 19-day ride.

Photograph by Michael Chow, The Arizona Republic.
Reprinted with permission by Gannett Company.

Just being out at the shooting range—where I was trying to qualify with my firearm again—was another miracle of my hand surgeries.

There's no question it was Suzie's presence, love and spirit that pulled me out of the abyss and back to life.

The legal duo who took on Ford Motor Company on my behalf. Above is Patrick J. McGroder III with me at an event. At right: David Perry from Texas.

Dr. Daniel Caruso, co-director of Arizona Burn Center at Maricopa Medical Center, led the initial surgeries that saved my life.

One of the strange outcomes of my new life is meeting high-profile athletes including professional golfer Fred Couples.

At left I am standing with 2013 British Open Champion Phil Mickelson. Above
I'm shaking hands with President George W. Bush.

My greatest gift is being here with my family (from left): Suzie, Masen, Kiley, and Zane.

Obviously everything's different now, but today Suzie and I still find a lot of gratitude and laughter.

My new passion and career: sharing my story as a professional speaker.

CHAPTER 13

The Trial Lawyers

AS THE GRIM DEATHWATCH at County continued, on the morning of March 27, 2001, lawyer Pat McGroder turned on the local six o'clock television news as part of his morning ritual. Working out at home, he watched in horror as the report relayed a car crash involving a taxi and yet another Ford Crown Victoria Police Interceptor (CVPI). A five-minute drive from where McGroder stood, the taxi had plowed into Phoenix PD Officer Jason Schechterle's 1996 cruiser, which erupted into a fireball and burned the officer to within seconds of death.

McGroder was aghast, shocked, and angered at this macabre confluence: For the past six months he'd been preparing possible lawsuits against the Ford Motor Company in these same sorts of fiery rear-enders involving the company's CVPI cruisers. This series of repeated crashes and subsequent deaths would be disturbing to anyone. But for a well-honed plaintiff's attorney, this was, in addition, a clear pattern of corporate negligence going back to the vehicle platform's introduction in 1978. After years of closer inspection and investigation, the lawyer was convinced the vehicle design was inherently flawed.

For starters, the fuel tank was located flush to the back wall and bottom of the vehicle's trunk. With the top of the tank extending up into the trunk area, and the lower part located behind the rear axle, there was nothing to protect the highly flammable tank on impact. During high-speed rear collisions, the back of the car collapsed, driving surrounding parts or trunk items into the fuel tank and puncturing it. The combination of fuel leaks and sparks created by the collision ignited the fuel vapors. Further, the force of impact often jammed the cars' doors shut, trapping occupants. A design that pushed gallons of fuel directly into sparking metal created time bombs waiting to burst into flames. McGroder's legal theory was that this vehicle platform, and Ford executives' knowledge of the design flaws, bordered on criminal negligence. One cop after another was burned alive and died in a Ford CVPI, with horrific consistency and heinous efficiency:

- 1983: Officer Drew Haynes Brown from Kennesaw, Georgia.
- 1992: Officer Ed Truelove of Cheshire, Connecticut.
- 1996: PFC Vincent Julia of Wilmington, Delaware.
- 1997: Trooper Robert Smith of Miami Shores, Florida.
- 1998: Trooper Hung Le of Ponchatowa, Louisiana.
- 2000: Trooper Lynn Ross of Tennessee.

In 1998 and 2000, closer to home in Arizona, there were the deaths, respectively, of Trooper Juan Cruz near Tucson and Trooper Floyd "Skip" Fink in Tempe, a Phoenix suburb. And now, minutes from where McGroder stood, Jason Schechterle was on the gurney after being cooked alive.

For McGroder, it was easy to see why Ford executives continued to dispute the claims despite the repeated occurrences: follow the money. By the 1990s, the Crown Victoria Police Interceptor had seized an enviable and profit-churning market share position, accounting for 85 percent of all police vehicles in the United States. The vast majority of the Crown Victoria fleet operating on the road, Ford lawyers contended, did so day in and day out without incident. Statistically, the burning deaths had occurred in a microscopic slice of the Ford Crown Victoria Police Interceptor sample pool.

Yeah, McGroder privately muttered. *Tell that to the families of the burned officers.*

Both the Fink and Cruz families would eventually retain McGroder, and by late 2000 he had filed wrongful death lawsuits on their behalf against Ford Motor Company. Co-counsel in the lawsuit included David Perry, the whip-smart, Texas-based personal injury lawyer who had already successfully taken on Ford in 1983 in *Durrill v. Ford Motor Company*. Perry was the two-decades-persistent bumblebee at the Ford Motor Company picnic that no one could squash. With McGroder joining the melee, the stingers were out and ready to do damage.

McGroder first met the Cruz family in August 2000 at what became an emotional meeting for all. All reiterated their commitment, through legal action, to force Ford to modify the production of the Crown Victoria police vehicles to make them safer. From the plaintiff's side, the problem with Ford's entire Panther line of cars—including the Crown Victoria, Lincoln Town Car, and Grand Marquis—was the fuel tank location outside the protection of the rear axle and within the car's crush zone.

Federal regulators, focusing mainly on police cases, counted sixteen fatalities in rear-impact fires in Ford cars built between 1992 and 2001. But the *Detroit Free Press* documented *thirty* deaths during that span, and a total of sixty-nine in the prior two decades, including at least eighteen officers.

On the defense side, Ford lawyers insisted the Crown Victoria was safe and met all federal standards, a view shared by regulators. Ford spokespeople also said the car had a comparable record to other big sedans in fatal fires resulting from all types of crashes. As a plaintiff's lawyer, McGroder knew Ford would never publicly disclose either the possibility of a design problem or the availability of protective shields to anyone other than dealers.

The entire ordeal was a complicated product-liability case that, by the time Schechterle's cruiser exploded on March 26, 2001, spanned more than two decades and involved taking on one of the bluest of blueblood American icons: Ford Motor Company. By the day of Schechterle's horrible ordeal, Pat McGroder and David Perry were trial lawyers at the height of their legal prowess, and luckily so: It would take a rare breed of plaintiff attorney to storm and breach the thick corporate walls surrounding Henry Ford's namesake concern.

By 2001, McGroder had already stacked up more than $300 million in settlements on behalf of his clients, a thirty-year career kicked off in 1970 under humble auspices. Two years before Schechterle was born, McGroder was a rookie lawyer doing criminal defense and red-light/green-light cases as he served his unofficial apprenticeship.

Eventually, by 2001, McGroder held his prominent post at the firm of Gallagher & Kennedy—just two miles from where Schechterle's police cruiser lit up the night sky—on the eighth floor of a glass and steel low-rise in one of the city's power corridors, the Biltmore area, which ran from Twentieth Street to Thirty-Second Street along Camelback Road, and where dealmakers shook hands over $30 baseball steaks in darkened booths. McGroder always drove the latest model BMW or Mercedes, always black, with a six-figure price tag. He lived five minutes from the office in the old-money exclusivity of Biltmore Estates, with a golf course as his backyard. His wife Susan, or Susie, was a beautiful and intelligent woman whose refinement was a good balance for the lawyer who liked to swear like a 1940s sailor. Together they produced three children—a boy and two girls, all strikingly attractive, intelligent, and well-mannered young adults who would do good things in the world. They'd attended the best private schools and then the universities of their choosing, and two would follow their father's footsteps into the legal profession.

Over his thirty-year career through 2001, McGroder had never become a book lawyer or professional legal scholar, like those who revered the practice of law as some holy sacrament. He wasn't going to change his stripes: He was still the fun-loving, scrappy Irish kid from Buffalo who loved a good dirty joke, dropped more f-bombs than a surly gang of longshoremen, and poked fun at his stuffed-shirt legal peers. But when it came to defending his clients—which meant exacting accountability from the misdeeds of overlords in big business and big government—McGroder was deadly serious. He was unmatched in his ability to circle, stalk, attack, and shred his opposition, all done with civility, humor, gentlemanly protocol, and pleasantness. McGroder was the legal equivalent of the Terminator: You could try to outrun, outgun, outspend, outprepare, and outsmart him—you could even rip his arms and legs off—and he would still come crawling after you to complete his mission.

As a great trial lawyer, McGroder understood that the law was simply a means to an end, and the end should always be solving complicated problems in a just, fair, and equitable way. Ultimately, the plaintiff's lawyer was the last line of defense against the unmatched wealth, power, and resources of giant corporations, municipalities, government agencies, and other well-appointed bodies.

Even so, many beat the drum of tort reform in response to public verdicts that seemed outlandish—*My freaking coffee is too hot!* But although tort reform might rid the system of sleazy ambulance chasers, class-action trawlers, and cheesy billboard quick-buck artists, who would stand up to challenge the true misdeeds and negligence by those hiding in profit-driven corporations and behind faceless bureaucracies? For McGroder, civil action was the last line of defense against unchecked human greed and incompetence.

In this way, long before sitting at a plaintiff's table, long before stumbling through his first case, long before all the tedious grinding through dusty case books at law school—even before stepping onto the Notre Dame campus for the first time—McGroder had always been a lawyer at heart. He was hardened, street-smart, and percolating with the focused rage of someone who hated seeing bullies get one over on the little guy. So on March 27, 2001, watching the news report about one of Phoenix's finest being burned alive right in his own neighborhood only infuriated McGroder and fanned his resolve. He was teeming with a visceral desire to right this wrong once and for all, a desire his practice of law had routinely honed into the blunt force of a gladiator's hammer.

Clients, McGroder liked to say, were just people with problems. His job was simply to untangle those problems—often complicated—and make certain the plaintiffs were treated fairly. Aside from those few huge plaintiff victories that made headlines and generated cries that the system was fatally flawed, most civil cases were legitimate instances of overt negligence and misdeeds. McGroder's cases were normally settled well out of the spotlight and, ultimately, held the responsible party accountable where no other recourse was available: another complicated problem solved with little fanfare. Money was not the best remedy, for it would not bring back the dead, reverse permanent disfigurement, or heal the permanently disabled. But it was the currency of resolution. And the basis for McGroder's life and career work was found right there at the end of the First Amendment to the U.S. Constitution: *Congress shall make no law… abridging the freedom… to petition the government for a redress of grievances.*

AS McGroder wiped away the sweat from his workout and thought about Jason Schechterle lying in Arizona Burn Center fighting for his life, he was undaunted by the enormity of the case against Ford Motor Company, the mind-bending complexity of corporate product-liability litigation, or the long odds of actually winning. Even so, although McGroder, along with his co-counsel Perry, packed a big legal punch, Ford was clearly still Goliath. But they had better get ready, McGroder thought, because a redress of grievances was coming hard and fast.

In that moment, a mantra and mission burned inside him with a white-hot intensity, and McGroder knew only one thing with absolute clarity: *Ford Motor Company needed to get its ass kicked.*

CHAPTER 14

From the Ashes

THE FIRST NIGHT after Schechterle's lifesaving surgery, the doctors assembled family, friends, police personnel, and fire department representatives to answer questions. After the briefing, Schechterle's father Fred stepped aside to talk to his son's partner Bryan Chapman. In his entire lifetime, Jason had never seen his father cry—the reserved man from a different era. And Jason would not see it on this night, either, as he lay in a medically induced coma. Fred Schechterle sobbed and leaned into Chapman for support.

Already, handling the logistics of helping Suzie Schechterle keep her household running and two children fed, bathed, and cared for was an around-the-clock effort. The long list of errands, coordinating pick-ups and drop-offs and food preparation and cleanup, fell to Chapman and Tuchfarber. At the moment of his greatest need, Pumpkin Head and Fatso stepped up in a noble way; they had their buddy's back no matter what.

True to their police training, the two cops divided their responsibilities into familial "beats." Shayne would cover the parents, Fred and Karen Schechterle, and their buddy's beloved maternal grandparents: grandmother Bette Earl (Clark) Oliver—the traditional Southern girl from Alabama who always espoused, "If it ain't fried, it ain't fit to eat"—and grandpa George Edward Oliver, born July 23, 1924, in Madisonville, Kentucky, the person who had largely shaped Jason's personality and demeanor. Chapman would be responsible for Suzie, the kids, and mother-in-law Louise Knowles, who had opened the door to Chapman's midnight pounding and had been the first in the family to learn about the crash.

For Big Head and Man Boobs, there were family members to pick up and drop off between home and hospital. The mortgage and other bills needed to be paid on time. There was home maintenance, and yard cleanup, and cars that needed gasoline. Chapman or Tuchfarber handled many of the family duties themselves and, when the list grew too long, delegated tasks to a long list of eager and willing police volunteers.

The two officers began meeting weekly with Central City Commander Joe Klima to provide detailed updates about family needs, Schechterle's medical progress, and all the tangential issues that arose. From there, Chapman and Tuchfarber rolled out to the other five precincts in Phoenix to provide similar updates that trickled down to all three thousand officers in Phoenix PD uniforms. On some days, to cover it all, they'd pick someone up at six o'clock in the morning for a bedside visit and not return to their own homes until two o'clock the next morning. Hours later, the cycle began again.

This duty assignment was a twin-shot roller coaster of adrenaline and emotional fatigue, especially through the initial days and weeks. The two officers had to repeat the same grim report to multiple people and groups: *He's probably not going to make it, and if he does we really don't know how functional he'll be.*

INITIALLY, Suzie was adamant about not wanting to see her husband in such a disfigured state; she did not want some bad B-movie image to be her last of him. But when her husband somehow survived the surgery, she changed her mind and pleaded with doctors Daniel Caruso and Kevin Foster to let her see what lay beneath her husband's bandages. They eventually agreed and, during one of the frequent dressing changes, allowed Suzie to stand bedside—with a doctor standing on each side in case she collapsed.

"I needed to know what Jason looked like," she said. "I needed to know what I was dealing with, and I was ready to deal with it."

With her first glimpse, her reaction was involuntary: *Holy shit, he's gone. OK, yeah, there's no resemblance to who Jason was prior to the crash.* Then, a split second later, she found the footstool near the bed and sat close to her husband. To Suzie, Jason's ears looked like burnt charcoal from a campfire.

"Can I get closer to him?" she asked.

"Yes," one of the doctors said. "Just don't touch him." Infection, the ever-present evil, was always lurking.

"Why do you still have these (ears) on?" Suzie asked. "They're dead."

The doctors went into a long explanation and explained they were waiting to see how much tissue might rejuvenate. When Suzie seemed OK with the morbid science—*she'd spent six hours with Mr. Lively!*—they started getting into more medical details.

"It was a turning point in my relationship with the doctors, because they knew I wouldn't be traumatized," Suzie said.

In the first seconds when she saw that her husband's face was completely gone, it knocked the wind out of her chest. But almost immediately, the feeling of horror faded and was replaced by resolve: *OK, so he's going to look different. Really different. How he looks is not who he is. So what's next?*

As the forty-eight-hour mark after the accident ticked by, Schechterle's doctors were astounded that their patient was still alive. They revised their prognosis yet again: Schechterle likely would not make it through the first week. Officially, he had suffered burns across 43 percent of his body.

"Draw a circle around your collar, and everything up just erase that," Schechterle later said. "Everything was fourth-degree, down to muscle and bone." His ears were completely gone, as was most of his nose. The searing heat had melted his entire head down to the skull. The fire flattened his corneas, too, which would prove to be one of the most severe and troublesome injuries.

Schechterle also had third-degree burns on his shoulders, arms, both hands, and the tops of each thigh. Mercifully, his chest, back, and mid-section were not burned because his body armor had withstood the flames. His lower legs, too, were not burned. His only other injuries were two cracked ribs and a concussion; it was the burns that were the cruel master of his fate.

"If it weren't for the burns, I probably would have spent a few hours in the hospital and went home," he said. Perhaps not back on active duty immediately, with a concussion, but home in a few hours, which is why lawyer Pat McGroder was on the trail; someone at Ford Motor Company had to answer to these heinous scenarios being repeatedly played out on law enforcement officers in the line of duty. McGroder had been called to the hospital by the police union attorney, who continued to play a role in the case. McGroder met Suzie Schechterle and her cousin at the police MAC van at the hospital.

The doctors' prognosis included other heartbreaking news: If Schechterle somehow survived, he might be blind. He *might* be able to speak, but the doctors said he would likely suffer diminished brain function from the lack of oxygen during the blaze. Family and friends were all left in a twisted limbo, wondering if they should pray for survival or a merciful death. If anything, given the prognosis, survival seemed the greater of two evils.

For every watchful minute of every hour and day, a uniformed Phoenix police officer stood guard at Schechterle's room. This was in small part a display of respect and ceremonial honor, but mainly a pragmatic standard procedure to protect Schechterle. No way would department heads leave one of their own police officers lying unprotected and unconscious in a hospital room. Someone would be on guard at Schechterle's door until he woke up and left the hospital.

THE horrible reality did provide odd and unlikely moments of dark-humor relief. The nurses had to change Schechterle's catheters regularly to prevent infection, which was the primary concern with such widespread trauma. It became routine for Suzie to chat with the nurse as the nurse handled her husband's penis and prepared to insert the new catheter.

It turned out that catheter insertion was easier when the penis was at least semierect, which explained the nurse giving Jason's member a few tugs. Later, Schechterle never heard the end of this one from his cop pals, who reminded him often that he'd slept through dozens of hand jobs.

Within days of the accident, Dr. Bill MacLeish, an oculoplastic surgeon, examined Schechterle. He, too, concluded that if Schechterle survived he would be blind. Each day and each diagnosis brought more bad news. Medically, other than his being alive, not a single bit of good news instilled hope for Schechterle in family, friends, and the larger police family. Instead, the convolution continued: Survival meant Schechterle might be blind and in a vegetative state. Death, at least, would spare him that suffering.

A week after the crash, Schechterle defied the odds again and left the doctors scratching their heads: He was somehow still alive. Doctors did not have any understanding of how he'd survived the crash, the surgery, the first night, and then days and now one week with fourth-degree burns. To survive this level and extent of skin loss and trauma seemed 100 percent impossible. Yet there he lay, heartbeat ticking. Once again, the doctors changed their prognosis to a more open-ended one: There still was no hope of a long-term recovery and, in all likelihood, at some point infection would end the ordeal for Jason Schechterle. That might happen in a day or a week, and most certainly within a matter of months. They reaffirmed to Suzie to get her affairs in order and prepare for her husband's eventual death.

And the doctors were mostly right: Day by day, Schechterle's body was fighting one infection after another. Each time family and friends watched and waited: Each new infection could be the one that did in the young police officer. But somehow Schechterle's deeper pulse to live brought him through each time, until he was beset by a new infection. This pattern repeated hourly and daily for weeks. And through each mini-victory of beating another infection, the only tangible sign of life within Schechterle was the beep and pulse of bedside monitors. Somehow, some way, hidden well beneath the hideous outer layers and ravaged body, the life force glowed, marching Schechterle forward a minute at a time.

THREE weeks after the accident, doctors were discussing new challenges with Suzie, Schechterle's wife, and his family: While not a certainty, Dr. Caruso communicated that there was an 80 percent chance they would need to amputate both of Schechterle's hands entirely. These frank, ongoing, and in-depth instructions were especially difficult for Suzie. But doctors were having tremendous difficulty controlling the unending onslaught of dangerous infections, and, in their assessment, neither hand would ever be functional again. Surgically removing the hands would eliminate a large open door for infections entering Schechterle's body. It was basically battlefield desperation: cut off the hands to save the man.

"There was a lot of discussion on amputating Jason's hands," said Caruso. "We never said that was the final straw. I desired to keep his hands attached to his body!"

What remained of Schechterle's hands looked more like mutilated claws. Each time tissue became necrotic, the doctors scheduled a surgery and removed another finger. His left hand was by far the worst. He had already had two fingers removed: his middle finger and index finger, at the knuckle. His thumb was completely gone. Schechterle's normally reserved father Fred knew his son's greatest love, playing golf, would be an impossibility. Suzie insistently told the doctors that full amputation of both hands would be considered only as a desperation last resort. From their silence, Suzie realized the doctors were already near that point. In the next hour, the next infection could end her husband's life.

Even so, the doctors continued researching other possible options. If they didn't find a suitable alternative quickly, then they'd schedule an emergency surgery to remove both of Schechterle's hands at the wrists. He'd never touch his wife or children again, nor would he be able to play golf, shoot a gun, or be a police officer. In those ways, his life would be essentially over. And he'd have no say in the matter, either.

"Thankfully," he said, "my family was very adamant: You do not amputate his hands."

Dr. Salvatore Lettieri, a plastic surgeon, presented an alternative he'd done previously that sounded to Suzie like something out of a direct-to-cable science-fiction flick.

"It was Dr. Lettieri alone who saved Jason's hands," said Caruso. "I was talking to him about the multiple amputations of fingers and the high likelihood of taking off Jason's hands in totality when he came up with the plan to save them."

Lettieri's proposal was to make two surgical slits on each side of Schechterle's stomach and insert the damaged hands into the abdominal wall. Specifically, the doctor would lift up the skin, fat and muscle and tuck each hand in this pocket surrounded by muscle and tissue. That surrounding tissue would then grow into the damaged hand tissue, forming a new layer of covering.

Then, they'd route the femoral artery from Schechterle's leg to the hands to infuse a steady, healing supply of blood. They'd close the incision and leave the hands inside Schechterle to incubate, like a fetus drawing sustenance from the mother ship. One night Suzie's husband had left for work, and now she was being asked whether to remove his hands or sew them inside his abdominal wall. As bizarre as it sounded, for her it was an easy decision if it meant not removing her husband's hands.

"I was adamant on them not taking Jason's hands," Suzie said. "He'd already lost his face and would have to reinvent himself. I didn't want Jason to have to live without his love of golf and any type of independence. I was able to block out emotion and focus on what was best for Jason. They're going to cut fingers off, OK, we're not going to cry and be sad. If this will help save his hands in the long term, then we had to do it."

The big plan to save the hands, however, had one big problem: It required keeping Schechterle fully sedated for more than a month. Otherwise, there was too much risk he'd wake up, see his hands disappearing into his own body, panic, and rip one or both his hands from the cozy and protective gut pocket. The patient's parents, siblings, and wife all had different inputs and ideas, but keeping him in a medically induced coma another month seemed extreme. The stress on Suzie was taking its toll.

"I can't make anyone happy," Suzie yelled. "You make the decisions." Looking back, she said, "I felt torn with all the roles I had to play—mother, wife, daughter-in-law, medical decision-maker—I didn't feel like I was doing any of them justice. I wasn't doing a good job anywhere. I just tried harder the next day. I hoped there was a light at the end of the tunnel, but I certainly didn't see it. I was on auto pilot."

Her father-in-law Fred came to Suzie: The family had agreed to support her decision whatever it was. Again, Suzie was adamant: save the hands. That meant her husband would remain in the medically induced coma. The doctors scheduled and then successfully performed the surgery as planned. All they could do now was wait and see if it worked.

"The doctors had already made Jason a guinea pig, so why not try anything they could think of to save his hands?" Suzie said. To her, the resultant aftermath was one of the more difficult things to see: her husband's hands disappearing above his groin into what looked like bulbous, yellow chicken fat.

Meanwhile, even as the medical staff pumped roughly 7,500 calories a day through Schechterle's feeding tube, his weight had plummeted from almost 200 pounds to 135. His body was in voracious calorie-demand mode as it tried to heal.

Unfortunately, both of Schechterle's hands became severely infected inside the abdominal wall pockets, which meant there was a strong possibility of the grafts failing, which would bring doctors back to square one: amputating both hands. It was a tense watch.

"Jason was going to die if we didn't get rid of that infection," Suzie said. "Every time we turned around he had another one. There were at least seven times I heard, 'We don't know if he's going to make it through the night.' The doctors were trying to save his body parts, but also battling these infections." Ultimately Lettieri was able to meet the challenge and eliminate the infection. The tension of it all, for Suzie, was unbearable.

In April, Caruso presented a plan to surgically apply Integra, a shark cartilage and bovine collagen used as a dermal replacement matrix. The solution would regrow a new, deeper layer of skin, called the dermis, on which surgeons would place skin grafts. The idea was not without family argument: while a common treatment on injured hands and face, there was serious risk of infection.

"It was very risky to use a synthetic product on Jason's face and hands due to the depth of his burns and the concern of how well his blood supply would return to the damaged tissue," Caruso said. "Also, there was the issue of the multiple infections he had on his face and hands throughout his hospital stay."

But as doctors also relayed how similar procedures had produced favorable results, Suzie insisted. Her guiding light was that her husband's case was extreme and required extreme measures. *Go ahead,* she told the doctors. *Just keep doing whatever you have to do to keep my husband alive.*

On April 26, Jason and Suzie's wedding anniversary, Suzie took their wedding album to County, sat bedside and went through the photographs with him. Later she sat outside Jason's room, showed the nurses the album and sat, sobbing.

"That's how we spent our fourth wedding anniversary," Suzie said. "When I look back I don't know how I did half the stuff I did. I just had a sense of peace that we were on the path of successful recovery. My faith helped me tremendously to be confident in my decisions."

VISITORS who came and sat bedside all started to notice a pattern. The only communicative link to Jason was the blood pressure reading on the monitor: As long as it was in the good zone things were progressing. But oddly, if someone changed the radio station from Schechterle's beloved country music, his blood pressure rose almost immediately. Despite the horrific crash, the burns, the surgeries, hands sewn in kangaroo pockets, and the medically induced coma, Schechterle's will and spirit—and taste in music—were indomitable. Once they learned of this telegraph wire into Schechterle's persona, of course, it became a source of endless amusement for all the cops. Even as he lay in a coma fighting for his life, his cop buddies could still tease him like fraternity brothers pranking a helpless pledge.

"We'd go into his room and mess with him by changing the radio station and watching his blood pressure go up," Tuchfarber said. It was Tuchfarber, too, who had come up with the password that would limit visitors and only allow pre-screened family and friends into Schechterle's room: "Chris P." Say it without pause, and the twisted sense of humor becomes apparent. The brief insertions of levity helped balance the dark reality that on any given day Schechterle could die. No one wanted to face that possibility.

On one particularly rough night, Tuchfarber and Suzie were bedside watching Schechterle thrash and struggle to pull his hands from his internal pockets. His body was drenched with sweat: Not even the medically induced coma could eliminate his suffering.

Although the patient they were visiting was comatose, family and friends passed along the intelligence they had gleaned: by watching the monitors one could tell whether Schechterle was awake or asleep, relatively speaking. Change the radio station from country to bubble-gum pop, and Schechterle's head would start jerking.

"What's wrong?" his mother would ask. Then she'd realize: "Your radio station?" After switching back to country, Schechterle was calm again.

If Schechterle's dad Fred relayed an unexpected PGA Tour event result, Schechterle's blood pressure spiked. Somewhere in the wiring of his subconscious Schechterle was still computing ball-to-green distances, checking the wind, and pondering club selection. Likewise, one day Schechterle's mom and siblings were in his room openly discussing his extensive and horrific injuries: He was likely blind, had no ears, and had lost fingers. Schechterle couldn't comment, but his blood pressure elevated immediately. Some ghost version of himself was there, fully cognizant and keeping watch.

On particularly rough nights when the nurses and doctors couldn't calm an agitated Schechterle, Suzie would get a 3 a.m. call. She'd get dressed, drive to County in a stupor, and sit with her husband, rubbing his feet. Almost immediately her voice and presence would calm him, and she could watch his heart rate drop on the bedside monitor. Twenty minutes later, when he started thrashing again, she'd calmly say, "Sweetie, I'm right here. You just need to go back to sleep." And his blood pressure and heart rate would drop again with an efficacy that modern medicine had been unable to achieve. Suzie would sit with Jason like that until the sun came up, kiss him goodbye on his unburned feet or chest, and then go home to get their two kids ready for school and day care.

Schechterle's right hand remained in the protective pouch for three weeks, his left hand for five weeks. Miraculously, the procedure worked: new tissue took hold and molded itself atop Schechterle's muscle, forming a foundation for all the subsequent surgeries to make both hands functional again. Another major hurdle had been cleared, but the finish line was so far away that no one even discussed when it might come into view. For now, it was still a day-to-day roller coaster of hope, emotion, and dread. Ever the stalwart, still there was only so much one woman could endure, and it all came to a head for Suzie on a rainy night in May.

Driving home in the early-evening dark, she calmly pulled into the parking lot of a big box store with no intention to leave her car, turned off the engine, and let it all out.

"I had a fit," she said. "I was banging the steering wheel and dashboard and screaming: 'Just take him. I can't do this anymore. He has no quality of life. He can't battle these infections. Please, God, don't make us suffer anymore.'"

Her screams were shrill and piercing. Once she'd unleashed the rage and frustration and sadness and fear, she sat there in silence, just listening to the rhythmic patter of raindrops. Then she wiped her eyes with some napkins from the glove box, checked her mascara in the rearview mirror, and drove home to cook dinner for their two kids.

"It was as though I just had to lose it," she said. "That was the only time I wanted Jason to die. It was probably one of the last infections he had to overcome."

CHAPTER 15

Wake-Up Call

WHEN JASON SCHECHTERLE woke up, as far as he knew it was the morning after his last shift, 513 Henry, and the 11:17 hot call on March 26, 2001. At least that was his perception of time, space, and events. In reality, it was actually June 12, 2001, and everything else in between was stamped out for him by an unassailable black void. The blank period included his fourth wedding anniversary (April 26), Memorial Day (May 28), and his son Zane's third birthday (June 2). The first thoughts of consciousness fluttered into the strange dark void. Sounds and smells identified his whereabouts.

I'm in a hospital. Why? And why can't I open my eyes?

The answer to the last question was that his eyes had been grafted over with skin harvested from elsewhere on his body, but now was not the time to learn such details. Unbelievably, Schechterle felt mostly clear-headed. Rapid-fire thoughts crashed into his mind. His wife Suzie started talking. Since the night of the crash-and-burn, someone, usually Suzie, Bryan Chapman, or Shayne Tuchfarber—especially after the vigil had turned from hours to days to weeks and months—had been parked at Schechterle's bedside 24/7. No one wanted him to be alone, and especially at this moment of first light. When they thought he was ready physically, the doctors began weaning him from the medications to allow Schechterle to wake up. The doctors, however, did not know exactly when that would happen. On this day his breathing changed rhythm, and Schechterle was awake. Suzie was the only person in the room. Even in the vague dark fog, Schechterle, like the cop he was, began establishing other immediate facts:

He was alive. Rene Descartes made it so: I think, therefore I am.

He was blind and swimming through some eerie netherworld.

His wife Suzie was by his side.

OK, how bad could it really be?

"Where am I?" he asked. "What happened?"

Weird… he had a clear memory of just being at work. *Last night, right?* But the last images he could conjure were of rolling by the domestic call and seeing Chapman flash code 4. Then the screen just went blank. *How in the hell do you end up here at the end of a code 4? Had some unseen maniac burst out of the house firing shots into the desert night? Really… what the hell?*

"You're in a hospital," Suzie said. "You had an accident."

"Which hospital?"

"County."

Schechterle recalled the grim joke among cops, about how they should take a black Sharpie to their body armor: *If found, take to County*. Clichés and dark humor; the truth cuts through everything.

"What kind of accident?"

"Jason, your patrol car caught on fire," Suzie said.

Before he could fully process that, Schechterle heard a familiar voice, and then he knew it was Bryan Chapman's hand gently patting his chest.

"Hey, buddy," Schechterle said. "What's going on?"

"Oh, just a few things here and there," Chapman said, smiling and—Schechterle could hear—fighting back tears. "But nothing to worry about. You just work on getting better."

Caught on fire. Schechterle felt lost and confused: He could not see or feel his injuries, but now he knew it was bad. But the mention of "fire" ended the conversation. He did not want any more details, and he sure did not want to ask why he couldn't see.

THE next weeks were a barrage of surgeries and, for Schechterle, a reluctant search for answers. He didn't have the inclination or energy to have visitors other than his wife, his partner, and a handful of others. Instead, the dozens of regular well-wishers piled up outside in the hallway, the lobby, and near the hospital entrance.

Schechterle was asking a lot of questions, but not getting many clear answers. He knew he was in rough shape, but he had no idea how tenuous his survival had been or how difficult the road ahead was going to be. He had no clue he was already a one-in-a-million miracle survivor.

Now that he was awake and moving to the next phase of recovery, Schechterle's doctors had to wean him off the powerful narcotic pain medication. But Schechterle's body was already addicted. The pain of losing his regular fix, combined with the searing burn pain he began to experience, was excruciating. Even so, he wasn't feeling sorry for himself or thinking he should just give up. Instead, he told his wife, partner, family, and friends that they had done the tough stuff; he just slept through it.

Not long after surfacing back to consciousness, Schechterle asked to speak to the firefighters from the Engine 5 crew. He wouldn't be able to see them, and he was starting to believe he'd never see anything again. When Darren Boyce, Rebecca Joy, Henry Narvaez, and Michael Ore walked into the room, Schechterle's father was sitting with his son. He said, "Hey, Jason, the crew from Engine 5 is here."

Schechterle had no warning of the onslaught of emotions to come, and he began sobbing uncontrollably. His father was immediately concerned that his son's shaking and movements might dislodge one or more of Schechterle's numerous bandages or IV lines. The firefighters discreetly bowed out to give Schechterle some time to process and be with his dad. The firefighters were equally moved just to see Schechterle back among the living. No one could believe that he had survived; they had been on scene and heard, smelled, watched, and felt the horror unfold. They did their jobs just as they had been trained to do, but there was no way a human being could survive what they saw that night. No way. And, yet, here he was asking to talk to his rescuers.

FOR Suzie, the situation was traumatic and often overwhelming: the long coma, the desperate surgeries, the ups and downs of thinking she had lost her husband more times than she could count, the disconnecting sterility surrounding her grotesquely burned husband.

"It broke my heart," she said. "I physically hurt for Jason and couldn't imagine what he was going through. What words could bring him any peace?"

So late at night when she knew they were alone, Suzie would slip off her shoes, put the bed rail down, crawl into bed beside Jason and put her arm over his chest. She cupped her hand on his unburned skin there, and just let him cry and cry. She knew the doctors were rightfully careful and paranoid about sterility, but she also knew equally important things.

"Jason just needed to be loved and held," she said. "We wouldn't talk. He just needed to cry and be loved."

Fellow police officers wrote entries in a spiral notebook kept by Schechterle's door. The various narratives were representative of what everyone was feeling:

"Jason indicated his strong desire to come back as a police officer. We reassured him he will always be a Phoenix police officer, and we will work out his assignment when he gets back. Jason was glad to hear that. His spirits were high. He was thankful for all the support of the police family. He was also appreciative of the officers staying outside his door."

"Jason's voice is very strong. He is alert and can carry a conversation. He is a tower of strength for us all."

"I was truly amazed at Jason's inner strength—not something I was prepared for. His strength actually took away some of my own anticipation about seeing him. Can't help but be proud of him. At lunch they had him trying to learn to feed himself. He was up walking a couple laps around the halls."

"Hospital staff raving about Jason being the perfect patient. They all just love him. After a hard morning of working out Jason went back to bed for a nap. What progress! What inspiration!"

"If you can spend ten minutes with this amazing human being and not be inspired to want to be a better person, you are missing a soul. This kid is amazing."

SARA Barron's first assignment as a primary care nurse was patient Jason Schechterle. She'd worked at County as a licensed practical nurse since 2000 and joined the Arizona Burn Center staff just before Schechterle's accident. Jason's case was challenging and high-profile as he was surrounded 24/7 by visiting uniformed cops, which added to the pressure she already felt.

In any burn facility, infection was a lethal and constant predator probing for access. The Arizona Burn Center at the Maricopa Medical Center was no different. Maintaining sterile conditions at the center, one of the top ten in the nation in terms of patient volume, was absolutely serious business. As part of protocol, all medical staff had to wear full protective gear, including surgical masks, gowns, gloves, and booties.

Barron pumped calories into Schechterle, but he despised what he was being fed. The steady flow of Ensure protein shakes were, in Schechterle's parlance, disgusting. The trachea port and tube in Schechterle's neck were to remain in place for one year, to create an airway during all his upcoming surgeries.

"Could I have some water?" he asked his nurse one day. Barron poured from a pitcher into a small cup and held it to his lips as he drank quickly.

"Could I have some more, please?"

"Absolutely."

They repeated the process several times until she said, "Have you had enough?"

"No," Schechterle said, "But I know you need to take care of other patients."

Nearly half of Schechterle's body was burned off, he couldn't see, and his hands were bandaged clumps, yet he was thinking of others.

FOUR months into his recovery, on July 30, 2001, Bryan Chapman was in Schechterle's room to bolster his partner's spirits and take his mind off what was going to be a long and grueling process. Schechterle was scheduled to start rehabilitation the next day at nearby Good Samaritan Hospital on McDowell

Road. The doctor who would be working with Schechterle at the next hospital stopped by the room.

"So I understand you've had some fingers amputated," were the first words from the doctor's mouth—but no one had told Schechterle yet about that grim reality. Each visitor was carefully vetted and warned: Do not talk about his hands or their current condition.

So, naturally, Schechterle thought the doctor had the wrong patient, but just for confirmation he turned to his partner and said, "Bryan?"

The quick-witted Chapman, the ever-affable cop who could think on his feet and had an effortless gift of gab, went speechless.

"Bryan? I didn't, did I?" Schechterle's voice was louder and infused with real panic. This was not the way to find out someone had removed his fingers as he lay comatose, just cut them off without permission. Beneath the heavy layers of white gauze on his left hand, Schechterle only had his ring finger and pinky. His index finger, middle finger, and thumb were gone. His right hand, similarly bandaged, was not missing fingers per se, but was more or less an unworkable blob of tissue not likely to become functional again.

"Bryan!"

The desperation in Schechterle's voice was crushing to his partner, who could only mutter, "Jason, um, well…"

Schechterle was livid: "How did you know this and not tell me?"

In reality, a psychologist had already told Schechterle during his wake-up, but in his grogginess he had not fully comprehended it. Since Schechterle hadn't brought it up to friends or family since, everyone thought it best not to talk about it until he was ready.

The horrific news—fingers amputated as he slept—meant the life he loved was over. Since he was 5, playing golf had been for him more than a simple game, diversion, or way to get out of the house for five hours. Golf held a deeper meaning and purpose for Schechterle. But that was all gone now: He'd never pick up, let alone swing, a golf club again.

Likewise, if he couldn't hold or shoot his .40-caliber Glock, his one-month turn on 513 Henry with Chapman was also over. He and Chapman would never patrol as partners again. Minus his fingers, Schechterle's life *and* career were over.

Over the next few weeks, as Schechterle struggled to understand it all, his mental state fluctuated wildly. Some days he was OK; other days he asked the nurse to post NO VISITORS. On the days he was more stable, his natural police curiosity returned, and whoever happened to be sitting bedside was barraged with a long list of questions.

Do I have any hair?

How bad do I look? Be honest.

Why did the car catch on fire?

What was I doing?

Did anyone else get hurt or killed?

How did they get me out?

Where was Chapman when this happened?

Did he go tell Suzie?

Will I ever be able to see again?

How much do Kiley and Zane know?

BY July 31, 2001, Schechterle had already defied every medical prediction and prognosis by simply living. He smashed another record by leaving the Arizona Burn Center a full six months earlier than predicted by the best doctors in the southwestern United States. The same ambulance crew that had saved his life March 26 returned for the momentous day to transport Schechterle across town for his next phase of recovery. More than a dozen officers in uniform showed up to see Schechterle leave.

Schechterle was still in the dark, with his eyelids sewn shut, and he was seventy pounds lighter than the day he'd arrived. His last solid food was Taco Bell takeout four months before. His wife, Bryan Chapman, and Shayne Tuchfarber helped him get ready.

"I had no hair, no nose, no ears, and my mouth hung open," Schechterle said of his condition that day. "So I was happy to be blind, too."

As Suzie gingerly helped stretch a T-shirt over his head, her husband screamed as though she'd dug a letter opener into his shoulder.

"Oh my God," she cried. "Did I hurt you?"

"No," he said, "don't mess up my hair."

The three cops had a good laugh. They helped him slip on shorts and shoes. In addition to the awaiting cops, there was a cluster of media people, brass from the Phoenix Police Department, and a variety of curious onlookers. His nurse Sara Barron arrived at the room with a wheelchair.

"You know what, Sara?" Schechterle told his nurse. "They brought me in here on wheels, but they aren't taking me out that way."

This from a man who could not even walk from his bed to the toilet under his own power. Regardless, with Bryan Chapman on one arm and Shayne Tuchfarber on the other, Schechterle shuffled out of County under his own power. The man who should have died a hundred times over was *walking* out of the hospital on his own terms. The July 31, 2001, entries into the spiral notebook journal emphasized the importance of the moment:

"Jason, this is one of the most memorable days in my life. Seeing you walk *out of the burn center was the best accomplishment I have ever seen. You are my biggest inspiration. You're the greatest, and I love you, pal."*

"It was a very emotional event for all of us. The courage Jason displayed was overwhelming. He insisted that he walk out of the burn center on his own. He walked by all the hospital staff and they were all so proud of him. There was many a wet eye. Jason continues to set the example for all of us. We are all so proud of him. God continues to bless him."

"The greatest moment I have ever been privileged to witness. Nothing else matters today— he is one step closer to home!"

"Jason, you are the most inspiring person I have met. You are the reason I do what I do. Continue to progress so you can go home. My days just won't be the same anymore."

"Jason, you're an inspiration to a lot of people. Never give up. We'll have to play some golf when you're feeling better."

"Lots of 'family' unity between fire and police. Very emotional departure from County Hospital. New room looks comfortable. Atmosphere is very positive and the outlook is optimistic."

ONCE in the ambulance, Schechterle's destination was Good Samaritan Hospital in Phoenix, where he began a rigorous in-patient rehabilitation routine including occupational, physical, and speech therapy. Nurses wheeled Schechterle from his room to the rehab area by eight o'clock in the morning, where he stayed until noon. During his lunch break he usually asked to be wheeled back to his room to rest. Then he had to do more hours of rehab until four o'clock in the afternoon.

Every aspect of his various therapies was painful. He had to work on regaining his balance. He still didn't know if he'd ever see again, so all the exercises were done in complete darkness. If moving his shoulders and arms was painful— and it was—moving his hands was excruciating. Both hands were completely nonfunctional. The fingers he still had were all sticking straight out and locked into place. Imagine trying to learn to pick up a spoon with a Frisbee duct-taped around each hand. About all he could do was squeeze objects between what were essentially paddles.

"There was not a part of therapy that didn't hurt," he said. Schechterle just did what he was told, because he was 100 percent dependent on others for his care and feeding. The first time he tried to eat cereal on his own, with a spoon inserted between two locked fingers, his arm was shaking horribly. When he finally got his hand to his face he couldn't find his mouth.

Progress was slow, but all the visitors kept his spirits up. Some days Schechterle was overwhelmed by the enormity of it all, and he'd break down and cry. When Suzie brought a cassette tape his two kids had recorded, a letter to Dad, he sobbed. On his worst days Schechterle was depressed and pissed off that he'd never be a cop again. On better days his will soared: *I'm going back to work.* And some days, he simply didn't care about anything and just wanted to go to sleep.

DURING the first week of August, Suzie brought Kiley and Zane to see their father. Kiley had come to Arizona Burn Center a couple times. The younger Zane, who had just turned 3 in June, had been shielded from seeing his disfigured father because no one knew how the young child would react.

"I had put Kiley into therapy immediately," said Suzie. "Regardless of whether Jason was going to live or die, Kiley was going to have to deal with a lot of issues. Zane was too young, but our therapist guided us on what to do, with age-appropriate descriptions that Daddy looked different."

As part of the preparation to see his father, Suzie showed Zane progressively closer-up Polaroid photographs, accompanied with lots of reminders: *Daddy looks different now*. When the trio arrived at Jason's room, Zane screamed, "That's not my daddy!"

"Hi Zane," Schechterle said, hoping his voice would trigger recognition. "It's Daddy." Zane seemed to recognize the voice, but wasn't making the connection. The little boy only became more inconsolable, which immediately made Jason start crying.

"Suzie, just take him home." Then Zane ran screaming out of the room and down the hallway.

"I didn't know who to go to," Suzie said. "My husband who's sobbing, or my child who's scared to death. It was so traumatic for both Jason and Zane, and me, too." The reality hit Suzie hard: *How in the hell are we going to do this?* At home, Zane continued to ask his mother where his daddy had gone and when he would be home.

In August, doctors cleared Schechterle to visit home for one night, and then he was allowed to go home for a weekend. It went well, except that anytime Schechterle was in the house, Zane hid in his room and refused to have anything to do with the unrecognizable monster. There was also a new dog licking the patriarch's leg.

Suzie told her husband she'd answered a classified ad. The owner said the pups had been born March 26. When Suzie heard the date—the night of the crash—she immediately drove to the house and brought home the first puppy that ran up to her.

One morning during therapy the skin graft on Schechterle's right eye split open slightly, allowing him to see some light, colors, and shadows for the first time. It was an incredible moment, and Schechterle was infused with new hope that he might regain his eyesight. He remained silent about the breakthrough, because he wondered if it was only temporary. He wanted to savor the blurry light for however long it might last. The doctors' prognosis had continued to be that Schechterle would be blind for the rest of his life.

In early August, Schechterle's grandparents were in a car crash that put his maternal grandmother at the same hospital where Jason was doing his rehabilitation work. Her condition slowly worsened as she developed hospital dementia. Schechterle was despondent over his grandmother's condition, but he was also fighting his own battles.

ON August 8, 2001, Schechterle visited Dr. Tony Smith, a hand surgeon at the Mayo Clinic in nearby Scottsdale. It was an emotional moment, because Schechterle had not yet seen either hand. Although Schechterle's surgeons at the Arizona Burn Center had saved his hands from amputation by sewing each of them into his abdominal wall for extended healing time, there had not been any reconstructive surgery yet to improve functionality.

As Smith unraveled the white gauze, Schechterle saw blurry images—through a tiny hole of a popped skin graft—of what remained of the hands he had last used to answer up the 11:17 hot call the night of March 26, 2001. He felt nauseous as he stared at the deformed clumps. Then he began crying: On the left hand, the only two fingers that were intact were the pinky and ring finger. The middle and index fingers were each stubs amputated at the first knuckle. The thumb was completely gone. Although he had two intact fingers, pinky and ring, they were each locked in a dead straight position. It was horrifying to see, when his last memory of his hands was of being at work doing what he most loved. He'd gone to sleep and someone cut off his fingers.

"At that time, I could have taken a dull butter knife and cut my pinky off and not felt it," he said. "I had no sensation in any of my fingers."

The right hand was in better shape and intact, but the index finger was becoming dislocated, with his thumb curling over the top of that adjacent finger in a locked position. Imagine making the "OK" sign with the tips of the index finger and thumb touching in a nice circle. In Schechterle's version, the thumb was all the way over the top of the index finger, rendering both digits unusable. The other three intact fingers were also locked in place.

Schechterle's crying turned into uncontrollable sobbing. The doctor quietly left the room while Suzie tried to comfort her husband. Eventually, after he had a chance to regain his composure, the doctor came back and described the surgery he wanted to perform.

His plan was to begin on the more seriously damaged left hand. First he would surgically remove the stub index finger by removing it all the way down into the palm to the base of the thumb—or, in this case, where the thumb used to be—which was called a "ray amputation." The width of Schechterle's left palm would then shrink from normal to that of just the three fingers above. Then Smith would transpose that appendage onto what would become a new, usable thumb. They scheduled this initial surgery for September 10, 2001.

Without a thumb, his hand was a meat paddle. Smith's best prognosis was that, after a lot of painful physical therapy, Schechterle's odds of full functionality were maybe 50/50. For Schechterle, it all centered on being able to hold and fire the Glock again with the proficiency to be a cop. Dreams die hard, and he was not giving his up.

"It made me feel a little better," Schechterle said. "At least here was a guy with a plan. But I still felt lost."

WHEN it was finally time for her husband to come home for good, on August 17, 2001, Suzie orchestrated a special maneuver: Operation Confidence Builder. The plan was to clear the house of children, get Schechterle home, and have an intimate encounter with her husband. With all the mental, emotional, and physical trauma he'd suffered, Suzie wanted to ensure him that he was still her same lovable Jason and, despite his appearance, he was whole as a man.

Shayne Tuchfarber met Schechterle at the rehabilitation center to drive him home. Tuchfarber had already bought some condoms: the absolute last possibility Suzie wanted at that particular moment was a new baby on the way. Shayne helped get his friend home and settled on the couch with a good channel selected on the television; Schechterle wouldn't be able to move from the couch or change the channel once his friend left. The kids were out of the house, ostensibly for reasons other than afternoon delight with the wife. With everything in order, Tuchfarber left without any mention to his pal about what was in the works. The new dog wandered up and sniffed around Schechterle.

Minutes after Schechterle had settled on the couch, Suzie made her entrance, cozied up to her husband, and whispered, "Let's make love."

Schechterle's first and primal reaction—even as he lay on the couch unable to see with his eyes sewn shut for healing purposes, with bandaged stumps for hands and trying to overcome major emotional and physical bodily trauma—was automatic and programmed from 100,000 years of the male species: *Great, let's go*. But then he was flooded with anxiety about his appearance and whether all the plumbing and mechanics would work. There had been no discussions about such possibilities by any of his doctors.

Jason still didn't fully know what he looked like, but he certainly knew he no longer resembled the Karate Kid, nor the man Suzie had married. Would his wife be repulsed by his appearance? But amid his rampant ruminations, his lithe young wife was already climbing on top of his gaunt 130-pound frame.

"He had no choice in the matter," she said. "So yes, I did take advantage of him."

Thankfully for both parties, no mental, emotional, or other issues occurred during the lovemaking: Operation Confidence Builder delivered on all fronts. As Schechterle would later famously repeat in public numerous times during his captivating forty-five-minute description of his odyssey: "Not everything burned."

ASSESSING Schechterle's appearance as he tottered around the house in August 2001, his loved ones were direct.

"To put it bluntly, he looked terrible," said Suzie. "Here was this man I loved with all my heart, and knew everything about, and he looked nothing like he had the last time I had seen him before the crash."

Partner Bryan Chapman provided an even more pointed assessment: "He was no Brad Pitt."

Indeed, Brad Pitt he was not: Schechterle had a skin mask on his face, with his lower teeth exposed. His "eyelids" were two surgical slits, and his "nose" was two breathing holes cut into tissue by his surgeons. Everywhere he'd been burned was now a crusty and oozing mixture of sores and scabs in various states of evolution. Only those in the innermost circle were allowed to see Schechterle.

His son Zane still didn't recognize the strange, monstrous man wandering the house, and wanted nothing to do with him. Daughter Kiley was warming up, although slowly. One night she edged near her stepdad and kissed the unburned spot on his wrist where he'd been wearing the watch his brother gave him.

On September 10, 2001, Dr. Smith was going to remove what was left of Schechterle's index finger on his left hand and reattach it to create a new usable thumb. It would be a fourteen-hour procedure that would largely determine whether Schechterle's left hand would be functional enough to play golf, pick up objects, and hold and shoot a gun. He was, after all, still a cop. The night before the big surgery, Suzie helped him into a wheelchair at the hospital and wheeled him to say goodbye to his ailing grandmother. He sat with her, held her hand, and spoke to her as though she was lucid and laughing as she used to do. But she was neither, and Schechterle wasn't sure if anything he was saying was reaching her. He, too, was awash in emotions, fears, and trepidation about the big surgery the next day. Although he said goodbye for the last time, as his wife wheeled him out of the room he felt an odd absence of closure. Perhaps, he thought, she'll pull through for a bit longer, and he'd get another chance to say goodbye when he was more together.

The next morning the surgery went off without any complications. The doctors were cautiously optimistic that they'd given Schechterle new hand functionality, but like everything else in this case, they'd just have to wait and see. When Schechterle came out of the fog of anesthesia, his wife let him know she was sitting bedside. He was weak and felt disconnected from his own emotions and world. The accident, the trauma, and twenty surgeries (the first fifteen were skin grafting), including the fourteen-hour session he had just undergone to repair his hand—it was all completely draining.

"Is grandma gone?" he asked.

"Yes," his wife said.

Schechterle was numb to what would have been, under normal circumstances, the worst news of his life. He had never lost a family member, and grandma Bette Earl (Clark) Oliver was one of his favorite people in the world. The Southern girl from Alabama—*If it ain't fried, it ain't fit to eat!*—was gone. He'd never again hear her laugh or taste her perfect fried chicken, biscuits, and gravy. Grandma was gone.

"I was so weak and still blind," he said. "I thought, 'What a terrible day this has been.' I was really feeling sorry for myself."

The next morning, his father Fred came to his hospital room early, which was a little unusual. While supportive and loving in his own way, Schechterle's father was a hard-core New Jersey guy. But on this morning, September 11, 2001, he was unusually emotional. The father told his son what had happened in New York and turned on the television so Schechterle could listen to the coverage of that dark day in American history. The exact details, chronology, and events were fuzzy because of the amount and strength of medications Schechterle was taking. When the towers collapsed, he was despondent about all the first responders who had just died. Hearing the events of 9/11 unfold on television gave Schechterle new perspective to counter his momentary lapse into self-pity.

"My grandmother had passed away," he said. "The next morning, I'm listening to the biggest tragedy America has ever known. It made me realize, I wasn't alone in pain and suffering. No matter what scenario you can dream up—like what happened to me—something far worse can happen. Like being trapped above the fire in one of those towers and having to choose whether to burn or jump. Compared to those people, I was doing OK."

His grandfather, ever the optimistic one, used his humor in a strangely morbid way. "Well," he said of his wife's passing the day before 9/11, "she beat the rush." His grandfather had always had a way of making Schechterle smile, and he had done it again.

As the nation collectively experienced that autumn, the full strength of the human spirit often lay in hiding until presented with something monumental. In Schechterle's private corner of the world, he was facing a monumental journey back, and everyone around him rose up. Volunteers showed up at his house, unannounced, spent hours doing all the yardwork, and quietly left. Dispatchers from the Phoenix Police Department arrived at the Schechterle home with enough food for family, parents, and grandparents.

Chapman and Tuchfarber went from working their regular forty hours a week to ninety, in support of their comrade and his family. Both officers knew Schechterle's parents, but as their duties expanded they got to meet Schechterle's grandparents, too.

"If you knew Grandpa George, he was the funniest guy I've met in my life," said Tuchfarber. "He took the burden off of me that I wasn't helping my buddy. And his wife Bette was a beautiful woman."

Tuchfarber's day began at 6 a.m. when he picked them up to take them to their grandson's hospital room. Tuchfarber updated them and relayed any new information he had. He drove them to PetSmart or Fry's, to get groceries, and anywhere else they needed to go. By the time Tuchfarber got home it was usually midnight or 1 a.m. After a few hours of sleep he'd start the process again.

"We bonded so fast," said Tuchfarber. "As far as I know, the Phoenix Police Department brass had never taken two officers off the street to be assigned to a family. It was awesome to be a part of that."

Chapman and Tuchfarber organized golf tournaments and car washes, too, with all the proceeds donated to the Schechterle family. The goal was to lay a financial foundation for what was going to be a long and painful recovery, a lifetime spent in hospitals and doctor offices and physical therapy sessions.

Amid all his progress, a big question loomed, unanswered: How did Jason Schechterle survive? He now had time to ponder, and he often wondered how he was still breathing. To be certain, he owed his life to a long and unlikely list of events. First, he was wearing his seat belt and bulletproof vest. The seat belt kept him from being hurtled through the windshield, lacerated, and crushed. The vest protected his core and vital organs from being incinerated by flames; a civilian in the same scenario would have likely died without the bulletproof body armor.

Second, miraculously, a fully equipped Phoenix Fire Department truck parked forty feet from where his cruiser came to rest. And—miraculous corollary—the emergency vehicle was only at that spot at the *exact* time required because Narvaez had overslept, which had delayed the crew by about thirty seconds. But take away those seconds, and the truck and crew would have been farther down the road and unable to respond with such immediacy. Even fifteen more seconds in those flames would have killed Schechterle.

Third, the Engine 5 crew—Darren Boyce, Rebecca Joy, Henry Narvaez, and Michael Ore—called for an ambulance and deployed in record time, with Boyce spraying life-saving water and oxygen into Schechterle's breathing space.

Fourth, the first two cops on scene acted swiftly: Kevin Chadwick was able to cut Schechterle's seat belt just in time, with Bryan Brooks there to untangle Jason's legs.

Fifth, also miraculously, Schechterle's accident happened two miles from the Arizona Burn Center, one of the best and most respected such facilities in the United States, where nurses and doctors were attending to him in record time: from explosion to treatment was just eight minutes.

"Add all that up, and it just does not happen," Schechterle said. "Everything except the collision went in my favor." In the line of duty, perhaps Jason Schechterle altered—or even saved—one or more people's lives, although no one will ever know for certain. People driving eastbound on Thomas Road, just ahead of where Schechterle's cruiser stopped the taxi death-missile, might have been next in the line of fire. Instead they drove home and have lived out their lives ever since, unaware that Schechterle took the bullet.

Suzie Schechterle believed sometimes bad things happen without rhyme or reason. Yes, perhaps her husband taking the hit had saved someone else's life farther east on Thomas Road. Then again, maybe the taxi driver would've slammed into a telephone pole instead and hurt no one. Given that, perhaps her husband's survival was just a one-in-a-million set of unbelievable circumstances. No one really knows or has any answers except one: *It's better to be lucky than good.*

For Schechterle, one of the biggest frustrations was being so dependent on Suzie for his care. Schechterle still couldn't hold a spoon; he had to be fed like a baby. He couldn't pick up simple objects, and would curse in anger. He couldn't even go to the toilet alone or clean himself after. His existence was a big and vague question mark: No one knew how or whether his health and functionality would progress.

Since moving was difficult, Schechterle mostly sat in his favorite recliner. Sleeping at night was fitful, so he'd try to rest sitting up, when he could, between doctor appointments. The eyelids that had been vaporized by flame were gone, replaced by two ever-open slits. Given his appearance, he preferred the shadows of his living room. He only went out in public when absolutely necessary. But sitting at home brought up the same recycled thoughts over and over.

Would he overcome his severe physical limitations? Regain his strength? Could his appearance at least be improved to be not quite so horrifying? And would Suzie, an attractive, vibrant woman in her 30s, stick around through it all?

Without his knowledge, one of Schechterle's doctors had already pulled Suzie aside and warned her of a disturbing reality backed up by data and his personal experience. In good-looking couples, when one person was horribly disfigured, the anxiety, stress, and medical demands often led to a divorce or split. If the walls at County had ears, the doctor had already heard rumblings about *when*, not if, Suzie would leave her husband. When told this, Suzie's tears turned into crystallized rage as she found her own resolve and spoke directly to the doctor: In sickness and in health, limitations or otherwise, she would *never* leave the man she loved. She might be a lot of things, but shallow was not on the list.

For Schechterle, his musings from his recliner always led him back to the fact that he should not have survived. It had taken a team of family members, cops, firefighters, and medical caregivers, who collectively marched Schechterle back from the grave. If nothing else, that love energy on its own was some sort of higher power that had intervened. Beyond that, even doctors who lived and worked within the hard empirical markers of science believed something intangible had been at work—providence moved—and one man lived where every other would have died. For Schechterle, to not be energized and inspired by that was impossible. That was why the tough days and dark moments never dragged him all the way down into the abyss of self-pity, anger, and even rage at his condition.

Schechterle was alive for a reason; his job now was to uncover that reason. Already, his ironclad determination was inspiring the very doctors and nurses entrusted with his care. Privately, they each doubted their own ability to find the same high level of mental toughness Schechterle's ordeal required. If he could walk out of County under his own power, then anything was possible again. To the well-trained medical team, it was awe-inspiring and equally humbling.

Of course, if the fire truck hadn't been rolling by with a crew ready to save him, a quick death would've been a whole hell of a lot easier—and would have relieved inordinate anguish, trauma, suffering, and grinding rehabilitation. But once his new reality was established, Schechterle never looked back, and his resolve solidified. He said, "I never thought about giving up."

Part III

To Protect and Serve

CHAPTER 16

The Fight Continues

FOR JASON SCHECHTERLE, finally back home in Avondale, a suburb west of Phoenix, the remaining months of 2001 were an exhausting blur of doctor appointments, visits with specialists, and excruciating physical therapy. He was still shuffling around like an 85-year-old man with three weeks to live. The long months in hospital beds had severely atrophied his muscles. Nothing worked right—shoulders, hips, knees—and every muscle, joint, and tendon was bound up, stiff and tight.

His hands were still essentially useless except as two big paddles that he could sort of use to pick up objects large enough to hold between his palms. They also never stopped hurting, and then during physical therapy they hurt more. Suzie, meanwhile, had to walk the delicate balance between loving support and appropriate ass-kicking. She certainly didn't mind feeding her husband his Froot Loops every morning, but she also knew at some point he was going to need a push toward independence. One morning she produced an ACE bandage, lashed the handle of his spoon to his right hand, and said she had to fold clothes while he ate.

"Suz, you know I can't do this. C'mon."

But as a mother of two she knew this was a critical tough-love moment. She retreated to the bedroom to, ostensibly, fold those clothes. But instead, she collapsed and silently sobbed as her husband screamed at her from across the house: "How can you not help me eat? You don't love me! Suz, c'mon, I can't do it. Please help me, please!" Emotionally, the "Thank God You're Alive!" phase was giving way to a new reality, the "How in the Hell Do We Do This?" portion of the program.

"I had to just swallow my pride and let other people take care of me," he said. "And start to figure out how to take care of myself."

Regular fights replaced the delicate decorum that had been in place since he'd woken up June 12. The roller coaster of Schechterle's psyche was a dark and daily thrill ride. At times he was actually OK. But at other times the gloom swept in and suffocated him. Through the cycles he remained mostly quiet, reserved, and pensive. Not knowing what the future held gnawed at him: He was a man who liked to be in control of his environment. He had arrived at the academy thirty minutes early *every* day to ensure he was not late. That was how he approached everything: full bore, throttle wide open, accelerator flattened. If there was a mouse turd to be jumped, he would train as an Olympic pole vault athlete to clear it. The nonsense of being laid up and disfigured was keeping him from the job he loved.

While he was so happy to be at home and still alive, he was still a stranger to his own 3-year-old son Zane, who moved around the house cautiously and was careful to give his father a wide berth. Daughter Kiley, 7, was faring better, but the ordeal and her father's appearance were intimidating. Mature for her age, she understood the severity of his injuries. While she had an overall sense that to be alive and home was miraculous, his appearance did affect their relationship. Even so, the communication lines were open, and she was very helpful in asking what he needed.

"Dying would have been easy," Schechterle said. "This path was not easy."

The re-ordered marriage celebrated bizarre new milestones: *Honey, you ate your Froot Loops and peed all by yourself today!* Amazingly, somehow Schechterle avoided the black abyss of self-pity and *wa-wa* wallowing. He mostly avoided *Why me?* thinking and never once regretted his decision to leave the power company to become a cop, even though it was that single decision that put him in the ticking time bomb March 26, 2001. Instead, he found a rare perspective, trapped as he was with no hand functionality in his emaciated and disfigured body. He was covered with scar tissue, oozing scabs, and open sores, with a mouth that was locked open and dripped saliva.

"Bad stuff happens to good people every day," he said. "I'm not immune to that. I just looked at it as my being hit prevented someone at the next traffic light from being killed by the taxi driver."

In the line of duty, that was his service and sacrifice. Yet he struggled with that notion. One of his strongest emotions was that of disappointment: His career as a patrol officer had come to an end not through some more honorable act of bravery and self-sacrificing glory in the line of duty: stepping in front of a bullet to save the life of an innocent. Racing into a house ablaze to rescue a screaming infant. Taking down dangerous thugs after a high-speed chase.

No, he thought, *he was permanently disabled because of a stupid auto accident.*

"This is life: I was due for some hard times and tragedy. I just got a big dose of it all at once. I always had an inner peace with everything that happened."

Stuck with plenty of time to contemplate the bigger questions, Schechterle, rather than following the road of self-pity, continued to be struck by the unlikely series of coincidences that had transpired to keep him alive. It was beyond coincidence, too, that he had been set ablaze exactly two years to the day after lowlifes ambushed, shot, and killed Marc Atkinson on March 26, 1999.

A tiny drop of water in a pond sends out ripples. What do these ripples mean? For what purpose was I spared?

"I believe in God, but I also believe we live our lives with free will and make our own choices," he said. But mostly what he thought about, and all he really wanted, was to go back to work, put on the dark blue uniform, and return to patrolling 513 Henry.

For Suzie, she might find herself folding laundry at 1 a.m. and thinking, *I am so tired.* Then she'd hear and see her husband Jason shuffling down the hallway, feeling the wall along the way, to attempt to go to the bathroom by himself.

"He was fighting so hard for me, for us, for our family," she said. "Who was I to say I was tired? He inspired me with his inner strength. Jason said the same thing—that, at his low times, I inspired him. We fed off of each other's strengths."

DR. Daniel Caruso put Schechterle on a low dose of the antidepressant Zoloft to help level out his emotions. Despite the odyssey he'd endured and the understandable challenges it brought, Schechterle was embarrassed. He didn't like popping pills to feel better, although the medication did help keep him from spiraling downward. Even so, after about a month Schechterle stopped taking the antidepressant.

"It got me over the hump," he said.

Suzie was also adjusting to her new full-time job: husband care. She'd quit her dental assistant job out of necessity, because someone had to shuttle Jason and help him through his daily medical appointments. Hourly and daily wound care at home—including changing bandages, applying ointments, and bathing and feeding her husband—was time-consuming, and the kids, too, needed care and attention. Suzie had three beings all completely dependent on her for around-the-clock care.

However, the biggest anxiety-producing factor was the unknown prognosis of Jason's eyesight. In the six months since the explosion, Schechterle's eyes remained surgically sealed shut by skin grafts.

"I just didn't know if I would ever see again," he said.

Doctors had been telling him that he'd likely need corneal transplants, a surgical procedure in which an ophthalmologist would replace Schechterle's damaged corneas with corneal tissue from a donor. The procedure was not without risks: graft rejection, detachment, or displacement of the transplants, or outright graft failure. The risk of infection, too, was ever-present, and particularly critical in Schechterle's weakened state. By the time he got home for good, he was down to 125 pounds.

At home, Suzie tried to infuse some normalcy one night by renting movies from Blockbuster. She picked up the latest animation romp for the kids and, for her and Jason, the highly touted new film *Castaway*. Given the circumstances, it might have been the single worst film she could have selected, short of a silent Charlie Chaplin classic.

"Jason still couldn't see," she said. "His eyes were sewn shut, and I was still feeding him. So I rent *Castaway,* about one man alone on an island with no one else. Talk about a movie with no dialogue. It was a complete disaster. It was me narrating the entire depressing film: 'Now he's knocking his tooth out with a rock.' It only accentuated the fact that Jason couldn't see."

But that was about to change.

"There just came a time when the doctor said we needed to open the skin grafts," Schechterle said.

Dr. Bill MacLeish performed the eye surgery to remove the skin grafts— and, everyone prayed—restore Schechterle's eyesight. Because he'd have to undergo general anesthesia, doctors also planned another hand surgery while Schechterle was out. The surgeries took place at Mayo Hospital in Scottsdale.

When he woke up, it was breathtaking to see light and color again. Although his view was blurry, like looking underwater at the other end of the pool, he felt an overwhelming sense of relief. Healthy eyes were shaped like a football: the heat had flattened Schechterle's corneas into pancakes. It was an unbelievable moment of hope: *I'm not blind. I can't see great, but at least I won't live in perpetual darkness.*

IN October 2001, Jason and Suzie Schechterle rode the elevator to the eighth floor of an office building on Camelback Road in the heart of the upscale Biltmore area, stepped off and walked through the double set of dark doors next to the glass emblazoned "Gallagher & Kennedy." They had an appointment with lawyer Pat McGroder, whom Jason had not yet met in person. The main offices of the legal firm were on the eleventh floor of the building; McGroder, in lockstep with his independent and outsider bent as voice for the common man, had taken up office space three floors below the firm's brass.

A self-described news junkie, Schechterle had carefully read and watched coverage of the two Crown Victoria cases closest to home in Arizona, those involving Juan Cruz in 1998 and Skip Fink in 2000. But with his long list of health challenges, unending doctor visits, surgeries, and physical therapy, he'd had neither time nor inclination to learn and understand the ongoing larger context surrounding the Crown Victoria Police Interceptor. He also did not yet understand how his own odyssey fit into a larger dark pattern. And he especially did not see how some high-flying ambulance chaser from Phoenix, in a tailored wool suit, was going to help anything.

"I just wanted to go back to work," Schechterle said.

Before meeting McGroder for the first time, Schechterle was a cop taken down in the line of duty; he simply wanted to be back among his crime-fighting peers. The larger court battles being waged against Ford Motor Company since David Perry's landmark case in 1983 had never appeared on Schechterle's radar. Schechterle had little energy or interest for pursuing a lawsuit against Ford Motor Company, but Suzie had met and talked with McGroder and recommended they at least meet and see what he had to say.

McGroder's longtime right-hand logistician, Debbie Francis, greeted the Schechterles, offered refreshments, and then led the couple into McGroder's spacious office, which faced north. That north wall was entirely glass, with spectacular views to the sparkling desert cityscape and brown horizon farther into the haze. McGroder's office had a line of sight directly toward the northeast; not in view was Schechterle's impact point to the southwest. For McGroder, that reality made the perceived negligence by Ford Motor Company especially egregious: The exploding Crown Victoria issue and subsequent human suffering had been brought, literally, right into McGroder's neighborhood where he lived and worked.

The office was clearly the operating base of a successful plaintiff's lawyer, that rare, eclectic, and *bon vivant* breed of attorney able to carefully balance a potentially volatile mix of acumen, ego, personality, skills, and traits that regularly toppled lesser craftsmen. Plaintiff's lawyers, at the core, were oddballs of the legal profession, more comfortable outside the castle walls where they could sling arrows at the big three establishments: corporations, big government, and big medicine.

These legal cowboys rode the plains, looking for action, taking cases on contingency and only drawing down dough at the end of a long process that ended with a case settlement, trial verdict, or zilch. In most plaintiff cases, that meant months and usually years of working without pay, on full contingency, with zero guarantee of a payday when the action came to a close. That high-stakes mentality belonged to a different breed of lawyer: part street hustler, part riverboat gambler, part self-righteous do-gooder, and part William Wallace warrior—willing to go it alone for a greater cause.

The best of these attorneys avoided the obvious low-rung whiplash cases and instead trolled for the whales, cases of absolute and clear negligence that harmed, maimed, and killed human beings. With those cases, plaintiff's lawyers such as McGroder could wrap themselves in a cloak of absolute righteousness—David slinging rocks at Goliath.

In reality, plaintiff's lawyers ran the spectrum from true altruistic servants righting societal wrongs to the sleaziest quick-buck artists clogging the system with the worst of ambulance-chasing clichés, cases that are nothing but sad money grabs. Their desire to end the macabre procession of burnings and deaths of police officers put McGroder and his team at Gallagher & Kennedy squarely in the former camp. Like other refined and top-rung lawyers, McGroder abhorred and refused to engage in the personal injury bottom-feeder realms of TV and billboard advertising; he sought high-profile cases with the potential to remediate corporate and governmental policy and behavior, which would in turn prevent future injuries and deaths.

In his office, the display of ego was strong, with numerous framed press clippings touting McGroder's success in other big cases, plaques and awards, and a Heisman-trophy-like statue capturing the attorney in a bronze boxing pose from his Notre Dame days. But balancing those brash displays were numerous other interesting sports collectibles, framed photos of his beautiful wife and three children, and "Love you daddy" artwork made by those same kids. The inscribed text on a small paperweight collectible at the edge of his massive desk gave a glimpse into this multifaceted human being: *I believe in Santa Claus*. The diplomas and inscribed accolades from the State Bar of Arizona were all there too, and, coupled with McGroder's confident stance and warm introduction, gave an overall effect that was comprehensive and immediate: Schechterle was impressed with the man.

Like Schechterle, McGroder stood six feet three inches tall. He wore a gray, tailored, double-breasted suit with a white custom-monogrammed shirt—$200 a pop—and a pink tie with an immaculate knot and tie bar. The two men, although living and operating under widely divergent budget scenarios—Schechterle had been unable to afford new training shorts at the academy even as his faded Schechter Shorts shrunk to obscene tightness levels—were obviously stamped from the same OCD mold of perfectionism. In cop and military parlance, McGroder was squared away. So despite originating from different spheres— McGroder from silver-spoon privilege and higher education, and Schechterle from the blue-collar byways of Tolleson, Hidalgo house, and law enforcement— the short meeting was off to a spectacular start of commonality.

McGroder always first inquired about his client's health, concerns, mental state, and all the other human elements. Major-league ego aside, this was where he differed from many other frothing plaintiff's lawyers, who dived immediately into case points and court actions and motions in their stampede to great riches. Some lawyers just could not quell their overwrought lawyerly instincts, nor stem the impulse to immediately share their high estimation of their overall greatness.

Instead, McGroder took in his new client for the first time. Schechterle was horrifically disfigured, had no eyelids, ears, or hair. His nose was virtually gone. The grafting of his face was obvious, and he only weighed about 120 pounds even though they were the same height. McGroder listened as Schechterle told him he was virtually blind and could only see blurry shapes. Appearance aside, McGroder was amazed by Schechterle's gentleness, spirit, and courage as he talked about wanting to return to work. McGroder was immediately hit with an overwhelming sense of urgency and purpose: *I need no further motivation in my case against Ford than Jason Schechterle.*

Once his client finished, McGroder verbally put forward his résumé, the cases he had championed and won, and what he and his co-counsel David Perry saw as the three fundamental design flaws with the Crown Victoria Police Interceptor:

1) By design, the fuel tank was precariously positioned behind the rear axle.

2) The fuel tank was surrounded by a hostile environment of various bolts and sharp metal edges that led to perforation of the tank when rearward materials were pushed forward.

3) The energy management system at the rear of the Crown Victoria was poorly conceived and designed: The components did not dissipate energy upon impact. Instead, the components just collapsed.

Following that technical listing, McGroder described what was happening on the road. The scenario began with a Crown Victoria rear-ended at highway speeds. At impact, the rear segment of the vehicle—namely the trunk and suspension components—was driven frontward. Because the fuel tank was behind the axle, the forward push engaged bolts, flanges, and sharp edges, which perforated the fuel tank. There were also components in the trunk—police equipment, tire irons, jacks, and other gear—being pushed through the trunk wall and likewise perforating the tank. As this was happening, the entire collided vehicle was being pushed along the asphalt, which created sparks from the dragging metal. Those sparks ignited fuel vapors and, seconds later, a conflagration of fire enveloped the passenger compartment, which was filled with flammable components and a live human being as driver.

McGroder concluded by coming full circle and explaining how those same elements repeated verbatim in Schechterle's incident and case. McGroder explained that the statute of limitations for a claim arising out of a workman's compensation incident required an initial filing within one year of the collision, or by March 26, 2002, which was about six months out.

"I am on a crusade as an advocate for police officers in these Crown Vics," the lawyer said with all the solemn conviction he felt.

It was a moment of clarity for the disfigured young police officer: *There has been a pattern of these incidents, then it happened to me, and it will happen again if we don't stop it. We have to get this fixed. This can't keep happening.*

As the end of the meeting approached, McGroder had not once mentioned money, so Schechterle broached the uncomfortable topic with his own direct question: "So you're going to make 33 percent of anything we get?"

McGroder paused, smiled, shook his head, and deadpanned: "No, I take 97 percent."

Schechterle smiled too, and knew they had found the right man. Schechterle had come to the meeting in a state of ambivalence. Now he was feeling an entirely different surge of purpose, and he felt energized to be in the fight against Ford Motor Company. Schechterle had wondered why he had survived. Now it seemed, at least in part, he had one answer. His new mission was to be a living, breathing, walking advocate to fix the Crown Victoria and prevent another police officer from being burned alive.

THAT same month, Schechterle's hometown Major League Baseball team, the Arizona Diamondbacks, advanced to the 2001 World Series. He watched every one of those seven World Series games, which stretched into November because of the delay caused by the events on 9/11. He had to sit inches from the TV and couldn't see the ball. Instead, he only saw blurry movements. But with his normal unbelievable take on things, he mused, "If this is all I can do the rest of my life, that's OK."

The Diamondbacks won the World Series in dramatic fashion by coming from behind in the bottom of the ninth inning off famed closer Mariano Rivera, who had not blown a save since Ford debuted the ill-fated Edsel in the 1950s (or so it seemed). Arizona pitchers Randy Johnson and Curt Schilling received co-Most Valuable Player honors, and the diversion, with its connection to New York, helped people rally around 9/11 survivors and find purpose again through America's pastime. Amid it all, Schechterle had no idea he'd soon be personally connected to one of those World Series MVPs in a dramatic way.

In early December, members of the Phoenix Police Department showed up at Jason and Suzie's house with a beautifully appointed Christmas tree that Jimmy Lawson, another burn survivor, had purchased for the family through the Burn and Trauma Foundation. The tree, decorated with numerous police ornaments, featured a photo of Schechterle in uniform at the top in an angel frame.

That same month, Schechterle and his wife made plans to attend the annual awards banquet put on by the Phoenix Police Department. Schechterle was still reluctant to appear anywhere in public, but he also knew the firefighters and police officers who had saved his life were being honored. From the moment he walked into the Orpheum Theater, the support and attention was overwhelming. The local media turned out and wanted to do interviews. Schechterle ended up doing an impromptu press conference before the event. It was the first time he had shown his face on television, and he felt very self-conscious. Later, when the officers and firefighters received their awards, Schechterle was moved emotionally. He was thankful for their service, which had saved his life.

"I remember the anxiety in Jason because of the public exposure," said Bryan Chapman. "I know there was a lot of apprehension. But it was also good because it forced him to get out there and face his fears. That was a tough moment."

After Christmas, when it was time to take down the tree, Suzie was busy carefully storing the ornaments, which would long be special family keepsakes. With the tree on its side on the floor, young Zane grabbed the photograph at the top, carried it to his father, and said, "Daddy, this is you."

It was the Hallmark moment, and the breakthrough Jason and Suzie had long sought. Jason was relieved and, more important, happy for his son, who had made the connection and no longer seemed afraid of his own father. Little Zane finally knew that his dad was home and still loved him. Suzie was overcome with emotion, and the tears flowed freely.

"I sobbed like a baby because I was so damn happy," Suzie said. "It was the first time through this whole thing that I felt I had done something right in how I helped Zane process everything. It was like angels had sung from above."

As powerful as it was for her husband, too, he had simply endured too much already. Said Schechterle, "After those ten months I had been through, I think I was completely out of tears."

The last time he had really cried was four months before, in August, when he first saw his mangled left hand through a peephole when his eye skin graft had popped open a bit. The hand looked atrocious. The next time he really sobbed would be less than six months later, on June 12, 2002—the one-year anniversary of the day Jason awoke from the coma. It would also be the day 25-year-old Robert Nielsen would be burned alive and die in his Crown Victoria cruiser. It would happen in metro Phoenix just forty miles from where Schechterle's son had finally recognized his disfigured father. Another officer burned in a Ford Crown Victoria, right in Schechterle's hometown, and it would sicken Jason to his core. He, too, would feel the full force of rage—righteous, crystallized anger—that propelled his lawyers Pat McGroder and David Perry.

CHAPTER 17

Carrying the Torch

ON JANUARY 10, 2002, Jason Schechterle was easy to find: just check a narrow list of local hospitals and doctor offices, because that's where he spent his days. On this day, he was back where it all began, at County, for yet another medical checkup. During the visit, a hospital staff member came into the room and asked Suzie to step out to take a phone call from someone at the Phoenix Police Department. Schechterle didn't give it a second thought. This was his life: He went to doctor appointments *every* day, had surgeries and, every day, people from the police department called about one thing or the other. This was the new normal.

Except this time, when Suzie came back into the room she was visibly emotional. Not tearful, but somehow moved. Schechterle's first thought was that they had lost another member of the police family and, momentarily, his heart sunk. If it was another Crown Victoria incident he might even come unglued; months earlier McGroder had stirred his fighting spirit and had further fanned the flames of outrage with regular updates on the various legal maneuvers against Ford. Schechterle had been trained in the immediate and life-or-death decision-making model of the police world. The civil litigation world, he was discovering, operated on an entirely different timetable. To Schechterle, it seemed two lawyers couldn't say "Hello" without writing and filing motions with the court. Fearing the worst, Schechterle braced for the bad news. The absolute last thing in the universe he expected his wife to say was, "They want you to carry the Olympic torch."

It took a few seconds for Jason's mind to process her words. Then he asked, "What? Who's 'they'?"

"The Olympic people want you to carry the torch when it passes through Phoenix."

When he grasped what she had said, he was first struck by the immense honor of such an invitation. But then, as he lay shirtless on the examination table, he quickly pointed out, "Suz, I can barely walk. I can't *run* with an Olympic torch."

"I know," she said, nodding. "You're right."

"And look at these hands; I can't even hold a spoon. I can barely eat Froot Loops. I'm a mess. How can I run with a lit torch? There's no way."

"I know," she said again, still nodding. "I know."

Then she gave him that look, the one that spoke without words. He laughed and shook his head. "You think I should do it?"

She nodded, smiling. "Yes I do. You cannot miss this opportunity. Embrace it."

She's crazy. He thought. *My wife is bat-shit crazy. And as usual, of course, she's right.*

"When?" he asked.

"In three days."

"Three days! Suz, that's nuts. There's no way. Maybe they should be looking for someone who can run, or even walk, and actually has hands to hold the damn thing, right?"

The idea had gone from the absurd to the impossible. If anything, he was thinking he'd have some weeks to consult with his doctors and therapists, which might allow time to figure out how to move his legs better and actually hold a torch with his mangled hands. Otherwise it was going to be like wearing boxing gloves and trying to pour tea without spilling as he ran. Not to mention that he could still barely see. No way.

"Three days?" he repeated.

"Yeah, three days. It's on Sunday."

Apparently, whoever had been slated for this four-hundred-yard leg of the torch carry was a last-minute scratch.

Jaleel White cancelled: We need a replacement. And FAST!

No way, Urkel's down? I'm on it. Now go back in there, chill those Olympic reps out, and wait for Jason Schechterle, who should be coming directly.

You sending Schechter Shorts?

You feel better?

Heck, sir, that's all you had to say!

It was someone at the Phoenix Police Department who put forth Schechterle's name as a late-inning pinch hitter. In early 2002, not even four full months had passed since 9/11. Firefighters injured in the line of duty were the new national heroes, along with, for the first time, rank-and-file police officers. Schechterle, too, had been struck down in the line of duty and had become a local hero. The Olympic flame would be traveling through Phoenix en route to nearby Salt Lake City, Utah, for the 2002 Winter Games. Schechterle would be a part of history. That was, if he didn't drop the sacred flame or fall on his face. And both of those unfortunate possibilities had a high degree of probability in his current condition.

On Saturday, a package arrived at the Schechterle home by overnight courier, containing the official white running suit Jason would wear during the torch carry event. He'd also found out he was to be the third-to-last person before the final torchbearer completed the Phoenix portion of the flame's journey by lighting the cauldron in Patriot's Square Park downtown. His nerves were already ramping up.

On Sunday, January 13, 2002, Schechterle awoke with a start and, although the event was not until that evening, was already buzzing with a nauseating blend of excitement and anxiety. Once again, he was struck by another odd milestone: He'd received his torch relay invitation on January 10, exactly two years to the day after he'd begun his field officer training program. Now here he was at 125 pounds, a tracheal tube hookup still in place, with mangled hands that were about to be called into duty well ahead of any timetable he or his doctors had devised. Schechterle would be among 11,000 or so torchbearers transporting the flame across the nation to the Games. The day was mostly agonizing; all he could do was sit, wait, stand, and pace. With his stomach in turmoil, he barely ate. Then, as dusk descended on a clear winter night in the desert, Schechterle climbed in the car with help from Suzie. The kids and Suzie's mom piled in, too, for the twenty-minute drive to downtown Phoenix.

By the time they'd parked and walked to the area where the small bus would pick him up, the scene was chaotic, with random well-wishers hailing Schechterle, loud crowds, and a feverish buzz of activity. For Schechterle, with his poor eyesight and with night fully settled, it was a blur of random shapes and unrecognizable faces. He was being pulled through a strange dream that was equal parts recognition—they were smack in the middle of Central City Precinct—and indecipherable faces and noise. He knew his family was all there somewhere, along with Bryan Chapman and Shayne Tuchfarber. Phoenix Mayor Skip Rimsza approached, with his 3-year-old triplets in tow, and told Schechterle he'd made the trip specifically to watch Jason run. Also in the crowd was his lawyer Pat McGroder with his wife Susie and their three children, ages 10, 13, and 15. The McGroders' two eldest children, Caroline and Patrick, would each later write their college entrance essay applications about Jason Schechterle.

"All the support, including the mayor, meant a lot to me," said Schechterle.

At the same time, the pressure to not screw up was intensifying. Things began to move quickly: The Olympic representative took Schechterle by the arm and led him to the bus. He explained the order of relay runners and told Schechterle where to get off the bus.

"I can't see," Schechterle said as he was being hustled onto the transport vehicle, a large white van. His vision afforded him a blurry view at best, as though trying to identify faces and objects underwater at the far end of a swimming pool—and, in this case, under cover of darkness. *Maybe this was all a horrible idea?* Suddenly Schechterle felt his heart rate spike, and he wondered if he was going to be on the national news and forever known as the idiot who dropped the Olympic torch.

"Don't worry," the Olympic representative said. "Somebody will tell you when it's your turn to get off."

Yeah, Schechterle thought. *Easy for you to say.*

His nervousness increased by the minute. Already shy by nature, this was only his second major public appearance. He was extremely self-conscious about his disfigured appearance. He also felt oddly out of place as the last-minute substitution. *Urkel's down!* Schechterle hated feeling so conspicuous in so many ways.

Not to mention that other nationally known sports figures and celebrities were seated around him on the same van, including former NBA basketball player Danny Ainge. And, even more incredible, just two months after the World Series victory over the Yankees, Curt Schilling was there, too. Schechterle could make him out sitting across the aisle and one seat up. Schechterle had once had his sights on a professional golf career, and he lived and breathed every down of Alabama Crimson Tide football on fall Saturdays. So to be sandwiched between two professional athletes he admired ramped up his emotions exponentially.

"I was completely in awe of this entire experience," he said. "Danny Ainge was a former Phoenix Suns player and NBA champion. Curt Schilling just won the World Series and was co-MVP. I was freaking out."

Then the Olympic representative on the van asked each torchbearer to quickly say their name and give a short introduction.

"My name's Jason Schechterle," he said. "I'm a Phoenix police officer. I was injured in the line of duty ten months ago. I'm honored to be here."

Introductions complete, the representative explained that each of the twenty participants would be dropped off every four hundred yards. Then came a quick flurry of instructions:

You will be given a torch. You do not pass the torch; you pass the flame. We will turn the gas on. Simply touch the tip of your torch to the next person's torch.

Schechterle was trying to process it all, but was more worried about not falling on his face and wondering if he had already missed his stop. Then came another bombshell to further heighten his anxiety: He'd be receiving the flame from NBA legend Danny Ainge and then, if he didn't embarrass himself and was able to complete his four-hundred-yard leg, passing the sacred Olympic flame to his hero Curt Schilling.

"That's when things ramped up for me," Schechterle said. "These guys are national superstars, and I'm sandwiched in the middle of them trying not to make a fool of myself."

The Major League Baseball pitcher, in turn, would complete his leg and pass the flame to the final participant, a young female Special Olympian who'd take the flame to the stage for the lighting of the cauldron. Within minutes, the van emptied until it was only Ainge, Schechterle, Schilling, and the young woman.

"How did you get injured?"

Schechterle realized it was the voice of Curt Schilling. *Yes, Curt Schilling is starting a conversation with you. Don't be an ass.*

Schechterle managed to answer and carry on a brief but intelligent conversation despite his nervousness. He told Schilling what watching the Diamondbacks win the World Series had meant to him in his weakened condition, and how he had to sit inches from the TV just to make out blurry shapes. At its best, watching athletes compete and win at the highest level helped regular people forget their problems for a bit.

"I wasn't going to ask some dumb question like, 'How do you throw a curve ball?'" Schechterle said. Mission accomplished. Then Danny Ainge stepped off at his stop.

"You're next," someone said to Schechterle.

If the moment could not get any bigger, somehow it did when Schilling laughed and said, "Holy shit, Jason, how many people are here for you? There are *a lot* of people out there."

Great, he thought. *And this from a man who pitches in front of 40,000 screaming fans.*

"I was completely naïve to the enormity of the moment," Schechterle said.

Then the van stopped, the doors popped open and the cheers echoed from out of the darkness and blurred lights.

"You're up."

Objective one, he thought: *Do not trip coming down these stairs.*

Once into the night, the loud roar increased. He could hear his name being yelled from every direction. *Friends? Family? Where's Suzie?*

"Here's your torch," a female voice said as Schechterle looked through his peepholes. As Schechterle readied himself, the young woman gave him the official safety lecture ending with, "And be sure to keep the flame away from your face."

Before he could censor himself, Schechterle smiled and said, "No shit?"

Schechterle knew Danny Ainge was already jogging this way; he only had a minute or so to ready himself. Schechterle was wearing a compression garment on his inoperable left hand; his right hand was also inoperable. He laid the long torch in the frozen crook of his left lobster claw and cupped the pointed end at the thin bottom with his right claw.

Do not drop this torch. You don't pass the torch; you pass the flame.

Schechterle looked northbound and could see them coming, a blur of headlights and flashing police lights moving slowly southbound toward him, the lone, lanky figure of Ainge jogging at the front. Then it was time, as the entourage led by Ainge enveloped Schechterle.

You do not pass the torch; you pass the flame.

Schechterle watched as Ainge gently took Jason's unlit torch, pulled it toward the flame, and made the transfer. The next thing that popped into Schechterle's head was *Damn, I'm tall, but this guy is* tall! And then he was back in the moment and beset by a rush of admonitions.

Do not screw this up.

You are the only person in the world holding the Olympic flame.

Do not fall on your face: The world is watching.

And don't worry about burning yourself: How much more damage could you really do?

Since learning of this duty three days earlier, Schechterle had been mapping his plan: He'd hold the torch as tight as he possibly could, walk down the street at his own pace, and pray the entire time. People would understand, right, if he couldn't run? Of course they would. The event planners had offered a wheelchair and/or a stand-in to carry the torch as Schechterle walked. Schechterle politely told the planners what they could do with each of those ideas. He had shuffled out of County hospital under his own power after being burned alive; he could certainly walk four hundred yards.

"When Danny Ainge lit the flame I was overcome with emotion," Schechterle said. He could barely see, but he felt a surge of energy from the crowd, an infusion of love and support that touched him deeply. To his left were Bryan

Chapman and Shayne Tuchfarber, in uniform, walking alongside and screaming encouragement. There were several Phoenix police motorcycles and patrol cruisers rolling slowly with lights flashing. There were other officers on foot and bicycle patrols. The Phoenix police force was standing by their man, including, of course, Schechterle's brother Michael in full uniform.

Schechterle turned and started south down Central Avenue toward where it merged into First Avenue. After taking a few steps, with no major mishaps, for reasons he still cannot explain, Schechterle started *jogging*. He had barely learned to walk again and now here he was, blind with two claws for hands, jogging down the street amid thousands of screaming people.

Do not trip.

Do not drop this thing.

He focused on what he could see of the black road; he never looked up. Schechterle heard his partner's voice to his left, clear as on Day One at the academy when Chapman had asked if Schechterle liked sprinkles on his cake: "Pick up those feet! You better run! Come on, Jason! Atta boy. Pick those legs up! Come on, buddy. You're almost there."

He heard other friends, family, fellow officers, and strangers shouting encouragement as though he was about to win the Olympic marathon at Panathenaic Stadium in Athens. In what seemed like a flash of seconds, he made it to Schilling. He did not drop the Olympic torch, fall down, or add new burn scars to his beaten body.

I'm done! I did it. Let's go home!

There was a pause as Schechterle waited to transfer the flame to Schilling's torch. The crowd noise swelled as Schechterle made the pass. Schilling's torch was lit: Schechterle could breathe easy. But the moment was to be extended. Suzie stepped in and hugged Schechterle for what seemed like minutes. She cried as he held her tight. The adrenaline dump he had learned about at the academy and experienced on patrol hit him hard. *What a moment. What a victory.* And again: *Let's go home! Back to the safety and solitude of the living room recliner.* Except Schechterle felt a tug and heard a voice saying, "C'mon, you're going with me." The voice was that of Schilling: He was taking Schechterle along for his leg of the relay, too.

Wait. What?

Minutes earlier, in the van, Schechterle had relayed to Schilling how powerful the unscripted moments in sports could be for people. And now Schechterle was no longer in the audience, but rather on that stage participating in one of those rare, special, and dramatic scenes that transcended the script.

With Schilling gripping his lit torch, Schechterle fell into rhythm to Schilling's right. Then Danny Ainge appeared from behind, came up on Schilling's left side, and walked along to form a band of brothers. The cheering intensified for the trio that included a public servant and two sports legends. But it was the beanpole cop getting all the encouragement.

Go, Jason!

C'mon, Jason.

You're the man, Jason. Go!

Schechterle was shuffling along in a slow jog that was an easy walk for Ainge with his long strides. By now Schechterle was numb, exhausted, energized, and overwhelmed. It was all too much.

"You all right?" Schilling asked.

"Yeah," Schechterle said. No one had any idea what an effort this had become; Schechterle was close in height to the two professional athletes, but he was absolutely gaunt, drained, and out of gas. In his Olympic tracksuit he looked like a boy wearing his father's clothes. The trio of Schechterle, Schilling, and Ainge eased into a slow and steady walk.

"I was so glad I accepted this opportunity," Schechterle said. "I had created a new good memory. Most of the stories from my previous ten months were not good ones."

When Schilling passed the flame to the young girl, in deference to her the three men dropped back, but continued to walk in what became a foursome. Patriots Square Park was abuzz and packed with people. Security guards appeared and ushered Schechterle and his new compatriots through the masses to the stage. They joined the other torchbearers on stage. The cauldron ignited into a glorious blaze, the glare from which further diminished any chance of Schechterle being able to see. Master of ceremonies Mark Curtis, a local television news anchor, asked Schilling to speak. And then Schechterle.

He was emotional, crying, and not a public speaker by any stretch. He felt vulnerable and exposed and physically weak. Like Rocky Balboa after fifteen rounds with Apollo Creed, he scanned the crowd. The first thing he said into the microphone was, "Suzie, where are you?"

Yo, Adrian!

The crowd noise quieted. Someone yelled, "She's back here, Jason. She's right here." Schechterle didn't hear her voice, but he felt her presence again. Then he said, "You're my rock, and I love you!"

Then the tears flowed, and he couldn't say another word. He was off the stage and surrounded by a massive rush of people. His grandfather George hugged him. Police officers came in from every angle with hugs and backslaps, many wiping tears of their own. A homeless guy produced a T-shirt and Sharpie and asked Schechterle for an autograph, his first of thousands. Grabbing the Sharpie triggered the old dark humor among Schechterle's cop pals that had become his own reality: *If found, please take to County.*

Later, as Schechterle and his wife and kids walked back to the car, Shayne Tuchfarber produced a baseball that Schilling had autographed.

"Chapman and I escorted Curt Schilling to his car to make sure he wasn't hassled," Tuchfarber said. "He signed the ball and said, 'You tell Jason if he needs anything to call me.'" Then Tuchfarber handed over the slip of paper with the number Schilling jotted down.

"Wow," Schechterle said. "This keeps getting better. Now I have Curt Schilling's cellphone number. In truth, I was just as moved by the homeless guy hugging me."

Around ten o'clock, Schechterle was back in the passenger seat for the drive back to Avondale. Suzie drove, with her mom and the kids in the back. They left downtown Phoenix, Suzie found I-10 westbound, and the interior of the car darkened as they left the bright lights behind. What a day. What a moment.

Then Schechterle asked, "What's tomorrow?"

"Monday," Suzie said.

Two months in a coma and eight more months in hospitals, doctor offices, physical therapy, and operating rooms did that to a person: Schechterle had no normal routine or timetable to mark days of the week.

"Monday," he repeated.

The start of the weekly grind: doctor appointments, physical therapy, and visits to specialists who continued to try to figure out how to get Schechterle's eyes and hands working again.

ON January 21, 2002, Schechterle underwent another surgery to repair his right hand. Dr. Tony Smith would perform three more hand surgeries during 2002, on May 23, June 21, and August 13. For Schechterle, all the hand surgeries, physical therapy, and pain and suffering had one primary goal: firing a gun again. If he could do that and re-qualify on the range—with a score of 210 or better—he could return to work in some capacity.

When he pondered such things, he was energized with the same feeling he first experienced in 1988: his awe and admiration for his older brother Michael in his crisp, clean dark blues. Back then, as now, all Jason Schechterle wanted was to be a Phoenix police officer. Back then, after bombing out of the hiring process twice, no analytical or logical facts supported the notion that Schechterle would triumph, in 1999, during his third attempt. Nor did they now.

But if Schechterle had learned one thing since the night of March 26, 2001, it was that analytics and logic were as relevant to his situation as the Fourth Amendment during a casual knock-and-talk: that is, zero relevance. So what science dictated held no bearing on what might be possible for Jason Schechterle. Make no mistake: He was going to be a cop again, because that was what he was meant to do. All he needed to do was figure out how to make that happen.

CHAPTER 18

More Miracles, More Tragedy

WINTER FINALLY ARRIVED in the desert in the early months of each year, as it did in 2002. Gone were the suffocating triple-digit temperatures and "cocoon living" in air-conditioned bubbles in homes, cars, and offices. The sky still burned a fierce blue, the sum total of "winter" a few weeks of rain and wisps of clouds. Maybe a handful of nights with freeze warnings, too. With the Olympic torch relay already in the books for the year, in these welcome cool months nothing on the horizon promised to equal or top that experience. But the life and times of Jason Schechterle had birthed a new reality: expect the unexpected.

Speaking of expecting, Jason and Suzie Schechterle got some news that was every bit as stunning as an Olympic torch relay invitation and bigger than anything that had already happened since March 26, 2001: Suzie was pregnant.

Wait. What? Schechterle said. *One more time, please?*

Yes, it was true. Not only had Schechterle survived, he had *procreated*! This would one day be the biggest punch line in the moving and emotional speech he'd give to many large audiences.

Not everything burned.

Just another miracle in a long line of miracles. The joke the couple shared was that taking care of her husband was, for Suzie, already like having an overgrown baby in the house. Now they needed to prepare for the mini-scale version of a dependent little human being.

Schechterle's days were otherwise the same unending blur of doctor appointments and physical therapy. To increase his odds for the best possible recovery, Schechterle had decided he needed to seek out the best plastic surgeon in the country.

"The doctors had stripped everything away," Schechterle said, "so it was time to start putting things back together."

Schechterle's decision to look outside Arizona for medical attention, however, would create other unintended consequences he'd only fully comprehend later. However, before leaving for his first scouting trip, another issue appeared on the docket during the same month. Rogelio Gutierrez, the illegal immigrant who'd started Schechterle's burn odyssey—and who, it turned out, was having an epileptic seizure when he crashed his taxi into the squad car—stood trial on two counts of aggravated assault for the injuries to Schechterle and the taxi passenger. The charges were Class 2 and Class 3 felonies, respectively. In preparation, Schechterle met weekly with Maricopa County prosecutors. He'd be called to testify, briefly, and planned to be in court for every minute of testimony, too.

During the trial, prosecutors argued that Gutierrez's history of recklessness regarding his epileptic medical condition was particularly troubling. He'd routinely failed to see a doctor regularly or take his prescribed medications. Prior to pummeling Schechterle's Crown Victoria and sending a fireball into the desert night sky, Gutierrez had caused four other previous crashes due to seizures.

Firefighter Rebecca Joy, the fire truck driver that night, testified, as well as Officer Wayne Scott, the first motorcycle officer on scene at Schechterle's crash site. Tommy Reyes, a detective from the vehicular crimes unit and the accident investigator, also took the stand.

Schechterle's testimony was necessary to establish his basic identity, his patrol area, and the facts of his whereabouts on the night of March 26, 2001. But because he had been knocked unconscious at the moment of impact, he couldn't offer much more and was only on the witness stand for about twenty minutes. Gutierrez's defense attorney had no questions for cross-examination, and the jury had only one: How far behind an emergency vehicle was one required to stay when lights and siren were activated?

"Five hundred feet," Schechterle told the jury. Arizona was one of only three states that allowed jurors to ask witnesses direct questions via the judge.

Prosecutors had more damning evidence: Gutierrez lied about his epilepsy and falsified driver's license applications with the Arizona Motor Vehicle Division. In his defense, Gutierrez, who'd suffered minor injuries and a broken leg in the collision, concocted a tale that Detective Reyes, the accident investigator, had come to Gutierrez's hospital room and broken his leg.

After closing arguments, the jury had the case on a Thursday afternoon, deliberated less than two hours, and had a verdict the following day. With Schechterle sitting in the packed courtroom, the jury foreman read the sentence: guilty on both counts. Bryan Chapman walked to his partner and patted Schechterle on the face. No words were needed.

"It was a moment of hustle and chaos," Bryan Chapman said. He'd been sprinting down the hall to reach the courtroom and walked in just as the jury foreman read the verdict. There was no hooting and hollering.

"I felt all along that this was a case that was going to come out in favor of the state and Jason," he said. "The actions and consequences that were played out by this guy driving the taxi were completely avoidable."

At sentencing, Gutierrez received two concurrent sentences: twelve years for Schechterle and seven years for the taxi passenger. Gutierrez served time until September 2011. When he was released, U.S. Bureau of Immigration and Customs Enforcement officials marched him back across the border in Nogales. In March 2002, as the one-year anniversary of being burned alive approached, the conviction of Gutierrez brought some closure to at least one part of Schechterle's night of terror.

WITH the trial in the books, Schechterle was ready to get his face fixed. He didn't have any illusions about ever looking remotely like the Karate Kid again.

Instead, his goal was to find out what skilled plastic surgeons saw as his best possible outcome, and proceed toward restoring some of his appearance.

Schechterle took Bryan Chapman and his dad Fred along to Virginia to meet Craig Dufresne, the chief of plastic surgery at Inova Fairfax Hospital. To round out the entourage, local Phoenix reporters Katy Raml and Judy Villa went along as well to document the trip for the ever-growing local audience that had been drawn in by Schechterle's horrific accident, amazing survival, and real-life triumph-of-the-spirit journey. From the Washington, D.C., area, the plan was to drive to New York City and meet with Elliot Rose, another plastic surgeon with a stellar reputation. The final leg was a quick stop farther north in Boston to meet a third burn reconstruction doctor.

"He was on a search to find someone to help fix him," said Chapman, who was less than enthusiastic about seeking medical care on the East Coast. That stance soured him on Dufresne, too, but Chapman knew his role and shut his hole in support of his friend.

In contrast, Schechterle immediately liked Dr. Dufresne; he partnered with Robert Barron, who'd worked as a disguise specialist for the Central Intelligence Agency. For more than two decades during the Cold War, Barron worked in the shadowy world of international espionage using custom-made prosthetics. An artistic genius, Barron had mastered the craft of disguising operatives to the point that they could move in and out of locations and through airports undetected. Now, under the banner of Custom Design Prosthetics, Inc., he was using his skills in the broader context of helping accident victims find a modicum of normalcy.

"I used to put people in hiding," Barron said. "Now I bring these people out of hiding through prosthetic devices."

After meeting Dufresne, the trio made the six-hour drive to Manhattan. Schechterle's academy instructor, Sergeant Lauri Williams, met the group for added support and sightseeing. Schechterle, however, was still shy, insecure, and reticent about his appearance, and less inclined to traipse around Manhattan gawking at skyscrapers. One Olympic torch relay was enough excitement for the year; he wanted to avoid being in public. But Williams was not having it.

"If we can hide your face, will you go?" she asked. They were gathered in their hotel room in midtown Manhattan.

"Yeah," Schechterle said, figuring he had an out, because how was she going to manage that?

"I'll be back," she said and left without consulting the others. Less than half an hour later she returned with a shopping bag and pulled out a bright red New York Fire Department hoodie. They helped Schechterle pull it over his head. Then she cinched up the strings until his face was hidden.

"Jason, it's New York City," Chapman said. "I hate to burst your bubble, pal, but there are so many freaks here no one will even notice you."

"All right," Schechterle said. "Let's go."

Even with the hoodie, Schechterle kept his head down and had to concentrate to keep from falling. He had a new contact lens for his left eye that improved his vision to 20-100. Not great, but a huge improvement over the underwater blur he had endured. His right eye, however, was still barely functional. Within minutes, they came upon a fire station entrance right on the street.

"Let's go in and say 'Thank you,'" Schechterle said. Not only did he have a new fondness for and connection to every firefighter in uniform, but this was only six months after 9/11. Reverence was the watchword at every turn. The firefighters inside received the impromptu visitors with ease and aplomb. The visitors from Phoenix were enamored with the immaculate NYFD fire trucks sitting at the ready.

"These are the most beautiful fire trucks I've ever seen," Schechterle whispered to Chapman.

"I know, no kidding," Chapman said. "I've never seen any city vehicle this shiny."

"Your trucks are beautiful," Schechterle said during the brief conversation. He was wondering if New Yorkers had some special cleaning formula or method to achieve such perfection. Schechterle was a lifelong student and devotee of the School of Attention to Detail.

"Yeah," the firefighter said solemnly. "They're brand-new. We just replaced the ones that were destroyed on 9/11. Those are all the guys from our station that died that day." He pointed to the wall covered with framed photos of the fallen firefighters.

"There's a big difference between East Coast and West Coast cops and firefighters," Chapman said. "Their camaraderie is much stronger. The last thing those guys saw before they rolled out on 9/11 was that firehouse and their neighborhood. It was a very humbling and reverent moment to be there." From the firehouse, the group rode the subway down to Ground Zero and spent a couple hours there.

At the next doctor on the list, as Schechterle sat there with Chapman and his father, he was hit with an intuition: *I cannot be in New York City for surgeries.* As he pondered that thought, he quickly realized there were too many logistics: long car rides into the city, and then more congestion and traffic to get to and from appointments. The noise, the unending sirens, the crush of people. Collectively, the entire notion just didn't feel right, nor was Manhattan a tranquil sea of healing calm. *Yeah, duh,* he thought to himself. But he was learning as he went.

"I was so worn out by then," Schechterle said. "I didn't even want to go to Boston." With that, the group cancelled their plans for Boston and instead took a flight from New York back to Phoenix.

ON a subsequent return trip east, Chapman and Schechterle rented a car at the airport and drove to an affluent suburban neighborhood in Virginia. They pulled up to a house where a man in his late 50s greeted them at the door. The host, who had a full head of salt-and-pepper hair and a mustache, was Robert Barron, the former CIA disguise specialist. Other than the presence of a small chunk of the Berlin Wall, the inside of the house looked like any other upper-middle-class home. After some pleasantries and small talk, Barron said, "Let's go down to my basement." Coming from the lips of a former CIA operative, this cloak-and-dagger invitation quickened pulses in both police officers.

In the basement, Barron hit a switch that flooded a workshop with clean, bright light. The hub of the disguise specialist's lair was a modern dental chair. There were cabinets and a counter workspace; it looked like a clean surgical ward. On the counter, a large magnifying glass was surrounded by a scattering of various prosthetics in different stages of process: ears, fingers, hands, and eyeballs. When Barron completed a gelatin prosthetic, it was clear. His mastery was the skin-tone matching process, with painstaking airbrushing.

"The realistic touches he put on were unbelievable," Schechterle said. "It was like walking into a museum. What an art to be able to configure that in real life."

Barron directed Schechterle to the dental chair to discuss his goals: to have normal-looking ears and a nice nose.

"I want the same ears as my dad," he said.

Barron nodded but explained how physical characteristics change with age. Then he looked at Chapman and sized him up like a blue-ribbon 4-H steer about to be led into the ring. Baron said, "Your buddy's ears and nose are actually perfect for you. Size and shape, everything."

Chapman didn't hesitate for one second in seizing that one: "Hear that, Schechter Shorts? I'm perfect for you."

Schechterle laughed. "Yeah, whatever." Then his tone got more serious. "Would you do it?"

"Yeah, of course," Chapman said.

Two years before, as they'd started class 333 together at the academy, neither could have imagined—even in the furthest-flung, twisted-tequila, sleep-deprivation experiment—that they'd be here, in a Virginia basement workshop with Chapman's appendages getting modeled up by an ex-CIA agent for his patrol partner's face. No, that potentiality had definitely never cropped up in their academy coursework: *Performance Objective 625.1.1, Modeling Patrol Partner Prosthetics for Body Part Replacement.*

"Sit down," Barron said.

"He put me in the chair of horror," Chapman later said. "That was the beginning and end of my modeling days."

Barron injected what looked like Silly Putty around Chapman's ears and nose and, thirty minutes later, had two clear Chapman-replica ears and a nose. Using the molds, Barron created clay molds and, eventually, the silicone prosthetics. Then the real magic would happen over the next weeks, as Barron painted the parts to match Schechterle's natural skin tone and coloring, which required another return trip with Suzie for the final match and fitting.

THE onset of spring and summer 2002 brought the famed desert heat and more stunning events that, in the long march of wild happenstance, had begun to appear normal to Schechterle. For starters, Schechterle had his right-hand index finger amputated. True to his nature, Schechterle tracked surgeries with his typical accuracy and methodical precision. So he knew the finger chop was surgery number twenty-seven—the first seventeen had occurred before July 31, 2001, the day he walked out of County. Another day, another surgery, another lost digit. *What's for lunch?*

What might topple most people all on its own—*We need to talk about removing your dominant-hand index finger, your trigger finger, due to painful seizing and dislocation*—was therefore just 1/27th of Schechterle's problems and surgical solutions so far. After fifteen months—from rousing in a burning car like a zombie from a 2 a.m. cable redux to staring down death dozens of times—Schechterle was amazingly calm. He might have been selecting pizza toppings when he said, "What if we just cut it off?" *And no anchovies!*

Dr. Tony Smith was immediately relieved. The pain in Schechterle's finger had been excruciating. The doctor had wanted to amputate, but hadn't known how to broach the delicate and difficult subject with a patient who'd already suffered so much loss.

Then, a month later, a representative from the Major League Baseball Arizona Diamondbacks called the Phoenix Police Department: The Diamondbacks' representative wanted to honor Schechterle with a suite at a game, as well as raise funds for his family. Then the idea evolved into also having Schechterle throw out the ceremonial first pitch at the June 23 regular-season game.

Schechterle had just had major hand surgery, lost his index finger, and couldn't even open or close his remaining fingers. His first thought was *How the hell would I hold a baseball?* So of course the first thing he said was, "I would be honored to throw out the first pitch."

Look, Urkel: You walked out of County on your own. You carried the Olympic torch with three days' notice. You'll just have to figure out how to grip and throw a baseball.

But first, the unthinkable happened. Again. And this time, Schechterle was enraged.

Officer Robert Nielsen, just 25 years old on June 12, 2002, was on his normal shift before 2 p.m. on a bright, blazing summer day in Chandler, Arizona, a suburb twenty-five minutes southeast of Phoenix PD headquarters. Nielsen was patrolling in a 1999 Ford Crown Victoria. It had been another uneventful shift until, in one swift moment, he was en route to a call at 70 miles per hour.

As he passed through the intersection at Chandler Boulevard and Pennington Drive, the driver of another vehicle failed to yield the right of way and made a left turn directly into Nielsen's path. The errant driver's vehicle struck the Crown Victoria and sent it careening into a utility pole. Upon impact, the patrol car burst into flames, trapping Officer Nielsen inside. Horrified witnesses stopped immediately, leaped from their vehicles, and attempted to pull the two-year veteran and husband from the blazing wreckage. But it was too late; Nielsen was soon consumed by the flames and, mercifully, dead.

When he got the news, Schechterle was with Shayne Tuchfarber, who'd taken him to yet another in a never-ending blur of doctor appointments. As usual they were laughing when Schechterle's cellphone rang. It was a local TV reporter who broke the news to Schechterle. The laughter immediately turned to rage. Schechterle hung up and called his lawyer Pat McGroder. McGroder had not heard the news.

"It happened again, Pat," Schechterle said. "This has to stop. What are we going to do? This has to stop!"

In that moment, something changed: The Crown Victoria issue was no longer about Schechterle's fight against Ford Motor Company. Now it was their duty to stop this from ever happening to another law enforcement officer again. For Schechterle, McGroder and Perry were the only people who had any chance of stopping the horror.

"You've got to be kidding me," McGroder said.

Schechterle was stunned and could only say, "I don't know, Pat. I just don't know."

It was official: The lawyers McGroder and Perry, and their client Jason Schechterle, were ramping up for a righteous fight against a corporate heavyweight unwilling to yield to reason or justice.

TRUE to the roller coaster of emotions his life had become, two weeks later Schechterle had to put aside the tears and rage and make his scheduled public appearance at the baseball game. Compartmentalizing the death, right across town, of Officer Nielsen, Schechterle focused on his special night. Flipping the switch off temporarily was difficult, but it was the only way he knew how to find a few hours of solace.

Schechterle invited to the game all the firefighters, officers, doctors, nurses, and therapists—some seventy people—who had brought him back to life. He'd asked his grandpa George and Suzie to go on the field with him for the pitch. For weeks in physical therapy he'd been practicing holding a ball. His practice throws were only ten feet across the room with a red rubber ball.

When it was time, a representative came to take the trio onto the field. Schechterle, his grandfather, and Suzie walked through the tunnels and onto the field. Along the way, stadium workers offered Schechterle well wishes and congratulations. Then Curt Schilling walked up; Schechterle hadn't seen him since the night of the historic Olympic torch relay.

"I'm going to catch this for you," the pitcher said.

"Can I go on the mound?"

"Most people stand on the flat part, but go ahead."

Schechterle had to wait through the national anthem, and as he waited his nervousness was ramping up. Schechterle was squeezing the baseball. Before he left the suite his cop pals had let him have it:

This better not hit the dirt.

Don't throw it underhanded.

Make sure your skirt's not too tight or it'll throw off your mechanics.

Hey Schechter Shorts, John Stockton called: He still wants his shorts back.

Bumble Bee tuna: Your balls are showing.

The Olympic torch experience had helped prepare him for this moment. Now, with a hard contact lens in his left eye, he could actually see people's faces, which added to his nervousness.

"Walk out to the mound," the representative said. Then the public address announcer said, "Ladies and gentlemen, please welcome Phoenix Police Officer Jason Schechterle."

A nice roar went up, but Schechterle didn't really hear it. He reared back, let the ball fly, and popped Schilling's glove with a decent effort. Relieved the moment was over—and that he'd not gone Bull Durham with the throw and taken down Baxter the mascot—Schechterle was ready to settle into the suite for the night and enjoy time with family and friends. But there, lodged in his mind, was the gnawing anxiety of Robert Nielsen's death, just across town, in a burning Crown Victoria Police Interceptor. Schechterle still wanted to know how this could have happened, again, to another one of his brothers.

ON June 26, Schechterle returned to Virginia for his first major medical procedure outside Arizona. Dr. Craig Dufresne's goal was to correct Schechterle's lowered head position and gaping mouth, which was locked open, as well as increase his neck mobility. To do so, Dufresne required two lengthy tissue-expansion surgeries, performed months apart. During the first surgery, Dufresne would insert two expander balloons in Schechterle's upper back and two more in his neck. Every two weeks, Schechterle would return to Fairfax so Dufresne could carefully monitor his patient. Meanwhile, back in Phoenix, Schechterle would see a local doctor who, three times a week, would insert a needle into ports installed by Dufresne and inject saline into the expanders. Over time, the subdermal balloons would expand and stretch the skin just like a woman's belly during pregnancy. Then, in a second surgery, Dufresne would remove the inflated balloons, raise Schechterle's head, and have enough slack in the newly stretched skin to pull it up and close the incision.

When Schechterle and his wife arrived at the Comfort Inn in Fairfax, they both smiled and shook their heads when they saw the room number: 326. As in 3/26, the day Marc Atkinson was killed in 1999 and, exactly two years later, the day of the collision. They both took it as a good omen.

A producer from a program called "Extreme Surgeries," an ongoing series on the Discovery Channel, had contacted Schechterle via Dufresne and asked whether Schechterle would be willing to have his surgery documented for the show. Schechterle reluctantly agreed, but later regretted the decision. The show's crew filmed him before, during, and after the first surgery; the operation was a success, but Schechterle didn't enjoy the experience. There were too many expectations and demands by the producer trailing a cameraman and sound engineer. Based on that experience, the Schechterles closed the circus freak tent and agreed that this would be their last medical documentary.

Back home, sleeping was impossible with the ever-expanding giant bulges in Schechterle's upper back and neck. It was like a double boob-job gone wrong, with four DD balloons all askew. With Suzie pregnant, the trips back and forth to Fairfax every two weeks were becoming tiresome and tedious. Schechterle would leave Phoenix on a red-eye flight with whoever his chaperone was that trip, make the thirty-minute drive from the airport straight to Dufresne's office in Fairfax, get his checkup, and then return to the airport for the flight home without setting foot in a hotel. Schechterle was starting to realize that out-of-state surgery was not a great idea.

In July, sixteen months after getting burned, Schechterle finally climbed in a patrol unit again for the first time. It was a moment he'd been envisioning since the day he woke up at County. The plan was to ride along with his partner Bryan Chapman for part of his regular shift. Foremost, Chapman made sure he didn't take a Crown Victoria that night.

"I was excited for him that he would be back to the sights, sounds, smells, and sensations of the police world," said Chapman. "Once you've been out on patrol, there's nothing else quite like it, and you miss what you can't get anywhere else."

On this night, they weren't assigned to any specific beat: They could go anywhere and respond to whatever calls they chose. Said Chapman, "Everyone in the precinct and in our squad was thrilled."

Being on patrol again reminded Schechterle how much he missed the street.

"I'd like to say it was like the good old days, but those days were gone," Schechterle said.

Being in a squad car also reminded him how much he missed chewing tobacco, a habit he'd started on Day One of his Field Training Officer program but couldn't do anymore because the wad would fall out of his damaged mouth. The nicotine itch was so agitating that Schechterle had been pondering taking up Marlboro Reds again. But Chapman quickly nixed that idea: "You already smoked too much at Twentieth Street and Thomas." Ultimately, Schechterle would use the small pouches of Skoal that kept everything in place.

Around 9 p.m., Chapman lit up a driver he suspected of DUI. While Chapman tried to perform an HGN test on the driver to determine whether he was impaired, the guy kept looking back toward the cruiser where Schechterle stood.

"Hey, aren't you that cop?" the suspect finally asked, pointing to Schechterle.

Chapman rolled his eyes. "Here we go."

The DUI suspect walked to Schechterle and extended his hand, saying, "Wow, I saw you on the news."

At that point, a motorcycle officer intervened and took over the suspect. Chapman shined his flashlight on Schechterle with a look of surprise.

"What?" Schechterle said.

"Dude, look."

When Schechterle looked down he saw that blood had soaked through his T-shirt. His entire chest was covered.

"Let's go," Chapman said as they both climbed back in the car.

"Can you believe this?" Schechterle said in frustration. "My first time back in a patrol car on a shift, and I'm headed back to County."

Doctors had to perform an emergency surgery to correct problems with the implants. Pockets had formed between the skin and muscle and were now pooling with blood. Schechterle was in the hospital for three days.

AT the end of the summer, Schechterle and Chapman flew to Los Angeles twice to meet with a "wigmaker to the stars." Schechterle had been referred to the specialist by Robert Barron, the former CIA specialist who had created the prosthetics. Schechterle had been trying his new prosthetic nose and ears, but the experiment was not going well.

"They looked great, and perfect, but they didn't look good on me," he said.

The color was a precise match to Schechterle, but with Schechterle's other skin graft scars and skin texture, Chapman's perfect ears and nose just didn't look right. And of course Chapman reminded his partner mercilessly that it would be *his* ears, Chapman's, that Suzie would be forever whispering sweet nothings into. The price tag on the prosthetics was $10,000. It only took Schechterle a couple minutes to put on the glue and lock everything into place. But in the Arizona heat, the glue loosened. He could only imagine the horror of having an ear fall off and traumatize a small child at the mall. Schechterle liked Robert Barron immensely and appreciated the incredible and painstaking work the artist had done to improve his appearance. But the prosthetics just didn't blend naturally on his newly scarred head.

Perhaps hair, Schechterle thought, would better complete the ensemble and provide a more balanced appearance. So on this day, he and Chapman flew into LAX and within an hour entered a cramped, cluttered shop in Hollywood, with wigs everywhere. Dozens of framed star photos lined the walls.

"Were you around with Frank Sinatra?" Schechterle asked the wigmaker, an older woman right out of central casting: tons of makeup, three-inch fingernails, and a sort of matronly, mad-scientist kinetic energy.

"Yeah, we did all his pieces."

One of Katey Sagal's wigs, from her role as Peg Bundy on "Married with Children," was there, too. Chapman said, "Dude, try that on."

"I'm not wearing that," he said.

"You can have hair again," the wigmaker told Schechterle, "And it's going to look real."

Schechterle liked what he was hearing. She carefully measured his head and asked, "What do you want?"

"Short dark hair to match my complexion." He showed her the pre-burn photograph she'd asked him to bring.

"Before the accident, his hair looked like a short brown Brillo pad," Chapman said later. "I'm thinking, 'Dude, don't show her that. You can have any hair you want now. You could be Fabio.'"

All the wigs were handcrafted from real hair. For the manufacture, fitting, and styling, the price tag was a hefty $15,000. An hour later the two cops were on their way back to LAX. Schechterle was thinking that if the wig helped him blend in a little better, then his appearance would be less shocking.

Two weeks later the pair took a return flight to Los Angeles for the fitting and moment of truth. The wigmaker unveiled her custom creation, fitted it perfectly to Schechterle's head, and trimmed and styled the wig until she was ready for him to turn and look into the mirror. By then, Schechterle had sky-high expectations. But when he looked, his immediate thought was, *This doesn't look right.*

"The wig just did not work on his head," Chapman said. "The hair itself was beautifully done, but it did not belong on his head." But instead Chapman said, "It looks good. You need to wear it. Give it a shot. You need to get used to it."

Schechterle wasn't so sure, but he nodded and reluctantly agreed. He wore it back to the airport, on the flight, let Suzie see it—once—and then threw the $15,000 wig in a box. He never wore it again.

"It was the most ridiculous thing ever," Schechterle said. Chapman's ears and nose soon joined the wig in the box, the Land of Misfit Body Parts, cast away and forgotten forever.

Who wants to play with a Charlie in the Box?

Schechterle would just have to get used to his new outer shell. He was horribly scarred and disfigured; it was who he was and always would be. There were worse fates, such as never waking up at all. Going forward, about all Schechterle would do to conceal his appearance was throw on a baseball cap and sunglasses, as much for sun protection as anything. And if his beautiful wife Suzie could still love him—wow!—then what else mattered? Still, in a sometimes vapid and largely superficial Western culture obsessed with appearance, it would take time for Schechterle to be 100 percent OK with his appearance. But one day he would. Later, when he stepped up to the podium to give his moving speech in a sharp suit and tie, his head, face, ears, and nose were all in plain view. He had nothing to hide.

But before that inner journey and evolution, in the immediate early years after the crash, Schechterle felt lost. According to Bryan Chapman, direct as ever, his partner looked heartbreakingly bizarre with his injuries, scars, skin grafts, and the puffy back and chest. Chapman could not have felt worse for his friend as they walked through airport concourses and felt the aghast stares. Schechterle's shrinking skin pulled his jaw down, exposing his bottom teeth and a gaping mouth. He was still skinny as a rail. He was horribly scarred, and his nose and ears looked like blobs of melted wax.

"He looked like a hunchback," Chapman said. "He was just trying to be normal. His appearance, per se, didn't matter to him. It's more that he wanted to lessen people's reaction to him and just blend in and be normal."

Indeed, although Schechterle knew on a deeper level that "normal" had been permanently obliterated March 26, 2001, he was still the unassuming Hidalgo kid who longed to just blend in with the crowd. Hence the search for any vehicle—prosthetic ears and nose and a professional handmade wig—that could return him to a time and place when he was just a fun-loving guy, doing what he loved.

ON September 5, 2002, Schechterle was back on the East Coast, on the operating table for the second of Dufresne's procedures. Schechterle's father had accompanied him. Suzie, very pregnant and unable to make the flight, stayed in Phoenix with the two kids. During the operation Dufresne scraped away scar tissue, removed the four expanders, and reattached the stretched skin to help Schechterle's mouth and neck mobility. The doctor was able to pull up six inches of stretched, healthy skin to replace the burned tissue on Schechterle's neck. He also removed scar tissue from the lower lip and harvested a flap of skin from Schechterle's abdomen to fashion a new upper lip. After more than eight hours in the operating room, the surgery came off without a hitch. However, within two days Schechterle had developed a staph infection.

It wasn't cataclysmic news, but in Schechterle's weakened condition the infection made for a few tense days until it fully resolved. Proceeding carefully, it also meant Schechterle was stuck in the hospital in Fairfax, Virginia, for more than ten days before Dufresne felt comfortable allowing him to travel back to Phoenix. That was the snapping point—when Schechterle verbalized what he'd already realized for some time.

"Never again will I have surgery out of state," he told his dad as they drove to the airport. True to his word, it was his last out-of-state procedure; the rest of the more than twenty-five surgeries he'd undergo would all be in metropolitan Phoenix.

On the one-year anniversary of his major hand surgery, September 10, Bryan Chapman called Schechterle with some bad news.

"About an hour ago Wayne Scott was killed on his motorcycle," Chapman said.

Beryl Wayne Scott.

He was the first motorcycle officer on scene the night of Schechterle's smashup. He'd also been the first to testify, six months before his death, at the trial of the taxi driver Rogelio Gutierrez. The news knocked the wind out of Schechterle.

"That's awful news," he said. "What happened?"

Chapman explained that Scott was en route to a hospital to assist with a fatal DUI investigation. A driver pulled out of a parking lot onto Seventh Street directly into Scott's path. With no time to react, Scott's motorcycle struck the passenger side of the vehicle, launching the officer over the vehicle. Eerily, the spot where Officer Scott landed was the same spot where Officer Patrick Briggs had died in a motorcycle accident on June 20, 1990. Scott, a ten-year police department veteran, died thirty minutes later at the hospital, leaving behind a pregnant wife.

THE fall of 2002 proved to be momentous and triumphant for Schechterle on two fronts. First, on October 29, 2002, Suzie gave birth to their son Masen, the miracle baby conceived after Schechterle's collision. *Not everything burned!* With Masen just a few hours old, one of the nurses said that another nurse, named Atkinson, wanted to come meet Schechterle. As a medical miracle and oddity of sorts, this was the new normal, so Schechterle didn't give the request a second thought. He also had a natural draw to anyone in the nursing profession because of all the wonderful care he'd received.

"Yeah, that's great," he said. "Tell her to come on in."

As he pondered the surname before she introduced herself, Schechterle made the connection and knew who she was: the wife of fallen Phoenix police Officer Marc Atkinson, whose funeral procession had inspired Schechterle to try one last time to make the force. Already emotional from the birth of his son, Schechterle held his emotions inside. Nurse Atkinson, too, knew that Schechterle's accident had occurred two years to the day from when her husband had been killed. But even after the brief introduction in the hospital room, she didn't know that it was her husband's funeral procession that had inspired Schechterle to pursue his dream of becoming a police officer. For Schechterle, it was too much to process and share in that moment.

Once Suzie and the new baby came home, Schechterle was the world's most loving father, but he wasn't much help in the diaper-and-infant-care department, with his hands still like two ping-pong paddles. So he did what a long line of patriarchs had done since time immemorial: He went back to work and left the kid duty to his wife.

"Masen's birth really confirmed that we were going to be OK," Jason said.

In November 2002, Schechterle slipped on dress slacks, tucked in his polo shirt, pulled on black leather shoes, and pushed his gold badge, #7110, into the waistband of his pants. Then he kissed his wife and new baby, got in his mid-sized Nissan truck, and *drove* forty minutes from their rented house in Avondale to 620 West Washington in downtown Phoenix. These pedestrian markers of normality—*He drove himself to work!*—were all a stunning succession of small miracles. That was why he found a cluster of media people waiting outside the door for his first day back at work. In twenty months, Schechterle had returned from the dead multiple times, walked out of County under his own power, and was now back at work.

Schechterle was working in the public information office with Lauri Williams, his academy sergeant and New York traveling companion, and two other public information officers. He felt a little weak physically, but overall was up for movement and activity. He didn't have any problems driving to work. The never-ending eye surgeries had proved helpful, and he could finally see out of his left eye. The job was a good fit, with light duty, to ease back into the working world after an almost two-year absence. He had no firearm affixed to his right hip, because he'd first have to re-qualify on the range.

"It just felt good to get dressed and go to work at eight in the morning," he said.

His job duties included answering phone calls, taking media requests, and coordinating the endless and heavy flow of information between officers, detectives, and the public.

Schechterle began 2002 carrying the Olympic torch when he could barely walk or use his hands. He'd thrown the first pitch at a professional baseball game. Now he had a new son and was back at work. But he still had several big items on his to-do list. First, with the help of his lawyers Pat McGroder and

David Perry, was to get Ford Motor Company executives to pull the plug on the Crown Victoria. In Schechterle's estimation, the company simply needed to stop manufacturing cars that were rolling time bombs. A troubling question that haunted the lawyers and their client: *Who would be next?* It was a cold and eerie waiting game.

Second, Schechterle needed to relearn how to shoot a gun. For that, surgeons would have to reconstruct two frozen claws into functioning hands. His new trigger finger on his dominant right hand would be his middle finger, since the index finger had been amputated in June. Once he could shoot again, Schechterle could take the qualification test to see if he could carry his service weapon again at work. That was the only way he'd ever move from light duty to being a full-authority cop again.

"I knew I would never be a patrol officer again," Schechterle said. "That was gone."

But the ultimate dream was still on the table: being a detective. The Hidalgo Kid did not understand simple words and phrases in the English language: *Quit. Give up. Impossible.* These did not appear on the screen of his consciousness.

CHAPTER 19

Legal Gunfight

BY EARLY 2003, Schechterle's medical team was continuing work on rebuilding his nose and ears and improving functionality in both hands. Because he was enduring the stress and recovery of dozens and dozens of surgeries, Schechterle's doctors came up with a genius strategy: two-for-one. Like happy hour in the OR, Schechterle would undergo one general anesthesia during which two different specialists would conduct separate operations. Dr. Bill Leighton was the plastic surgeon responsible for Schechterle's head and face; Dr. Don Sheridan would work on the hands.

After Schechterle decided to see local doctors only, his lawyer Pat McGroder referred him to Leighton, an aesthetic and reconstructive plastic surgeon who was an expert in soft-tissue expansion and burn reconstruction. McGroder and Leighton were both cut from the same mold: consummate professionals in their respective fields who could each make sailors on shore leave blush with their salty language and offbeat humor.

During his first meeting with Leighton, Schechterle walked into the doctor's office, sat down, and sighed. Then he simply said, "Doc, I am fucked up. And I'm aware of that."

Leighton put on his best poker face, nodded and said, "Yeah, you are."

The laughter put both at ease and was the start of a strong bond between doctor and patient. Schechterle was adamant about Leighton not using expanders, which had caused so much discomfort and an even more freakish appearance during the process. This admonition put the surgeon at an immediate disadvantage, because he'd have to develop another plan to harvest enough skin. So instead he told Schechterle he'd excise scar tissue from the scalp behind his ears, fashion that skin into rolls, and attach that as new ears.

The plan for building a new nose was similar: Leighton would take flaps from the cheeks and upper lip and construct a new appendage. He'd also have to move Schechterle's septum down to correctly shape the tip of the nose. Harvested skin had to be grafted over with skin taken from elsewhere on Schechterle's body. At one point, Leighton had an inspired idea: to construct a new nose using biceps tissue—except this would require sewing Schechterle's face to his arm and leaving it like that for six weeks.

"Fuck you," Schechterle said, half-jokingly and 100 percent seriously. "You're crazy. There's no way we're doing that."

Leighton's response: "So I take it that's a 'no,' then?"

The jokes continued throughout the session; as Leighton would later say, all Schechterle wanted was a place to hang his sunglasses so he could look cool. That and the ability to hold and eat an Ultimate Cheeseburger from Jack in the Box, because his hands were so jacked up and his mouth contracted.

In turn, Leighton referred Schechterle to his friend Don Sheridan, an orthopedic surgeon who was the team hand specialist for the local Major League Baseball Arizona Diamondbacks. When Sheridan met Schechterle for the first time in early 2003 and saw his hands, he was looking at the worst case he had ever seen. The hands were still just claws. While sewing them into Schechterle's abdominal wall had saved them from being amputated, the procedure had allowed so much skin and fat to grow that the hands had tripled in thickness. Although imperative at the time as a last-ditch maneuver, that new growth was now limiting movement. Leighton performed a reconstructive liposuction to remove the excess tissue and then sent Schechterle to Sheridan for the real work of reshaping the hands into something functional.

Schechterle communicated his two burning desires to Sheridan: to return to police work (i.e., to be able to fire his gun again), and to play golf. From where he was starting, those were both tall orders. Schechterle's hands had severe contractures, which meant they were frozen into unusable positions. Almost immediately, Sheridan knew and conveyed to Schechterle that he'd never have two fully functioning hands again. There was simply too much damage. He did, however, have an idea that might deliver on both of Schechterle's goals.

When joint contracture is corrected, patients almost never end up with full extension. But within the limited arc of movement, Sheridan could center the range of motion into the most functional position needed. For Jason, that position would be the grip to hold a pistol. If he could hold the gun and learn to pull the trigger with his middle finger (since his index finger was gone), he might have an outside chance at re-qualifying on the range. Even if he could do all that, the big question would be whether Schechterle could draw, point, and shoot with speed and precision, because every test on the range was timed. Some elements were as short as three seconds: target turned, draw, *pop pop*, holster, target flipped back. *Maybe*, Sheridan thought, *but not likely*. But he'd do everything in his power to help.

Knowing the goal, Sheridan had Schechterle bring him a molded rubber replica, a so-called red gun, of Schechterle's service weapon, a .40-caliber Glock. Red guns were 100 percent safe, while duplicating the size and weight of real guns by different manufacturers and in various calibers. On them, police recruits could learn all the essentials of firearm carrying, safety, and operation during academy and other training scenarios, with zero risk of accidental discharges, injuries, or death, since red guns were nonfunctioning blocks of heavy rubber.

Red gun in hand, Sheridan sterilized it, took it into the operating room, and used it as a prop to mold Schechterle's hand around as he operated. Sheridan released the joints in Schechterle's hands with incisions, molded the grip around the red gun, and pinned Schechterle's fingers in place. Sheridan would eventually perform four more surgeries on Schechterle's hands. Meanwhile, often under the same general anesthesia, Dr. Leighton was undertaking other tasks, including sanding Schechterle's face off, which, although it initially worsened Schechterle's appearance and was intensely painful, eventually made a big improvement in his skin surface and texture.

"Blue Gatorade and morphine," said Leighton, in reference to Schechterle's preferred post-op thirst quencher and pain reliever. "That's all he ever wanted."

ON December 19, 2002, Trooper Robert Ambrose, 31, was sitting in his Ford Crown Victoria on the shoulder of I-87 in Yonkers, New York. It was 8:35 p.m. He was writing an accident report for a minor accident, as he had done numerous times in his five-year career with the New York State Police. He was badge 198, assigned to Troop T in Tarrytown.

Behind Ambrose, a driver attempted to switch lanes in the winter darkness, struck another vehicle, and then veered onto the shoulder and smashed into the rear of the Crown Victoria. The Ford police cruiser burst into flames, which enveloped Trooper Ambrose and gave him no chance to survive. The driver of the vehicle that struck Ambrose, who was driving on a suspended license, would also die. The fire consuming Ambrose was so intense that rounds from his service weapon began to discharge. The eerie pops of gunfire shattered the cold tranquility—and would reverberate all the way to the state Senate in Albany. Ambrose's fiery death, coupled with the ongoing string of similar incidents, had finally caught the attention of New York's political power brokers. State Senator Mick Spano convened a subcommittee to conduct a hearing into the safety issues of the Crown Victoria Police Interceptor. Invited to the hearing were Pat McGroder and his client Jason Schechterle, Ty Rupert from Fuel Safe, Bill Chisholm from Fire Panel, and McGroder's expert Mark Arndt. Schechterle was once again enraged. *There it was again: How can this keep happening?* Lawyers McGroder and David Perry would assist counsel in the Ambrose case and were also co-representing the Nielsen family.

On a January Sunday morning in 2003, Schechterle boarded a plane at Sky Harbor Airport in Phoenix. Accompanying him were his two sidekicks: partner Bryan Chapman and McGroder. Their destination was Albany, New York. Schechterle was making the trip to testify at the New York state Senate hearing being convened on the Crown Victoria. The six-day trip to the East

Coast would also include a stop in Atlantic City, New Jersey, where Schechterle would speak to a gathering of a hundred people at a New Jersey State Police function.

Schechterle and his compatriots were all sickened and livid that another officer had died a heinous death inside a rolling Ford time bomb. Schechterle was energized to go public with his own experience and advocate for changes to the Crown Victoria. Getting the attention of lawmakers, it seemed, was a huge step toward forcing Ford executives and engineers to redesign the Crown Victoria fuel tank position and construction.

"We also wanted to show support for the guy that agency lost," Schechterle said.

When the group stepped from the cozy confines of the Albany airport, they were blasted with a cold wind that chilled to the bones.

"Jesus Christ," said McGroder, a Buffalo native softened by three decades in the desert.

"You got that right," added Chapman, an Ohio native also reacclimated by his desert migration.

"Did your husbands make the trip, too?" Schechterle offered. He was shivering too, but he wasn't going to whine like these two softies.

"Why don't you make yourself useful and build us a fire to keep warm," McGroder said.

"Yeah, a nice big, bright blaze—you're good at that," Chapman said.

"What are we looking for, McGroder?" Schechterle asked as they headed out to the rental car lot. "You book us a Lincoln Town Car? Crown Victoria? Pinto?" Schechterle had bought two new suits and a trench coat for the trip, to better fit his new lean frame. Due to the voracious calorie demands of healing, it would take a full three years for Jason to get back to his normal weight.

"Yeah," McGroder said. "And just to be sure, I asked for one pulling a U-Haul trailer full of gasoline barrels."

"With extra C-4 in the trunk, right?" Chapman said.

When the black sedan rolled up, the trio quickly piled into the warm interior and sped off toward the hotel in downtown Albany.

"With Pat, it's not like we were staying at Motel 6," Schechterle said of the well-appointed travel arrangements. "But I'm sure he billed that to me, and I ended up paying for it anyway. During that trip I got to know him in a way that brought him down to earth."

Once checked in, they were met by Dan DeFedericis, the president of the New York State Troopers Police Benevolent Association (PBA). Like McGroder and Schechterle, DeFedericis had become a great advocate in the cause to fix the Crown Victoria. Also like McGroder, DeFedericis was a Buffalo native; his father was chief of police in the nearby suburb of Cheektowaga. DeFedericis himself had been a trooper for seventeen years and had finished law school, although he'd not sat for the bar exam. Like so many others, DeFedericis was captivated by Schechterle's saga of survival and his indomitable spirit of courage. DeFedericis had used his leverage with the PBA to apply political pressure that led to these Senate hearings.

Their first morning in Albany, Schechterle sat with a local reporter for an interview arranged by DeFedericis. She was a feature writer and, at one point in the interview, asked Jason if he'd gone to the hospital after he was caught in the fire. Speechless, Schechterle looked at McGroder, who just shrugged his shoulders. Chapman, too, was dumbfounded by the inane question.

"Yeah," Schechterle finally offered. "I did have to go to the hospital for a bit."

Even in Albany, New York, strangers would approach and ask Schechterle, "Aren't you that cop from Phoenix?" And then they would say something along the lines of, "You really are an inspiration."

In one instance, a homeless man recognized Schechterle and said, "Aren't you that cop from Arizona?"

Schechterle smiled, nodded, and said, "Yeah."

The man was wearing dirty, torn mittens. He removed one and offered his bare hand in the cold saying, "God bless you."

Schechterle shook his hand without saying anything else.

Chapman, McGroder, and Schechterle went to Senator Spano's office to give him a preview of their planned presentation. During the rushed preview Spano had to step out, so McGroder continued with the PowerPoint slides as he educated the senator's staff. Although he knew the hearing was well-intended, McGroder began to wonder whether he'd be given a chance to discuss real solutions to the Crown Victoria issues, or if the hearing was more of a political play without much depth.

Then the trio had to rush back to an afternoon press conference arranged by DeFedericis at the New York State PBA office. The press turned out in good numbers and listened to DeFedericis as he explained they wouldn't tolerate any more officer deaths and wanted all Crown Victorias in the fleet remediated at any cost. He announced his intention to ask the state legislature for enough money to fix the patrol cars.

Schechterle spoke for about ten minutes, and McGroder followed him to answer the various technical questions about the Crown Victoria issues and litigation. It was DeFedericis' intent to use the press conference to preempt any attempt by Ford representatives to spin the Senate hearing the next day. The strategy seemed to work well.

After the press conference, the trio from Arizona went to the state legislature building to meet senators who might sit on the panel. The three waited in an area where lobbyists gathered to corner lawmakers and pitch pet projects. Led by McGroder, the men met several senators, some of whom were dubious that anyone could survive a high-speed rear collision in any vehicle.

The trio grabbed lunch at a huge, crowded cafeteria that served the entire governmental complex of buildings.

"I don't want to go in there," Schechterle said, as he lingered back in the hallway that opened into the massive room.

His lawyer nodded, thinking, *He's embarrassed about his appearance. And that's OK.*

Schechterle waited in the corridor while the lawyer and his partner took trays and returned with lunch. The three found a large janitorial closet and sat in the dingy room eating with the janitors.

"I need to be more considerate toward you, Jason," McGroder said.

"What?" Schechterle said.

"About the cafeteria," McGroder said. "I didn't even stop to think how difficult that would be for you."

Schechterle smiled. "You got it wrong: I didn't want to go in there because I didn't want to ruin anyone's lunch by them seeing me."

With some surprise, the trio from Phoenix discovered that Jake Jacobson—Chapman's and Schechterle's union president—was also in Albany. Shockingly, however, he was there to speak on behalf of Ford Motor Company. It was like Tinker Bell taking up with Captain Hook: It made absolutely no sense.

"You don't fly across the country on Ford's dime and testify on their behalf when one of the officers in your union was nearly killed in a Crown Vic fire," Chapman said. "In the end, the testifying turned out to be more theatrical than substantive. Jason, of course, was a good ambassador and could talk about the real-world effects of these cars exploding."

Even at the agency that employed Schechterle, Phoenix cops had minimal awareness of the wider issues with the Crown Victoria Police Interceptor. The only visibility at all was due to the three Arizona deaths of officers Juan Cruz, Skip Fink, and Robert Nielsen. Even so, Crown Victoria Police Interceptors comprised 90 percent or more of the Phoenix Police Department fleet, with a smattering of Chevrolet Caprices. Eventually the city would spend $1 million to outfit the Crown Victoria cruisers with fire panels and bladder technology.

Next up was the five-hour drive from Albany to Atlantic City, a unique chance for the lawyer to bond with the two police officers on a more personal level.

"We laughed for five hours," Schechterle said.

In Atlantic City, the trio met with the Police Benevolent Association union representatives, all of whom treated the visitors as family members.

"We got the real sense that this was a big issue for the guys involved," Chapman said.

McGroder had other business in the area, so Schechterle and Chapman took a flight home from Atlantic City.

CHAPTER 20

A Civil Action

IN 2003, in anticipation of filing the formal suit against Ford Motor Company
on behalf of Schechterle, lawyer Pat McGroder began drafting the disclosure
statement. To do so, he spent untold hours with his client and Suzie, as well as
Schechterle's parents, brother, sister, and friends. The resulting profile was an
amazing recounting of courage in action. Hearing Schechterle's story in such
gripping detail, chronologically for the first time, reaffirmed to McGroder just
how far his client had come.

What an inspiration!

McGroder also met with representatives from the city of Phoenix and,
specifically, the supervisors within the workers' compensation area. All
Schechterle's medical bills were being paid by the city because he'd been
injured in the line of duty, with the understanding that Schechterle would
repay the fund from any eventual financial settlement from Ford. By early
2003, the total tab was already at $1.2 million, including Schechterle's
medical expenses and lost wages. McGroder also interviewed the key medical

personnel treating Schechterle, including Dr. Bill McLeish, the eye surgeon. These details would be documented in the formal civil suit against Ford Motor Company.

Through the legal process, McGroder and Perry would bring the facts to light. To begin, Schechterle's eyelids had been burned off, with severe burns to his corneas and pupils; McLeish created new eyelids. In addition, Schechterle had been blind for more than eight months, with much talk of corneal transplants and the likelihood he would never see again. If McGroder could prove Ford was negligent in causing these injuries, how much was a good pair of eyeballs worth? Those injuries alone would have Ford over a financial barrel, but the medical narrative of the suit would document every other injury and surgery Schechterle had suffered and undergone. No savvy defense lawyer would want those gritty details marched before a jury.

McGroder's firm also ponied up a sizable sum to have a scale model of the crash scene built by a specialized company, Graphic Law. The model was seven feet long and showed in exact detail the position of each vehicle and how things had transpired the night of March 26, 2001. The model would illustrate the facts of the case for a jury, should the suit go to trial. McGroder also had to finish an accident reconstruction, but was awaiting skid-testing data from the county attorney. McGroder's target was to finish and file the lawsuit by mid-March.

Concurrently, McGroder was preparing a similar suit in the case of Robert Nielsen, the 25-year-old Chandler Police Department officer who had been burned alive. As was protocol in preparing these types of cases, McGroder had purchased the wreckage, including the gas tank, from the city of Chandler for $500. Before having it transported, McGroder and Mark Arndt wanted to inspect the vehicle. It had struck the utility pole on the far right rear quarter panel. Using a tape measure, the lawyer noted about fifty inches of crush from the rear quarter on through the fuel tank. There were several tears in the tank, including one caused by the tank strap. Their assessment: Upon initial impact with the other vehicle, a frame weld failed and the rear axle disengaged from the frame.

McGroder knew several issues the defense would raise, including Nielsen's high speed, no lights, and no siren, which comprised several violations of general orders of the Chandler Police Department. Undeterred, McGroder's strategy was to first go after the offending driver, to the tune of millions, and then go after Ford Motor Company for wrongful death. McGroder would employ the plaintiff's standard platform: excessive speed, lights, and siren or otherwise, police cruisers should not explode upon impact.

McGroder learned from the medical examiner, Phil Keen, that Nielsen's body showed no signs of traumatic injury. In other words, fire, not the collision, killed Nielsen, as it had in many other Crown Victoria cases. McGroder had the medical examiner walk him through all the gruesome details of the autopsy, including soot in Nielsen's bronchial tree, which was evidence he was alive and breathing as the fire consumed the interior of the Ford Crown Victoria.

McGroder hired Bill Ernyei, an accident reconstructionist, to determine Nielsen's speed at the time of impact. The expert estimated the speed to be somewhere between 73 and 75 miles per hour, which didn't help McGroder's case. McGroder would have to concentrate on the other driver's negligence.

The lawyer had also carefully gathered witness testimony from four different people, including one woman who claimed to be psychic and had had a premonition right before the accident that something bad was about to happen. Although not admissible in court, it was an interesting and odd side note in the case.

Depending on how far along the case moved, McGroder was also prepared to pay for crash tests using remedial measures on the Crown Victoria test cars to see if bladders and/or a fire panel would have saved Nielsen's life. Throughout his preparation of the Nielsen case, McGroder repeatedly thought: *There but for the grace of God goes Jason Schechterle. How close had he come to being another casualty? Inches and seconds.*

As planned, in March 2003 McGroder and Schechterle held a press conference in Phoenix to announce the formal suit against Ford Motor Company. Schechterle wanted to make the public appearance so he'd only have to do it once and not sit for numerous interviews with various media outlets. McGroder made some introductory remarks and then introduced his client. Schechterle read a prepared statement and answered a few questions, which McGroder restricted to non-case-specific queries.

Meanwhile, McGroder was awaiting word on a motion to allow a tear-down of Schechterle's Crown Victoria. They first needed court approval, but once underway the tear-down would be essential to assess puncture sources in the fuel tank. Proving how and where the fuel tank was penetrated was critical to a successful outcome in the case. Ford lawyers would contend that it was unreasonable to expect any vehicle to be able to withstand a 100-mile-per-hour rear impact. McGroder would present his argument about the fuel tank position and design on the Crown Victoria.

Further down McGroder's list of priorities was the taxicab company itself, which might have a pot of insurance money. However, their lawyers were contending that Rogelio Gutierrez, the epileptic who seized and struck Schechterle, had no authority to drive the cab, let alone drive for the cab company. The taxi company was cutting loose their former employee to let him twist in the legal wind of civil liability all on his own. Whatever transpired, Ford Motor Company remained the primary target for McGroder.

McGroder was also in contact with the attorney for the family of Trooper Robert Ambrose, 31, whose death in New York in a Crown Victoria just six months after Nielsen's had precipitated the state Senate hearings. McGroder and Ambrose's attorney were sharing information and discussing possible co-counsel scenarios, such as sharing costs, experts, and any eventual settlements, but nothing formal had been arranged.

In 2003, Jim Feeney from Ford Motor Company took Jason Schechterle's deposition in a conference room at McGroder's firm.

"Jim Feeney from Ford was a worthy advocate for whom I had tremendous respect," said McGroder. "He was a perfect gentleman and left the deposition, I believe, with the realization that Jason Schechterle is an American hero."

IN December 2003, the Detroit Free Press newspaper documented that sixty-nine people had died in fiery rear-end crashes in the Crown Victoria since the Panther platform was introduced in 1979. According to the article, at least eighteen officers had died as the result of Crown Victoria police car fires, more than reported by the government. And those deaths did not include the long list of serious burn injuries such as those that beset Schechterle.

By the end of 2003, almost two years into his long recovery, Schechterle would have made a strong argument that cases such as his were every bit as egregious, if not more so, than death itself. Something had to be done, and he and his lawyers were determined to pressure Ford executives into changing the design of the Crown Victoria Police Interceptor.

CHAPTER 21

The World's Greatest Job

JACK BALLENTINE joined the Phoenix Police Department in 1978, the same year Ford Motor Company introduced the 1979 Crown Victoria Police Interceptor. At the time, Jason Schechterle was 6 years old. When Ballentine joined the force, his mother gave him a wallet-size illustration of St. Michael, patron saint of cops, with an inscription: *Pray for us and cast into hell Satan and all the evil spirits who wander through the world seeking the ruin of souls.* He carried that card on patrol always, long after it became thin and tattered.

After working patrol in the Maryvale Precinct for six months, he moved to the then-new South Mountain Precinct. His first assignment was investigating gangs. From there he moved to a walking beat through the housing projects in South Phoenix. In 1980, he went undercover with a special government-funded operation.

"I was lucky," Ballentine said. "It was a unique set of circumstances that I was allowed to go to these specialty assignments. It was really kind of a charmed existence for me."

In 1986, he went even deeper undercover by crawling into the seedy underworld of contract killing. As an undercover operative, his mission was to arrange a murder-for-hire and capture the suspect fully committing to the act on audio and video surveillance. With that evidence, the suspect could be arrested and charged, and some unsuspecting person's life spared. This was the highest form of law enforcement protection and public service: stopping crimes and violent acts *before* they were committed. To move the case past wily defense attorneys to a conviction, Ballentine would have to carefully tiptoe around the boundaries of entrapment, which required several key factors to be a valid defense.

As a state-certified peace officer, Ballentine had legal leeway to use deception to obtain evidence and combat crime. On a bar stool in a strip bar with topless women rubbing on his leg, he could pretend to be a drug addict or a biker gang hit-man-for-hire, or act like he was several eights short of a full deck. He could pretend to be strung out on trucker candy, or a convicted felon who'd done hard time, or a mob-connected thug who'd take a life for ten large in two equal payments. *Half upfront, the other half in a bus station locker.* He could pretty much tell people anything he wanted in creating a believable sleazeball character.

He could not, however, try to lure a suspect into hiring him for murder if the person had not previously considered the crime. In other words, the *idea* for the crime had to originate with the suspect, not Ballentine. The detective, therefore, couldn't peddle his wares like a salesman: *Hey, have you ever thought of just having the lousy husband/cheating wife/business partner/rival gang member killed?* That would be entrapment: no conviction.

Nor could Ballentine urge, induce, or cajole the suspect into committing the offense. The last element of proving entrapment was predisposition: the suspect had to be fully capable of committing the offense and ordering the hit before Ballentine ever came along.

However, if Ballentine merely created an opportunity for someone who already had a contract hit in mind to commit the crime, then the entrapment defense didn't apply. Even if the idea originated with the suspect, Ballentine had to remain careful not to push the suspect into action. The intent and commitment to follow through with the crime all had to come from the suspect, not Ballentine.

But before ever meeting with a potential suspect in a restaurant parking lot to arrange a killing and worrying about avoiding entrapment, Ballentine had to first get into his role.

"I played seven different characters," he said.

His looming six-foot-five-inch physical presence and pumped-up 285-pound frame already gave Ballentine a good head start on playing the part of criminal thug intimidator. To add believability to his nefarious bad-ass biker and ex-con-type roles, he grew his hair halfway down his back, stopped shaving and showering, and prowled the sun-glinted streets and dark dens of Phoenix on a rat-bike Harley-Davidson, a mutt-cycle cobbled together from various police-seized motorcycles. Ballentine couldn't run the risk of rolling up to meet a potential murder-for-hire suspect on a bike pulled straight from the impound lot: The suspect might recognize it as his own or that of one of his fellow thugs: *Hey, that's Lefty's hog!*

Interestingly, even as he worked one of the most dangerous details, Ballentine was never a gun lover and rarely carried a piece. And, no, it was not because he couldn't shoot straight: He qualified as an expert-level shooter.

"I have nothing against them," he said. "I just never had an interest in weapons."

Sure, the odd time or two he'd carried a small-caliber piece, rolled up in a bandana and tucked into one of his boots. But otherwise, he relied solely on his ability to physically, mentally, and emotionally intimidate everyone around him when he was in character. And, if need be, his fists and tenacity completed a pretty good triumvirate of defense.

Ballentine was one of six operatives in his undercover unit, which was largely autonomous and operated separate from police headquarters at 620. The main safe house was an anonymous warehouse on the west side of Phoenix, in an industrial area that smelled like burning roofing tar and diesel fuel, directly below the flight path to Sky Harbor International Airport; the unending drone of commercial jets echoed overhead day and night. Several sets of train tracks also cut through the area, adding the constant rattle and clack of commerce and industry to the din. The first rule was to make sure no one was following when returning to the warehouse.

"You didn't want to bring anything back there," Ballentine said. "You never wanted to burn that place."

Given that he was usually riding there at night, with no sign of human activity through the endless clusters of chain-link junkyards and windowless industrial buildings, it was easy to spot a tail. That is, any single set of headlights did not belong.

The warehouse had bay doors that rolled up and high ceilings, with an area to park. Ballentine could wheel his salvaged Harley right into the space next to the other unmarked vehicles, including the special vans outfitted with full audio and video surveillance platforms. The unfinished concrete floors meant the space was cold in summer and colder in winter. Inside, several rooms were built out and partitioned off from each other. The command center was a large room with desks around the perimeter and a cluster of tables in the center to meet, spread out paperwork and photographs, and plan operations.

The warehouse had space for the administrative staff, offices for the sergeants who oversaw the operation, a workout room, a pool table, and a basketball hoop. Lining the walls were seized video arcade games set up so the operatives could become adept at all the various bar games. To make themselves believable in seedy bars, these detectives became some of the best pool players and Space Invaders marksmen their unsuspecting cohorts would ever encounter. Some of the detectives who were bow hunters set up an indoor archery range as a way to practice and unwind.

From that nondescript hideout, Ballentine rolled out on the hog to loiter in the dark nooks and crannies of Phoenix where questionable people knew worse people who were willing to pay to have someone killed. Ballentine built a street network of informants, topless dancers, bartenders, drunks, ex-cons, drug addicts, and dealers. Only the informants knew he was a cop; everyone else in his make-believe hierarchy thought Ballentine was the real deal, a hardened thug who killed for cash. He met with hundreds of people who casually talked about having someone killed, but he only followed through on those cases where he sensed the suspect was absolutely, 100 percent committed to the deed. Ballentine's rule: *If not me, then someone else.* That is, if Ballentine didn't stop the bloodthirsty maniac, then that person would simply move on and find a real hit man. Over the course of his time undercover, Ballentine would narrow his bar trawling down to three to five of those lockdown cases each year.

Working deep undercover, Ballentine prowled, breathed, and lived the sights, sounds, and smells of the city's gutter subculture. Moving in that subterranean world exposed him firsthand to the unthinkable, the bizarre, the laughable, and the unbelievable. During one setup, as he sat in his truck near the airport with a stripper who'd just returned from Las Vegas, Ballentine watched as she reached under her short skirt—no underwear, of course—and pulled a baggie of methamphetamine from her secret stash box. *The only way to fly!*

A depraved couple wanted to hire Ballentine to off their own son, who they said had become a bothersome annoyance. *Kids these days.*

A woman who'd attempted and failed to kill her husband on her own wanted to hire a professional to do the job right. *And you should hear his snoring!*

A man with *GQ* good looks and a bipolar bent for exploding violence wanted Ballentine to kill his equally attractive girlfriend so she couldn't testify against him for dangling her out a second-story apartment window. *Women: Can't live with 'em, can't live without 'em.*

On and on it went, one dirty deal after another conducted in broad daylight in the parking lots of Denny's restaurants and other civilian establishments under sunny Phoenix skies. Particularly troubling was the fact that business was booming for such misdeeds; it demanded Ballentine's full attention to stop these crimes before they occurred.

"You don't emotionally process what you encounter in the grand scheme," he said. "If you do you could get pretty bitter and simply stop believing in people and individuals. I always avoided generalizations and dealt with each case on an individual basis. The vast majority of time, those particular people were so self-consumed and greedy that they were willing to do whatever they could do to make it happen. If it meant taking another person's life, then they were going to do it."

In 1988, concurrent with his murder-for-hire cases, Ballentine worked with the Organized Crime Bureau (OCB), which included a number of different squads with different investigative specialties. Ballentine's squad investigated motorcycle and prison gangs, which was a good fit for the ongoing hit-man cases he continued to work. His squad was also charged with dignitary protection, in conjunction with U.S. Secret Service agents, for any heads of state visiting the Phoenix metropolitan area: U.S. presidents and vice presidents, along with kings, queens, and other foreign royals.

"While I was protecting the first President Bush, I was knee-deep in a murder-for-hire case," Ballentine said.

He worked OCB and did murder-for-hire for twelve years. In total, over a span of fifteen years, Ballentine sifted through hundreds of murder-for-hire cases, followed through with twenty-four cases, carefully avoided those legal snares of entrapment, and saw prosecutors get convictions in every case.

But it was a dark and dirty business, with a cumulative and rising emotional toll. Ballentine was always scrambling to avoid detection and come up with new characters capable of murder for hire, always walking the dangerous line between believability as a scumbag and, flipping the switch, back to normal for his wife, two boys, and Little League baseball games. One minute he'd be on the phone with his wife about a leaky toilet that needed fixing, and the next he'd have a 19-year-old stripper rubbing her hot mound on his knee and pointing out Ballentine's next hit-man client. Also complicating the situation, strippers with kids at home were always looking for a decent man, and despite his Oscar-worthy performances as a heartless worm, the women prancing around in dirty stilettos and neon-green bikini bottoms—and nothing else—could always intuit the core of goodness within Ballentine.

I know he's a criminal, she'd tell her friends as they put on makeup before their shift. *Even so, there's just something different about this guy.*

No one, not once, ever suspected the truth: *Yeah, no shit: He's a cop!*

Ballentine never succumbed to the constant courting and offers of companionship, which in that world would have meant a hot loin slap in a dirty stall. All factors considered, the job simply became all-consuming. Even the best men could eventually be broken.

Finally, in 2000, to preserve his sanity and not spin away into the dark world he'd grown quite comfortable prowling, Ballentine left undercover duty. Like Rocky Marciano, he retired his hit-man post undefeated: 24-0.

"I wanted a different challenge," he said. "It was time for a change."

He would become a homicide detective, which would be his final post with the Phoenix Police Department. As part of his new duties, Ballentine taught a detective qualification course at Rio Salado College in Phoenix to young police officers looking to one day promote. In early 2001, an eager young rookie named Jason Schechterle was one of the forty-five or so new students in Ballentine's class. It didn't take the young cop long to make an impression on the twenty-six-year police veteran.

Early on in the course, Ballentine walked to his city-issued unmarked truck after class one night with thoughts of finally getting some quiet time at home with his wife. Instead, Ballentine was greeted by his new student, Jason Schechterle, who just wanted to ask a quick question. There in the parking lot, standing truck-side, Ballentine obliged. Then came a second question. Ballentine obliged again. Then questions three, four, and five. With each answer Ballentine offered, Schechterle came up with more questions. This process didn't happen just once or twice during the course: Every night, after every class, Schechterle was waiting by Ballentine's truck for the private post-class session. Ballentine, ever patient, might nevertheless have pondered an order of protection against his own student.

"Yeah, basically he drove me nuts," Ballentine said. "*Every* night after class he was waiting for me."

And the interrogations by Schechterle were not five or ten minutes: His inquisitiveness often extended to an hour or more, as Schechterle asked and absorbed everything he could from the seasoned pro.

"He was so eager to learn and wanted to be so good," Ballentine said. "I was so impressed with him. He's a smart guy, and so friendly and willing to learn. He was like a sponge. He was at first annoying, and then turned out to be such a likable guy."

During the next seventeen weeks, a special bond formed between the veteran and rookie cop. Ballentine admired that Schechterle was not waiting for things to come to him: He was going after what he wanted to move forward.

"When you see someone new who wants to do well, you give him whatever you can," Ballentine said.

"He was someone I looked up to with a tremendous amount of respect," Schechterle said.

Eventually, in late 2002, after the crash and long recovery, once Schechterle was able to start back to work in the public information office, he and Ballentine were both working in the headquarters building at 620. Ballentine, homicide detective, would call Schechterle and ask him to come up to his office on the third floor. There they'd sit and talk or go to lunch. When Ballentine had some case-related errand or paperwork to run around town, he took Schechterle along. The veteran and young cop quickly bonded further and became good friends.

"He always seemed to be there and be concerned," Schechterle said.

As grateful as he was to be back at work, Schechterle realized his heart wasn't in being a public information officer. He was going to work at the police department building and had a badge, but it just didn't compare to the energy and feel of being on street patrol. Career-wise, 2003 had been a bit like being put out to pasture. During one of their confabs, Schechterle expressed his mixed emotions to Ballentine—grateful to be given a job but not loving it—and said that he was thinking of retiring.

"They were so kind to him, but he wanted to be a cop," Ballentine said. "That's all he wanted to do."

From the first time he'd met Schechterle, the kid's effusive energy and dedication to police work had made an impact on the old pro. Ballentine had really worked the street in his hit-man role, so he knew the energy, pang, and longing Schechterle missed. It was why the kid had tried not once or twice, but *three* times to make the force. It was why he'd traded in a steady paycheck with a blue-chip company and pursued being a cop, at a 50-percent-plus pay cut, after watching Marc Atkinson's funeral procession. It was why he couldn't sit in a cubicle and answer phones for the next eighteen years of his career. Schechterle was born to be a cop, and Ballentine was cut from the same bolt of fabric.

Ballentine floated an idea that sounded to Schechterle like Santa Claus himself asking a kid if he wants a new Daisy Red Ryder BB gun under the tree: What if he could get Schechterle transferred to the homicide squad?

Schechterle thought, *Is the Pope Catholic? Hell yeah!* Being a homicide detective was his dream job all along. This would be a delicate maneuver, however, requiring deft diplomacy and timing. It certainly wasn't a done deal at

Ballentine's suggestion. In the hierarchy of detective jobs, being assigned to the homicide unit was, for many, the top of the list, where only the elite of the elite were allowed to work cases and solve murders. Competition for the limited slots was fierce and, once on the squad, many detectives rode the job to retirement. It was very difficult to get assigned to a homicide unit. Ballentine also knew there might be a major uproar if Schechterle was simply handed one of the coveted slots, taking away the job of someone who'd been patiently waiting in line. Without Schechterle knowing, Ballentine began quietly talking to different people in the police command hierarchy. He made his case: *Schechterle was already detective-certified. He was smart, capable, and motivated. He could do the job. We don't assign him as next on list and take someone's spot; we bring him on as an assistant outside the normal hiring hierarchy. That way no one's feathers get ruffled.*

"There were political concerns we had to talk about," Ballentine said. That included talking to the powerful police union representatives. "Our goal was to give Jason someplace to feel useful. He was completely capable of doing the job."

Ballentine used his veteran capital and checked off the various bureaucratic boxes on behalf of his protégé. One bright day in early 2004, Schechterle was out playing golf with his lawyer Pat McGroder. That alone was another major milestone: His doctor's breakthrough work on Schechterle's hands had given him the ability to hold and swing a golf club again. Not only that, Schechterle was posting scores right around par, which only infuriated his lawyer, a lifelong hack and frustrated golfer himself.

Out of cellphone range that day, Schechterle wouldn't retrieve the message left by Ballentine until later that afternoon. He quickly called back.

"Hey, where have you been?" Ballentine asked.

"I was out playing golf."

"I'll cut right to it: How would you like your business card to read, 'Jason Schechterle, homicide detective?'"

"That would mean everything to me. But don't screw with me. Seriously?"

"Seriously. We're going to have you transferred up here. Can you start tomorrow?"

Schechterle said yes and hung up. Then the emotion of the moment overwhelmed him, and he cried. It was March 2004; it had been three years since the night of the crash, and now he was a homicide detective.

In his case, he'd remain on light-duty status—no weapon—until he could pass the gun range qualification test again with his reconstructed hands. Even though Schechterle had passed his detective certification course, he'd only worked patrol for fifteen months before being burned up. So while the job promotion was partly special consideration, it was not a charity post either.

Ballentine warned Schechterle that he'd only be accepted if he carried his own weight. No one was going to cut him any slack because of his health issues, poor eyesight, mangled hands, or any of the rest of it. If anything, those handicaps would be easy fodder to deride the rookie without mercy. Hobbled or healthy, being on the homicide squad was an overwhelming, demanding, and stressful post. Each new workday started with one or more dead bodies and inched along from there. Case loads piled up; families demanded closure.

Schechterle would be expected to perform, and his primary role initially was to help the seasoned detectives investigate their cases. Schechterle was assigned to Ballentine and his partner Alex Femenia. No one pretended that Schechterle had been trained to investigate homicides: he hadn't. Nor did he test into the position per normal protocol. He'd start as a glorified grunt, and if he didn't screw that up he might get a chance to start learning the craft.

His new boss was Sergeant Carl Richardson, who was firm, fair, and direct: *You're not a charity case. You're here to learn how to do this job and be productive. And you're going to have to work harder than everyone else to keep pace. You up for it?*

Yes, sir, Schechterle said. *Yes, sir, I am.*

Ballentine's plan, which he communicated to the squad, was to set aside how Schechterle looked and not treat him any differently than anyone else. Said Ballentine, "Detectives are hard on each other. If there's a weakness, they will expose that weakness." It did not take the detectives long to jump on the first thing they noticed about their new squad mate.

"When Jason first came he was dressed like a kid who just climbed off a tractor," Ballentine said. "It just wasn't going to work. To work homicide you had to dress snappy. He didn't meet that standard when he first arrived. We rode him like a bad habit."

Schechterle got the message and went shopping. He bought a number of new silk shirts, dress pants, and black leather shoes. A suit and tie was not the protocol, but nice shirts, dress slacks, and polished shoes were. Said Ballentine, "He turned out to be the best-dressed guy out of everybody. He took all of it really well."

To make sure Schechterle understood his place in the hierarchy of murder-solving, his duties were arranged so that for the first month he barely left the office. When he did, it was to walk to court and get a subpoena signed or help shuffle other legal paperwork. Other times he'd sit and listen to hours of taped prisoner phone calls, with the outside chance a murder suspect might spill something incriminating that the detectives could use to bolster a case. Schechterle ran errands, filed papers, and did any other task that would free up time for the detectives working active cases. Schechterle knew he was being accepted when a Mr. Potato Head toy started appearing on his desk, minus ears and a nose. Or Mr. Potato Head's ears would be dangling by string on the office door.

"Everyone was very welcoming to me," Schechterle said. "I'd never seen a homicide victim." That changed on April 7, 2004.

"Hey, we got a murder," Ballentine said. "Let's go."

Schechterle was at 620 in his third-floor cubicle when Ballentine called with that news. It was almost noon; Ballentine had caught the case as scene agent and was taking Schechterle along for the real deal. Schechterle didn't need to be told twice: He was up and on his way to the scene, which Ballentine had relayed was near Sixteenth Street and Thomas Road, in Schechterle's old 513 Henry beat where he'd been blown up.

Once there, the first patrol officer on scene briefed Ballentine and Schechterle. *One victim, male, early 40s. A woman, the spouse of the deceased, said two men broke into her house and tied her up. After she broke free, she called 911 and found her husband dead in his bed. There was no obvious physical evidence: No gun shell casings. No other murder weapon. No sign of forced entry into the house. No blood or other evidence of struggle anywhere except in the bedroom where the deceased's body lay in bed in only his underwear.*

Schechterle couldn't deny the anticipation and energy coursing through his body as he followed Ballentine into the house for an initial survey. Contrary to the depiction of murder investigations on big and small screens—wherein detectives arrive, walk to the dead body, poke around for some evidence and then rush off to apprehend their first suspect—the reality was painfully slow and tedious… before becoming even slower and more tedious.

"Jason took to it immediately," Ballentine said. "He always wanted to help, train, and learn."

On this, his first real-life homicide investigation, Ballentine and Schechterle wouldn't even begin to start nosing around the body for another eight hours. And as far as rushing off to interview suspects, the case agent *never* left the scene until the house or apartment was properly measured, diagrammed, and photographed, and all the evidence marked, photographed, and collected. He didn't know it then, as they walked into the house for the first time sometime after noon, but Ballentine and Schechterle would be on that property until three o'clock the next morning.

"I learned more about investigating a crime scene on that one call than any other time," Schechterle said.

There was no dramatic speech from Ballentine to the rookie, and no formal listing of official rules. Ballentine simply told Schechterle that he needed to listen and watch what each detective was doing, and when there was something they needed, he had to make sure it got done. Period.

"We knew he'd get it," said Ballentine. "Jason is observant and paid attention to what was happening."

It was also impossible to convey to a new homicide detective just how difficult, demanding, and overwhelming the job was; Schechterle would quickly figure that one out all on his own. From the first call, homicide detectives were under enormous pressure from multiple sources. And everything had to be done exactly right so the case was not later lost in court. Homicide detectives became emotionally involved in the loss of life as the voice for the victim through the investigation.

The first walkthrough of the crime scene was only a cursory look. Before going in, Ballentine reminded Schechterle to be mindful and watch where he stepped. Two of the three admonitions scribbled on the grease board the first day of the academy applied here: *Don't touch anything. Be quiet.*

Ballentine walked slowly and spoke aloud, making observations that might or might not turn out to later have evidentiary value: "Feels like the AC is on. Shades are pulled. Kitchen light is on."

At the bedroom, he looked toward the bed: "Deceased male. Appears to be mid-40s, Hispanic. Bloody head and face." Then they carefully retraced their steps and backed out of the house.

"OK," Ballentine said. "Now we process the scene. We'll start outside and do a grid search. Every square inch of this yard, front and back. Check each window and point of entry for any signs of tampering. Look for anything and mark it whether you think it's helpful or not: a piece of discarded gum. Blood evidence. Weapons if we're so lucky. Tossed receipts. Shell casings. Crumpled papers. Anything. We don't even know how he was killed yet."

For the next two hours, Ballentine and Schechterle scoured the grounds outside the home and came up goose-eggs. While they were doing so, the lead detective, or case agent, called Ballentine at the scene.

"Hey, I've been talking to the wife of the deceased," the detective said. "My interview with her doesn't add up. Their kids are saying she had an affair. They think she's involved."

This was interesting news, but to seasoned detective Ballentine it was just another possibility in a long list of possibilities. He filed it away in his mind and continued working. Once they had processed the perimeter outside the house, Ballentine and Schechterle carefully moved inside to repeat a similar process. By then the police photographer had arrived and was documenting every square foot of floor and wall space, every room, every piece of furniture.

Ballentine and Schechterle were running a tape measure together and documenting and diagramming the house; Ballentine typed the measurements into a laptop computer. The more they documented and looked, the less they found. Lack of certain evidence could turn the train toward other motives and possibilities:

- No obvious forced entry at any door or window.
- No collection of the ties the intruders had supposedly used to bind and gag the wife.
- No blood evidence or signs of struggle anywhere. No toppled chairs, crooked rugs, broken framed photographs. Nothing out of place.
- No shell casings or bullet holes.

The only evidence of violence and murder was in the bedroom, on and around the victim. Still, as they processed the scene, Ballentine was careful to remind Schechterle not to form any opinions. *Keep processing the scene, collecting evidence, and eventually the evidence will lead us to our case theory.*

After hours and hours outside and inside searching, marking, and measuring, darkness had fallen. Sometime around nine o'clock that night, Schechterle finally examined his first body. Another difference between make-believe police shows and reality was that no one touched the body until an investigator from the Maricopa County Medical Examiner's Office made an official assessment. The ME investigator finally pulled back the covers to reveal the corpse fully and rolled the body to assess injuries.

Earlier, Ballentine had already shared one possibility: "I don't think he was shot."

The blood splatter in the room was high up on the wall, not directly behind or near the head. That pattern of blood, instead, was likely someone hitting the victim with a blunt object, once, and then on the upswing of the second hit casting off blood higher up on the wall. The ME confirmed Ballentine's early intuition: no gunshot entry or exit wounds anywhere on the body. The ME packaged the body for transport, including brown paper bags on each hand to preserve any fingernail evidence.

Ballentine and Schechterle finally left the scene around 3 a.m. It had been almost twenty-four hours since Schechterle arrived at 620 for his normal shift, and he'd had no warning that he'd be going out on an actual investigation. He'd be expected back at work at the usual time, now only a few hours away.

Welcome to homicide.

"The job is like a 7,000-pound elephant sitting on your shoulders," Ballentine said. "You dream about the case while you're asleep and think about it while you're awake. You own it."

Over the next weeks and months, Schechterle discussed the case nonstop with the lead detective. That detective had interviewed the wife several times, as well as the guy with whom she'd been having the affair. All the circumstantial evidence pointed to those same two as perpetrators, but there was nothing solid to hang a murder charge on. The detective's theory was that they planned to take out the husband as he slept. The wife let the boyfriend into the house early one morning (no forced entry); he walked to the bedroom and clubbed the husband to death in bed (no gunshot, high blood splatter near the ceiling). Then they staged her being tied up, waited a couple hours, and called 911. Like the detectives, no one in the victim's entire family was buying the story. For now, the case had gone cold.

IN August 2004, Schechterle worked a triple homicide with Alex Femenia as the case agent, which meant Femenia was the lead detective. Initially there was shock—triple homicides were rare.

"All murders are big deals, but three at once is an overwhelming scene," Schechterle said. "It's one crime scene with three different bodies in three different places."

Everything that could be involved in a murder case was part of this one. There were two male victims and a female victim, all in their 20s. The initial theory was that it was a drug deal gone bad, because one of the victims was clutching a scorched glass meth pipe. However, the case took an ominous turn when a Phoenix police officer called Detective Femenia and implicated his own son, who was indeed involved with another suspect. Both were eventually arrested and charged with felony murder.

Six months after Schechterle had gone to his first homicide crime scene, the lead detective from that case walked up to Schechterle's desk around 4 p.m. and said, "You're not going to believe this."

"What?"

"You know our fake home invasion case, right?"

"Right."

"Another detective just got called out on a murder-suicide. He called and said he was looking at the two bodies. Our cheating wife and her boyfriend."

"No."

"Yeah, it's them all right. Looks like he shot her and then killed himself." It happened in a small, ratty house on the west side of Phoenix, two bodies on a bloodied kitchen floor.

"I guess your case is solved," Schechterle said, knowing the larger truth.

The detective nodded and smiled. "More or less."

Technically, with no evidence to connect the two crime scenes, the original case remained open. Cold case. But in the larger karmic realm, it seemed justice had been served in Schechterle's first homicide, which would forever remain with him because the man killed was a true victim. Many homicides turned out to be connected through bad intentions, dark actions, and misdeeds—criminals killing criminals before, during, or after crimes committed. Or civilians exacting revenge on other civilians, both parties with questionable ethics, actions, and choices. Not that anyone deserved to be murdered, but in many homicide investigations the road to that dead end was littered with ominous warning signs that most reasonable people avoid.

But a man clubbed to death as he lay asleep in bed—with no evidence to show that he even knew his wife had wandered into the arms of another man—was truly an innocent victim. As a homicide detective, Jason didn't have the time or luxury to wallow in sadness for the victim, but each time a true innocent was taken it was especially bothersome.

CHAPTER 22

Showtime

BY JUNE 2004, a trial date had been set in *Schechterle v. Ford Motor Company*. Although a trial was a roll of the dice for both the plaintiff and defense, any real prospect of settling between the two sides had become unlikely. In fact, where there had once been settlement attempts and mediation, there now blew a cold, silent wind of disdain.

Six months prior, the two sides had sat down to negotiate a settlement at the offices of Gallagher & Kennedy in central Phoenix. On the plaintiff's side of the conference room table was lawyer Pat McGroder, his client Jason Schechterle, and the freewheeling Texan and anti-Ford crusader David Perry. On the other side of the table were three attorneys representing Ford Motor Company. Acting as referee was a retired judge named Dan Nastro, the neutral go-between.

Nastro's eloquent opening and explanation laid out the risks and rewards in both settling and going to trial; there were pros and cons to each for both sides. For both sides, a settlement eliminated the biggest wild card of the trial arena: the jury. For the defense side, Jason Schechterle presented a legal nightmare at trial. He was a U.S. military veteran, police officer, and detective who'd been taken down in his prime while on duty. His attorneys McGroder and Perry would relay Jason's horrific injuries, miraculous survival, and triumph against all odds in such a way that it would be captivating human theater and riveting drama. And the attorneys would skillfully draw a bull's-eye for the jury on the defense lawyers, seated in the courtroom, representing a corporation that in 2003 logged revenues exceeding $164 billion.

Both sides knew that, to the jury, it would look like this: *In this corner, Jason Schechterle, an American hero and survivor, horribly scarred and disabled for the rest of his life through no fault of his own. He was burned alive by the defendant's product defect, which the defendant has known about for more than thirty years but has done nothing to remediate. All Jason Schechterle was trying to do was his job, which was to protect and serve. And in this corner, a team of lawyers from a company that made a net income of $495 million last year.*

The specter of a huge jury verdict could motivate the defense side to settle. Likewise, for the plaintiff, a guaranteed settlement amount, to provide for Schechterle's long-term life care, could also be motivation to avoid the vagaries of a jury decision. Yes, the plaintiff might settle for less than a jury would award—but jury awards were also open to the appeal process, which would add many more years as the Ford defense team used all its final stall tactics. Ford's skillful lawyers could probably run another five or more years off the clock without having to pay Schechterle a single cent. Also a consideration was the cost of a trial for both sides: mentally, physically, emotionally, and financially. In general, an agreed settlement that avoided all the swirling uncertainty of jury trials and lengthy resolution was in the interest of both parties.

But McGroder and Perry weren't going to take a bag of peanuts to let the Ford attorneys walk, and those same attorneys were not going to hand over the keys to the kingdom to ambulance-chasers from dusty blips on the map. Spoken or not, there was no love lost between the plaintiff and corporate defense attorneys. These were men bonded by the same profession who lived in such different worlds they might as well have been two warring tribes divided by language, tradition, and customs. The legal system was their venue, their version of slaughter without remorse; settlements and jury verdicts were the legal equivalents of trophy scalps. The victor drank the opponents' blood and danced under the moon; the vanquished retreated, retooled, and attacked again with even fiercer determination. On both sides, it took a big ego, razor savvy, and rare strength to enter and win these warrior battles.

For McGroder, the corporate attorneys were stuffed-shirt "yes men" who stood behind thick corporate walls of denial and issued settlement checks with no true accountability for the death and mayhem McGroder believed their product inflicted on human beings.

For the defense attorneys, McGroder and Perry were the bottom rung of their profession, snake-oil slicksters in $2,000 tailored suits who used the blanket allegation of negligence to personally profit from human suffering and death.

In this particular mediation, the plaintiff's side kicked off the proceedings, in late 2003, with Perry presenting a series of PowerPoint slides that so offended the other side that the three Ford attorneys got up and left the room. Judge Nastro was able to race out of the room and talk the defense side into staying.

"It started off bad the first minute and got worse," Schechterle said. "I didn't want to go to trial. If we won, the jury could come back with some ridiculously large verdict, which would then get appealed and drag on for years. And going to trial was not going to advance our advocacy any further with trying to make the Crown Victoria safer for police officers."

"I had left all the negotiations in Pat McGroder's hands," said Perry. "He knew Jason Schechterle, his injuries, and the venue much better than I, and was in a much better position to actually negotiate the numbers. At the same time, it was obvious to me that Ford *had* to settle. They could not afford to go to trial against a totally innocent plaintiff with Jason's local-hero status and our evidence of the fix Ford engineers could have easily used—which, according to Ford's own crash tests, would have prevented the fire. We were going to try the case as a fraud case. Ford's lawyers resorted to their bullying tactics and threatening to blow up the mediation, but it didn't work."

Before Schechterle's crash, expert witnesses in other similar cases had testified that shields would protect the fuel tanks of Ford Crown Victoria Police Interceptors. After Schechterle's crash, but before his case was ready for trial,

Ford engineers designed and tested a shield to protect CVPI fuel tanks. The engineers tested multiple vehicles during seventy-five-mile-per-hour impacts; the shields successfully prevented fuel leakage. Ford executives authorized shield installation on all new CVPIs beginning in the 2003 model year and provided, at no cost to police agencies, shields for retrofitting onto earlier-model CVPIs. McGroder and Perry's expert witnesses testified prior to trial that the new shields should have been developed earlier, to be on Schechterle's police car when it was built, which would have prevented the fire.

The Ford lawyers' defense was that the Schechterle crash involved a taxi traveling at an extreme speed, which would have rendered any shields ineffective. Ford engineers conducted two 100-mph crash tests to prove their theory. However, when Perry's and McGroder's expert witness examined the crash-test vehicles in preparation for trial, he found that both fuel tanks were intact and neither had been punctured. The shield had been successful in the 100-mph test!

Therefore, with the specter of a trial looming, Ford lawyers had three big problems. First, the company was still manufacturing a vehicle with the same defect as the Pinto going back to the 1970s. Second, although engineers had successfully designed a shield to fix the Pinto problem more than twenty-five years previously, the same fix never appeared on Mustang IIs (as Perry had successfully proved in *Durrill v. Ford* in 1983) or any vehicle with the Panther platform. Finally, Ford engineers, through their own crash testing, had proved they were capable of properly designing a shield for the CVPI that would have prevented Jason Schechterle from being burned at all.

"It was an untenable legal position for Ford," Perry said.

Just two weeks before the final mediation and showdown with Ford lawyers, Schechterle had a nose surgery. Until the day before the proceedings, Schechterle had two plugs in his nose that looked like small rubber hoses. The tubes kept his airway open and allowed the nose to heal without collapsing. However, Jason didn't want to attend the big settlement conference in his suit and tie with rubber plugs sticking out of each nostril. Against the advice of Dr. Bill Leighton, Schechterle had him remove the plugs the day before.

Toward 5 p.m. during the settlement conference with Ford, McGroder noticed Schechterle's nose was bleeding. The blood started as a trickle and quickly turned into a gush. Schechterle tipped his head back, but it wouldn't stop bleeding. He was getting nauseated from swallowing so much blood. His shirt and tie were splattered with blood. When a tissue was soaked, Schechterle threw it down on McGroder's office floor and started another. The Ford attorneys, who were parked in a conference room down the hall, had no idea what was happening to their opponent. McGroder called Leighton, who arrived thirty minutes later. Leighton examined Schechterle and said there wasn't much he could do to help Jason; they'd just have to wait it out. With that, the doctor left.

Two hours later, the bleeding still hadn't stopped, and the negotiations had gone nowhere. The two sides had been in separate rooms and hadn't spoken in person for the previous twelve hours of negotiations. In the end, there was no progress toward a middle ground.

At 9 p.m., Leighton asked McGroder to bring Schechterle to his office in north Scottsdale. McGroder called off the negotiations with Ford and drove Schechterle, admonishing his client, jokingly, not to bleed all over the soft leather interior of the Mercedes-Benz. Leighton examined Schechterle again, applied some ointment to clot the blood, and inserted gauze to finally stop the bleeding.

"Tonight I had my doctor in my lawyer's office, and now my lawyer is in my doctor's office," Schechterle said. "I'm feeling pretty special."

With any hope of settlement apparently at a dead end, Schechterle was dejected. He didn't want the public spectacle of a jury trial, nor did he want any eventual verdict appealed and dragged through the legal process for years and years to come.

Meanwhile, in the grand scheme of the Ford Motor Company universe, the cost of the Crown Victoria Police Interceptor outcome was a tiny sliver of the behemoth's billions. And with some 350,000 police cars operating on the road and "only" twenty or so officers burned alive, that was .006 percent of all Crown Victoria Police Interceptors involved in fatal rear-enders. The highly capable corporate defense attorneys could stand behind that tiny percentage with unwavering confidence. Likewise, the savvy plaintiff's attorney would continue to beat the drum that any such death, let alone multiple such deaths, was egregious negligence.

"Whatever the logic," Schechterle said, "They just didn't seem to care."

IN June, McGroder called his client at police headquarters.

"I immediately heard something different in his voice," Schechterle said.

All McGroder said was, "Will you take [x] amount?" For Schechterle, the number was one he'd told his lawyer would be acceptable. The money would never give him his hands or eyesight back, or his old life, but would ensure he could pay for the lifetime of medical care that loomed ahead.

Schechterle didn't need any time to ponder. "Yes."

"OK, just come down to the court."

"We spent $100,000 producing an animation showing all of Jason's injuries, surgeries, medical records, treating physicians, surgeons, and specialists," McGroder said. "We wanted to preserve Jason's dignity during any potential trial, which can be a traumatic process. My belief is that the animation had a dramatic impact on Ford's position in this case."

For the plaintiff, the two biggest hurdles were the high speed of the taxi at impact and, under Arizona law, the percentage of fault that would be assigned to Ford Motor Company (rather than the taxi driver). There were already hearings underway to determine whether other Crown Victoria incidents would be admissible as evidence at Schechterle's trial. During those hearings one afternoon, Schechterle leaned over to McGroder and said: "Do you know who would be most disappointed with a $100 or $200 million verdict from a jury trial?"

"Ford," McGroder said without hesitation.

"No, me."

McGroder looked stunned.

"Pat, I have to go home and look in the mirror. I live in a rental home. I have three kids, a detective's salary and an uncertain financial future. I have to worry about my health. I know if this case goes to trial and we win, Ford Motor Company will appeal and we'll be another five to seven years down the road before it's resolved. If Ford's lawyers are willing to be reasonable, then I want to settle."

For McGroder and Perry alike, this news was an immediate letdown. The trial lawyers were locked in a battle with a very real potential for a nine-figure verdict on behalf of Jason Schechterle, and nine-figure verdicts didn't come along too often in any career. No matter how one sliced it, $100 to $200 million was a shit-ton of dough. But in the end, what Schechterle wanted most was resolution and closure, and the lawyers had to heed their client's wishes.

McGroder arranged a meeting with Ford attorney Jim Feeney at an Irish pub, Rosie McCafferty's. They each had a couple drinks and talked, as both lawyers and human beings. That discussion led to subsequent and more serious discussions over the next few days. Perry was in Phoenix too, for the hearings in preparation for trial, but hadn't gone along to the meeting with Feeney. From those talks, the two sides reached a settlement. The judge stopped the evidentiary proceedings and announced the case had settled.

On that day, Schechterle walked out of the old courthouse, just blocks from Phoenix police headquarters, and breathed an immense sigh of relief. As he turned and started to cross the street, there was Jim Feeney, the opposing side attorney. Feeney smiled, extended his hand, and said, "Good luck."

Schechterle shook his hand, nodded, and walked back to work. The legal chess match had concluded, but more importantly, the legal fight had moved Ford Motor Company executives to action. At least partially as a result of Schechterle's advocacy, new safety features were soon implemented for the Crown Victoria Police Interceptor.

IN July 2004 Schechterle bought a new house in Phoenix to be closer to work and family. That same month he traveled to St. Louis to testify in another Crown Victoria case for David Perry, who was in his trademark tailored suit and cowboy boots in the courtroom.

In the end, as part of Schechterle's own confidential settlement, Ford attorneys had neither publicly accepted responsibility for Schechterle's injuries nor publicly acknowledged any fault. A wire transfer from a corporate Ford account to Schechterle's lawyers' designated holding account (for later transfer to Schechterle less expenses and a contingency fee) erased the direct fiduciary responsibility of "Jason Schechterle" from Ford's ledger. Schechterle's private victory, however, would not be a hollow one.

"I believe Jason Schechterle changed the way Ford Motor Company did business," McGroder said.

For years, McGroder and Perry had been working to come up with solutions to protect police officers patrolling in Crown Victorias. Using their own money and research and development team, they championed a puncture-proof bladder technology to stand as a buffer around the vulnerable fuel tank. Until then, this technology had only been used in high-performance racing vehicles. A company called Fuel Safe developed the prototype, which was then installed on every city of Phoenix police vehicle. The original design engineer, Ty Rupert, was so inspired by Schechterle's story that he became a police officer.

Then, in conjunction with the Scottsdale company Fire Panel, McGroder and Perry oversaw development and crash testing of a similar fire-retardant panel that found its way onto thousands of police vehicles across the United States.

"We were putting a lot of pressure on Ford to recall those Crown Victoria vehicles," Perry said.

To that end, in 2002 Ford safety engineers conducted their own Crown Victoria crash tests and identified failure modes in the fuel tank. The company developed plastic shields for the bolts so they couldn't puncture the fuel tank during a rear-end impact. Beginning with the 2003 model year, those shields went on all new Crown Victoria Police Interceptor vehicles. Concurrently, Ford executives also made that upgrade safety kit available as a retrofit for all existing CVPIs. The company offered the kit to all law enforcement agencies at no charge, and it was eventually installed on 300,000 police cars. Ford engineers also created a trunk pack to allow police officers to store their gear in a puncture-proof pack, which they offered to police agencies for a fee.

"In the end, as a result of these continuing tragedies, Ford representatives did take responsible steps," McGroder said. Ford engineers eventually evolved their own fire-retardant retrofit system, similar to Fire Panel's version, to be put on the Crown Victoria Police Interceptors, which they offered to police agencies at $2,500 per vehicle.

McGroder said. "We took the position that the Fire Panel was cheaper and better, based on our crash testing. There were two real-world crashes where the Fire Panel worked perfectly."

316

The civil action had wielded enough leverage to force Ford executives and engineers to do something about Crown Victoria Police Interceptors. In the end, everything Schechterle had suffered through for five years—being cooked alive, dozens of painful surgeries, mangled hands, shot eyesight, ear and nose prosthetic specialists, wig makers, and horrific disfigurement for life—hadn't been for nothing. For a person trained to protect, serve, and uphold justice, there was now something positive and tangible: two wild-card ambulance chasers and one determined cop from Phoenix had moved Ford's brass to action.

But as much as they had done, it was still madness to Schechterle that every Crown Victoria wasn't pulled from service with a complete redesign of the vehicle. Not every agency could afford the $2,500 tab to retrofit each Crown Victoria Police Interceptor in service. And so, unfortunately, it continued: the ominous ticking of the clock, the countdown to the next police officer being burned alive in a Crown Victoria Police Interceptor. Tragically, the next occurred only three months after Schechterle's settlement with Ford.

On September 26, 2004, Officer Christopher Sobieski, of the Prairie View Police Department in Texas, had just finished issuing a summons and was sitting inside his 1999 Crown Victoria on the shoulder of Highway 290. A pickup truck driven by a drunk driver slammed into the back of Sobieski's patrol car, which exploded. Fire quickly consumed the 39-year-old Sobieski.

CHAPTER 23

Wild, Wild West

ON AUGUST 23, 2004, Schechterle's homicide squad got called out to a double murder in a quiet suburban neighborhood in north Phoenix. Jerry Laird was the scene investigator; Schechterle was helping him process the scene, the most gruesome one he had encountered yet.

The two bodies had been husband and wife. While she was on the phone with a 911 operator because she feared for her safety, the husband shot her and then slashed her throat with a knife. With the line still open to the 911 operator, the deranged husband walked around screaming and stabbing the knife into his own chest. When the police arrived and the husband pointed a gun at officers, the cops shot and killed him inside his home near Tenth Street and Thunderbird.

"We got called at 10:30 that night," Schechterle said. "I was in that house for sixteen hours. It was the most blood I have ever seen."

The case resonated, too, as one of his sadder ones. As he worked the scene, thoughts and questions bubbled up. *Here were two happy, healthy people living the American dream. A spacious home with a Mercedes-Benz in the garage and other niceties. What was their first date like? Their wedding day? Five years before, the couple had lost a child to cancer. But murder-suicide? Did they ever foresee the dark winds that would come?* Schechterle wondered as he tiptoed around the bodies and blood.

For Schechterle, working as a homicide detective obliterated the TV and movie versions often portrayed of investigations. For the most part, investigating murders was slow, boring, tedious work. Also, once he'd seen his first dead body, all the rest looked more or less the same. Not that there wasn't a certain reverence for each victim and empathy for the families, but the shock of seeing a cold stiff was long gone. *If you've seen one dead body, you've pretty much seen them all.* Schechterle rolled up to homicide crime scenes not in a sleek, unmarked sedan but in a white pickup truck with tonneau cover, which held the variety of evidence markers, tools, and equipment he needed.

"I just loved every aspect of this job," he said. "I never had a bad day in homicide. And I was learning to play golf again."

"I loved what Jason did and wanted to hear his stories," Suzie said. "I was intrigued by what he did. It gave us more to share. He didn't have to shield me from it in any way."

ON another front, by fall 2004 Schechterle was still determined to re-qualify with his weapon. To do so, he switched from the .40-caliber Glock 22 semiautomatic to a seven-shot Smith & Wesson revolver that fit his hand better. The revolver could fire either .38- or .357-caliber bullets. Officers had the freedom to choose from a number of different service weapons on an official approved list.

"I had to relearn how to get the gun in and out of my holster with the shape of my surgically repaired right hand, and how to hold it," Schechterle said. Eventually, grabbing and shooting would become second nature with the new hand and new gun. But for the time being he was still assigned as light duty: no service weapon on his hip. It was time to start the process, so Schechterle went with a couple guys from the Phoenix SWAT unit to the Ben Avery shooting range in the desert hills on I-17.

"It was the first time I'd pulled a trigger in three and a half years," he said.

It was difficult—as though he'd never shot before in his life. He kept repositioning the gun in search of a safe hold so the hammer mechanism didn't rip his skin. He also didn't want to drop the gun during kickback.

"I realized this was going to be a very slow, tedious process," he said. He started practicing regularly at the academy range in South Phoenix near the mountains. With his original index finger gone, his new trigger finger was his middle finger. The .38-caliber revolver was a bit smaller, fit his hand better, and allowed him to use a speed-loader rather than trying to plug bullets into a magazine cartridge. After months of practice, he was ready to take the qualification test. To carry his duty weapon again, Schechterle would be taking the same qualification course that every peace officer in the state of Arizona had to pass annually, with a score of 210 or better. Scoring 240 and above was "Expert."

The test consisted of fifty rounds fired during a series of timed events, at distances ranging from three to twenty-five feet—the range of almost all real-world police shootings. For the test, there were two instructors on site, with rows of various targets displaying an upper-body silhouette, with no arms, containing a large square and a smaller square. Putting every shot in the smaller square was ideal.

For the test, the target turned, the shooter drew the weapon from its holster, fired two rounds center-mass, and replaced the weapon into the holster—all of which had to conclude within the time limit for that portion, which might be as short as three seconds.

Target, draw, BANG, BANG, holster. Three seconds.

Other longer scenarios required the shooter to draw, fire three shots, drop, replace the magazine (or speed-load the cylinder), and fire three more shots to re-create a reload scenario during an active shooting. In 2005 Schechterle took the qualification test twice in two days, unofficially, to measure his progress, which detective Alex Femenia helped arrange. Schechterle, however, was landing in the 180s, well below the required 210.

"I was hitting the targets dead-on, but my issue was always the time element," he said. "The fact that I was even firing a gun, with my messed-up hands and eyes, was huge."

Sadly, qualifying with his gun again just wasn't realistic. When he made that realization, he accepted the new reality with his normal ease.

"I was OK with it," he said. "There are time requirements for a reason, because in a real shooting scenario, every second is precious. Police officers can't be fumbling around with their gun. I was going to be a light-duty guy for the rest of my career."

Not carrying a gun on duty was not a deal-breaker as a detective. His mentor, Jack Ballentine, was an expert shooter who didn't really like guns and rarely carried his duty weapon. When Schechterle asked on calls, "Do you have your gun?" Ballentine would say, "Yeah, it's in my briefcase." But Schechterle was always suspicious that the weapon was actually at Ballentine's house or in a desk drawer at 620, untouched since his last qualification test.

"I always thought it would be good if at least one of us were carrying if we ever got in a bind," Schechterle said. "But it sure wasn't going to be me."

IN 2005 someone flipped a master switch, and the year went beyond crazy. Ballentine and Femenia, along with Schechterle, worked fifteen murders that year. With such a heavy caseload, how many would they be able to solve? In the end, all of them.

By then, Schechterle was mostly done with surgeries—through number forty-seven—had plenty of energy, and was logging the long hours of a homicide detective. He had the clothes and the look, and was developing more and more confidence in his abilities. He was finding the pace and rhythm of the job and what it entailed, and was very proficient at processing homicide scenes. In a relatively short time, Schechterle was becoming an adept homicide detective.

In early 2005, Sergeant Carl Richardson retired and was replaced by Sergeant Patrick Kotecki. In March that year, with Jack Ballentine giving the greenhorn a nod to superiors, homicide Lieutenant Benny Pina increased Schechterle's responsibilities. For Schechterle, there was no dramatic speech or new directives. He just kept his head down and worked as hard as he possibly could every day on the job.

There were four homicide squads at the Phoenix Police Department, with eight detectives in each squad. Everyone worked more or less business hours Monday through Friday. Each detective was also then on call for a twenty-four hour period and then off for seventy-two hours. It was only during the on-call period that the squad caught new cases.

Schechterle's C-32 homicide squad, led by Sergeant Patrick Kotecki, included Jack Ballentine, Carl Caruso, Tom D'Aguano, Alex Femenia, Jerry Laird, and Steve Orona. On all of Jack Ballentine's cases Schechterle worked as his assistant. He also worked with the other detectives on their cases. The only consistency in being a homicide detective was that the job was stressful and unpredictable. On some shifts the phone never rang, which freed up time to work on open cases or go back even further to cold ones. On other shifts there might be three murders in one night. There was never a week Schechterle didn't log at least sixty hours. Some weeks might be eighty hours, with the squad sergeant tracking everyone's time. Depending on years of service and overtime, the homicide detectives on the squad were each making $60,000 to $80,000 a year.

"When you're working a murder really hard and making progress, it might get interrupted by another murder," Schechterle said.

Tuesdays were body-tag day—the lower-priority deaths that one detective could investigate alone. Any suspicious death that was not necessarily a homicide got bumped to body-tag day and to the junior detective, which in his squad was Schechterle. Suicides, workplace accidents, and SIDS (sudden infant death syndrome) cases all fell into the body-tag-day bucket. Detectives from all four squads also had to volunteer to cover Saturday and Sunday. During one month, Schechterle was awakened by his desk sergeant three Saturdays in a row for three separate SIDS cases.

"Somebody found their baby dead, so you have to be very sensitive," Schechterle said. He'd have to interview the family, the first responders, the treating physician, and the medical examiner. "Emotionally, those SIDS cases were horrible. If there was a part of the job I didn't like, it was investigating a SIDS death. It was just tragic."

Suicides could also be handled by one detective. While on the squad, Schechterle investigated some thirty-five suicides. "I had a few that looked suspicious at first, but every one I investigated was ruled a suicide," he said. Then came a case that would send Schechterle and his squad on a wild investigative ride that would run nonstop for nineteen days.

EARLY on the morning of Thursday, March 3, 2005, a farm worker made a gruesome discovery in a field near Ninety-Ninth Avenue and Lower Buckeye

Road. The discovery was that of a deceased young male, lying on a dirt road on his right side with one arm curled beneath his body. The large amount of blood around the body and three expended 12-gauge shotgun casings were ominous markers of murder. The first Phoenix officers on scene also discovered one unspent shotgun shell, an automobile fuse-box cover, and nine $1 bills on the road near the cornfield. It was rural but within Phoenix city limits, and Schechterle's C-32 homicide squad caught the case. Around 8:30 that morning Schechterle met his supervisor, Sergeant Pat Kotecki, plus Jack Ballentine and Detective Alex Femenia, at the scene.

"The scene was less than a half-mile from not being our case," Schechterle said. He'd received the call at home, from Ballentine, and drove to the scene in his white Chevy truck. "It was definitely the wildest and most interesting case I worked."

As the detectives talked, Schechterle scanned the rural expanses: It was the middle of nowhere and, seeing nothing, his initial thought was, *Wow. This is going to go nowhere.*

Indeed, there was no wallet. No identification. Little evidence. And no suspects, motive, rhyme, or reason. Even so, this homicide squad was top-shelf.

"Jack Ballentine had the Midas touch," Schechterle said. "Things would fall into his lap. I knew we'd catch a break."

The detectives were going to need some special pixie dust to solve this case. *Who was the victim? How did he get here? Why was he here?*

The blood evidence pointed to the victim being shot on the road and then pushed down the dirt embankment. The scraped dirt meant the victim struggled to get back up to the road before dying. Schechterle examined the gray fuse-box cover, which was spattered with blood. The detectives knew this piece of evidence might be critical in leading them to the make and model of the vehicle that was at the scene.

"This murder case was a defining time for Jason, because it was so difficult for him physically and everything was happening so fast," said Ballentine.

Back at 620, Schechterle and his peers were still working without a name for the victim. The victim's fingerprints didn't yield any hits on NCIC, the National Crime Information Center database, or in the Arizona system. Schechterle called a local auto-parts store and used the number of the fuse box to get a make and model for the vehicle on scene: 1999 Chevy Cavalier.

"We knew the make and model but, obviously, not the color," Schechterle said. An autopsy the next day confirmed cause of death: three shotgun wounds to the neck and torso from close range.

Meanwhile, across town Chris Ferschke was concerned that no one had seen his friend Valentin Cruz-Gabriel. Other friends learned that Cruz-Gabriel's white Cavalier had been discovered parked on the Gila River Reservation. On March 5, Ferschke drove out to the reservation with friends to post missing-person fliers. The next day they returned with a large group to search the area and knock on doors on the reservation. Asking questions about the white Cavalier led the searchers to the door of Lolita Carlisle, who had a daughter named Samantha Somegustava. The 21-year-old Somegustava would soon be in Schechterle and Ballentine's cross hairs.

On March 7, Ferschke put out a wider plea to ask law enforcement agencies to help find his friend Cruz-Gabriel. On March 8, Ferschke contacted the Maricopa County Medical Examiner's office to inquire about any recent "John Does" brought to the morgue. The ME investigator, indeed, had two young Latino men fitting the description of Cruz-Gabriel. When the ME investigator called Ballentine with a heads-up about Ferschke's inquiries, Ballentine immediately contacted Ferschke to learn more.

Meanwhile, the Chevrolet Cavalier was sitting in the impound lot. Because they couldn't search the vehicle until they got a signed warrant, Schechterle peeked through the window to confirm what the detectives were hoping. In the parlance of Fourth Amendment search-and-seizure rules, Schechterle's look through the window was authorized under the "plain view" doctrine. Schechterle's heart rate quickened: the fuse-box cover inside the car was missing. Although not definite, this was strong evidence that the white Chevrolet Cavalier had been at the crime scene and might yield further clues.

"I remember that being such a cool feeling, like you see on TV, as the puzzle pieces fit together," he said. Because the white Cavalier was found on tribal land, the Gila River police were now involved.

On the morning of March 9, Ballentine met Ferschke and finally had a potential name for the victim: Valentin Cruz-Gabriel. That same day Phoenix police crime lab analysts positively identified the victim through a set of prints taken by Mesa police for a prior traffic incident.

Ballentine and Schechterle later drove to a casino on the sovereign nation of the Gila River Indian Reservation. They were tracking the movements and activity of whoever was using Cruz's credit card *after* the murder. Of course, everywhere they went, Schechterle heard, "Hey, you're that cop!" and "Glad you're doing OK."

"Being at work, wearing my badge, and doing an important job took away a lot of my worries and apprehensions," Schechterle said. "My appearance did not matter. I was focused on the victims, suspects, and families."

Unbelievably, while at the casino, a security guard told Schechterle that Lolita Carlisle was playing the slot machines; she was a person of interest for the detectives. The tribal police soon detained her. She immediately copped to taking the credit card, but said she didn't do anything else. Ballentine pressed her for more information about her daughter, Somegustava. Following the trail, in another interview Ballentine and Schechterle got a gem: The man being questioned told the detectives that Somegustava and another person had jacked some fool driving a white convertible—same make, model, and style as Cruz-Gabriel's car.

Ballentine and Schechterle formed a case theory: Samantha Somegustava and a second assailant robbed and murdered Cruz-Gabriel. One week into the investigation, the detectives released a photograph of Somegustava to the media; she had a tattoo on her neck: R.I.P.

On March 14, Ballentine and Schechterle were back on the reservation to do more canvassing. Somegustava was still at large, but the detectives were confident her time was almost up. At 5:30 p.m., they met two Gila River police officers to coordinate the search. Ballentine asked if the tribal police would accompany them into the housing project to conduct interviews. An hour later, as they were leaving, Ballentine's Midas touch manifested: At an intersection, the detectives watched two tribal police cars swoop in and surround a red Jeep Cherokee. Guns drawn, the cops rushed the vehicle and took Somegustava into custody.

"It was a very magical ride for a few weeks, getting to the resolution," Schechterle said. Because the arrest was made on tribal land, Ballentine had to conduct his interview within the borders of the sovereign nation. Schechterle sat back to enjoy the show.

"Jack Ballentine had a real knack for doing interviews," he said. "Our sergeant used to say he used Jedi mind tricks."

Before Ballentine started the interview, he offered Somegustava food. Then he asked that her handcuffs be removed. Ballentine hit her with the straight scoop: She'd better get on board and be honest. He'd been a cop for thirty years and had already done his homework on this case. That meant she just needed to come clean now, because it was over. Then he said, "Let's start with when you got the car."

Somegustava's first version was that Cruz-Gabriel kidnapped her in the Cavalier, drove to the cornfields along Ninety-Ninth Avenue, and said he intended to rape her. So she used the shotgun she found in his backseat and shot him three times in self-defense.

Ballentine was unimpressed: try again. "The only thing that's going to make it right for you right now is your telling the truth."

Somegustava's second version was that she was with a friend at Circle K when Cruz-Gabriel drove up in his white Cavalier and solicited sex from the two women. The story got wilder from there: The friend convinced the victim to drop her off at a hotel to get drugs, but she never returned. Then Somegustava convinced Cruz-Gabriel to swing by the house of her friend Richard Enos, which made no sense to the detective. *Why would Cruz-Gabriel agree to go pick up a guy if he was interested in sex with Somegustava?* With Enos now involved, a struggle later ensued in which Enos ordered her to shoot Cruz-Gabriel, so she did.

She's getting warmer, Schechterle thought as he watched Ballentine lead her into the spider web.

Ballentine's interview with Somegustava ended at 9 p.m. She had pawned the blame onto the two men in the car, first onto the victim and then onto her accomplice Enos. Regardless, she had also unknowingly waded into a confession of first-degree robbery-murder, a death-penalty-eligible case in Arizona. Ballentine and Schechterle were pumped, but they still had to get their suspect off the reservation legally. It was a Gila River sergeant who persuaded Somegustava to sign a waiver of extradition.

Straight out of the movies, just before 10 p.m. a tribal police car kicked up a cloud of dust as Somegustava was whisked toward the "border," which in this case was a Circle K at Thirty-Fifth Avenue and Baseline Road, just beyond the reach of reservation lands, jurisdiction, and laws. One of Schechterle's own, a uniformed Phoenix officer, awaited the transfer of the prisoner to a Phoenix PD squad car. Once inside, Somegustava was subject to the legal authority of the state of Arizona and shepherded downtown to the Maricopa County jail complex.

As they drove back toward 620, Ballentine called Sergeant Kotecki as Schechterle listened. It was an unbelievable turn, as the suspect accounted for every piece of evidence at the scene, including the live shotgun shell and the money on the ground. Ballentine confidently told his boss: "She's done."

The detectives talked shop all the way back to downtown Phoenix. *How did Somegustava talk her way into Cruz-Gabriel's car? Why would he be on the prowl for a quickie, in the middle of the night, when his girlfriend awaited his arrival after work? Maybe he wheeled into the convenience store looking for a little cocaine or ecstasy to fuel his sex weekend with his girl? Or maybe Somegustava pleaded some nonsense about needing assistance and appealed to the victim's good nature to help?*

By 10:30 p.m., Schechterle was watching the monitor again with a feed from the interview room that held Somegustava. On another monitor was a male suspect in another interview room, Somegustava's boyfriend, who turned out to be innocent of any wrongdoing.

Detectives knew there was a second assailant.

Richard Enos, street name "Troll," was soon in custody and filling in the final piece of the Somegustava case: He was in the backseat of the Cavalier early on the morning of March 3. He said a man he didn't know was behind the wheel (Cruz-Gabriel), and Somegustava was in the front passenger's seat. Somegustava was after the victim's cash, his tip money from work as a bar-back at Graham Central Station. That explained the scattered $1 bills found at the scene.

At some point, Somegustava and Enos moved to the front passenger seat with Cruz-Gabriel in back. She drove down the desolate dirt road as dawn broke. Cruz-Gabriel grabbed her hair and tried to choke her. Enos says he jumped into the back and fought with Cruz-Gabriel, fisticuffs that continued outside the car and onto the road. Somegustava ran to the back of the car; Enos said he heard three shots. Just like that, Cruz-Gabriel was no more. Blood splatter hit Enos.

"Jack always told me that everyone has good in them," Schechterle said. "They inherently want to do the right thing. If he gave them a chance and took them down the right path in an interview, they would confess."

Samantha Somegustava and Richard Enos were both booked on charges of first-degree murder. Ballentine and Schechterle finalized their case theory: Skilled car thief Somegustava had conned her way into Cruz-Gabriel's Chevrolet Cavalier to rob his money and car. She stopped to pick up Enos, both for muscle and to settle a debt she had with Enos' brother. From there it just went bad.

Friends and families memorialized the victim at two services in Mesa, one for the friends he'd worked with at Graham Central Station and the other for family. He was buried in Oaxaca, Mexico. No one will ever know exactly what happened from the time Cruz-Gabriel encountered Somegustava in the Circle K parking lot in the wee hours until he was brutally murdered just an hour or so later.

"We had a truly innocent victim, a good person who was well loved," said Schechterle. "That was my first time experiencing the satisfaction of putting someone away who needed to go away."

After a trial, a jury found Richard Enos guilty of first-degree murder for the shooting death of 24-year-old Valentin Cruz-Gabriel. On October 12, 2007, Enos received a sentence of life in prison. In May 2009, Samantha Angela Somegustava, 26, was sentenced to life in prison without the possibility of parole for her role in the murder.

"Jason was such a quick study that he progressed really quickly," Ballentine said. "His writing skills were very good, which was a tribute to how smart he is.

The only downside was his eyesight was a challenge. The job was brutal on him because we wouldn't sleep for days."

For weeks during the case, Schechterle had been rolling home at midnight or later and then was back at work by six-thirty or seven o'clock the same morning. Those grinding hours as a homicide detective started to chip away at Schechterle's already weakened health and body. His injured eyes, especially—corneas flattened by the 2001 fire—started to deteriorate under the stress of the job. He didn't realize it yet, but the clock on his dream job and career was now ticking.

CHAPTER 24

999: Officer Down

EARLY ON THE MORNING of May 10, 2005, the phone rang at Schechterle's house just after 5 a.m. In the split second before he answered, four words flashed through his mind: *Tuesday... body-tag day.* Before he picked up the phone, he knew within the hour he'd be standing over a dead body somewhere in Phoenix, most likely another SIDS death or suicide. He prayed for the latter; he hated the small dead bodies more than anything.

"I've got one for you," said the voice of Sergeant Pat Kotecki.

"All right, Sarge. What do you have?"

"Jumper. Female. Hotel at Forty-Fourth Street and Van Buren. Get there within the hour."

"Yes sir."

Thank God, Schechterle thought as he hung up and pushed back the covers. It was another of the many oddly macabre reactions that only other police officers truly understood. *A suicide before breakfast: yes! Things are looking up. I'll take that every day and twice on Sunday over a SIDS case.*

Within twenty minutes, Schechterle was up and dressed, badge clipped on his waistband and driving toward the scene. Once there, around 5:45 a.m., he began his investigation where the victim had landed. The uniformed sergeant on scene gave Schechterle the briefing: the initial call, the officers who'd arrived first on scene, what they saw, and who they interviewed. The crime-scene-specialist photographer also listened to the briefing. The investigation had already turned up two interesting facts: Witnesses had begged the woman not to jump. Even so, Schechterle couldn't assume it was a suicide and had to investigate the crime. And the woman was not registered to the room with the balcony from which she jumped.

"Let me take a quick look at her," Schechterle said to the photographer, "And then you can start documenting the scene."

Schechterle walked slowly to the body, which was not covered. She was wearing pants and a T-shirt. Her hair was tousled and blood-soaked. The entire time, Schechterle made careful notes on a brand-new yellow legal pad, which would eventually total ten to twenty pages of handwriting. By now, he was mastering the ability to write with his surgically repaired hands. The latex gloves he wore were built for four fingers and a thumb, which meant they didn't fit well, with empty slots flopping around as he worked: no index finger on his right hand, first two fingers on his left hand empty, and half a thumb.

"I was shocked at how much writing police officers do," Schechterle said.

The initial assessment was a cursory look to corroborate what he'd been told so far. This scene in particular—the parking lot of a busy hotel on a business day with the sun up—presented a subtle pressure to clean up the scene more quickly, especially out of respect for the fallen woman as she lay in public view under what would soon be a glaring Arizona sun.

"People drive by and see a dead body in the parking lot, they're probably not going to want to stay at the hotel," Schechterle said. "This would turn out to be one of the longer suicide scenes I investigated."

From there, he talked to three construction workers who'd been nearby and witnessed the jump around 4:45 a.m. They had begged her not to make the fateful decision. From their vantage point, they saw her jump and fall. They couldn't see the impact from where they stood. Then Schechterle interviewed the hotel manager, who escorted him to the room: no female clothes, no luggage, no signs of drug or alcohol use. No forced entry on the door. The bed was made. It was not adding up to a normal suicide.

At 7:30 a.m., while Schechterle was standing in the hotel parking lot, Kotecki's cellphone rang. The sergeant had been on scene and standing nearby. He answered, made some notes, and hung up.

"We just got a hanging at the Biltmore."

"It's going to be a busy day," Schechterle said, knowing that the case would be assigned to someone else in C-32 squad, which ended up being Tom D'Aguanno. Not that Schechterle was heartless, but he was in the middle of his own death investigation. It was the way of murder in the big city; each detective needed to focus on his own investigation and let go of everything else.

At 9 a.m., while Schechterle was diagramming the scene in the parking lot, Kotecki's phone rang again. Although Tuesday was body-tag day, on this particular day the C-32 squad was also on homicide call. Schechterle's ears perked up, thinking they might be catching a murder case.

"We got another one."

"Holy shit," Schechterle said. "Where is it?"

"Nine hundred," Kotecki said, which meant Cactus Park Precinct. Three suicides in three hours: It was an ominous sign on a day that was about to turn even darker.

By 11:30 a.m., Schechterle had wrapped up his scene investigation at the hotel, which he'd rule a suicide. Sergeant Kotecki was still on scene. Schechterle had discovered that one of the hotel employees had given the deceased a key to the room when she had pleaded for a place to freshen up. That explained the undisturbed room with no forced entry. There were no other indications of foul play or involvement of anyone else in the death. Multiple witnesses had seen her jump to her death by her own volition. He'd been able to identify the woman, who was in her late 30s, via the purse found in the room. Schechterle would have to include every painstaking detail in his report. But as it turned out, he wouldn't be writing that report immediately as planned.

It was cooler than usual for an early May morning, with the temperature only in the high 70s. But the status of the current weather was nowhere on

Schechterle's radar as he meticulously wrapped up his investigation. He didn't want to think of the amount of paperwork he now had stacked up: His report ended up being twenty pages, and took hours to write. The last line read: *This case is pending the medical examiner's report.*

Almost noon, and he hadn't even been to his desk at 620. As he climbed in his unmarked truck and turned out of the hotel parking lot, his cellphone rang: It was Sergeant Kotecki, just ahead of him in his own unmarked car as they both drove back to headquarters. When Schechterle saw it was Kotecki, he wondered why he was calling, as they had just spent the last four hours side by side. *Oh shit*, Schechterle thought. *This will not be good.*

"We have a 999. Thirty-Four-Hundred West Cactus. I'll see you there."

A cold chill shot through Schechterle: 998 was an officer-involved shooting; 999 was an officer down. When any cop heard "999" it was like a vicious gut-shot.

"Yes, sir." Schechterle turned his radio to channel 9, which broadcast calls for the 900 Precinct where the incident had occurred, which had begun with a routine traffic stop. Schechterle's thought as he raced to the scene: *What an ugly day.*

AT 11:10 that morning, as Schechterle investigated the suicide at the hotel, Phoenix police Officer David Uribe ran a license-plate check through his MDT. He was behind a Chevy Monte Carlo. Less than a minute later he got a bingo on felony: The plate came back as stolen from a local car dealership.

Uribe called the dispatcher and told her he was going to stop the car on West Cactus Road. Forty seconds later, he radioed that the vehicle was occupied times two, white males. The dispatcher requested a 10-20, to note Uribe's exact location. Uribe did not respond. She tried his unit ID again—*nine two three bravo*—with no response.

At 11:12 a.m., a flurry of 911 calls flooded dispatch: officer down. The voices were all panicked: *He got shot. He's lying on the street. There's blood. He does not look alive!*

A U.S. Postal Service worker on duty was the first to reach the fallen officer and frantically tried to clear Uribe's airway. Blood gushed from Uribe's head in horrifying torrents. Another citizen tried to help. The good Samaritan attempts to perform chest compressions on Uribe only pumped more blood from the gaping holes in the officer's right temple and neck. Mouth-to-mouth resuscitation proved just as futile.

Soon Phoenix police officers took over the scene and rescue efforts, but Uribe was slipping away fast. Uribe's gun was still holstered, which meant one thing to the officers on scene: *This was a straight ambush job. God help the perpetrators of this grisly offense.*

"You don't get to kill a police officer on duty in broad daylight," said Schechterle. "How many cars did I walk up to in my short career on patrol?"

Sadly, Uribe's son was also on duty this bright morning and heard the call. The son was patrolling in the neighboring 800 Precinct, Maryvale, while his dad worked Cactus Park. Likewise, Uribe's wife was a police dispatcher with Glendale PD.

Sergeant Pat Kotecki's first task: assign a lead detective for what promised to be a high-profile case and investigation. The 39-year-old Kotecki chose the wily veteran Jack Ballentine. His partner Alex Femenia was tasked with analyzing the crime scene.

Eight minutes after the first 911 call, officers and detectives already had a bead on the Monte Carlo, which the suspects dumped with its motor still running just one mile south of the shooting, near Metrocenter Mall. For whatever reason, one or both took the time to pop the hood and rip out coolant and vacuum hoses. There were two spent .38-caliber shell casings under the tail end of the car. Back at the scene, there were twenty-one witnesses waiting to be interviewed by detectives.

Just before 1 p.m., Femenia was ready to scour the scene in detail with crime-scene tech Elaine Finlay, who was another key part of the C-32 squad. Like his partner Ballentine, Femenia rarely carried a gun. And just as his squad partner Schechterle had done right up to field officer training (when he switched to chewless tobacco), Femenia's bad habit of choice was burning Marlboros.

At John C. Lincoln Hospital, a vigil of family and fellow police officers assembled for Officer Uribe. The large contingent was eerily similar to that of the night of March 26, 2001. Just as they had for Jason Schechterle, family, friends, and fellow officers hoped, cried, and prayed for the best, and prepared for the worst. Uribe suffered devastating gunshot wounds to his forehead, upper lip, and neck. Sadly, at 3:50 p.m., he was dead. When Schechterle heard the news, his mood plummeted.

About the same time, detectives had a possible lead into what was now a full-bore murder investigation: a Denny's restaurant receipt found during the search of the Monte Carlo. Dated the previous day, the receipt specified table number and server. Perhaps there was also a security camera that might have captured images of one or both of the suspects.

When detectives checked it out, they hit pay dirt: two men caught on tape paying at a cash register. Another camera caught the two males with three other males and a woman at the table specified on the receipt. Additionally, the two men seen at the cash register fit the general description of the murder suspects. Still photos captured from the video made it onto the local 6 p.m. television news.

Another tip came in: A Phoenix woman told detectives her 21-year-old daughter had been in the Monte Carlo shortly before the Uribe shooting. She also relayed a potential bombshell: Her daughter told her that a friend, Donnie Delahanty, 18, had been bragging for days about shooting any cop who pulled him over. Another name came up: Christopher Wilson, who had been with Delahanty earlier in the day. The puzzle pieces were coming together.

The pace of the investigation intensified with each new lead: Around 9 p.m. Matt Watson, 22, called Phoenix police saying he needed to talk. By 10 p.m. he was sitting in an interview room at 620 West Washington, staring at the imposing figure of Jack Ballentine.

"You seem to be having a hard time with this," Ballentine told him. "But everything you can tell me right now is really important."

Watson spilled: He and the daughter of the earlier tipster had been running methamphetamine back and forth from Tucson with none other than Donnie Delahanty and Chris Wilson, the two names that had already come up in the investigation. He admitted hitting the pipe with the suspects and others the previous night, and offered that Delahanty normally carried a Smith & Wesson 9-mm handgun in a holster. And for days, he said, Delahanty had been ranting about shooting any cop who came to his car window.

In a glimpse into his own twisted world, Watson seemed especially upset that his stereo equipment, skateboard, tool bag, and clothes were still in the trunk of the seized Monte Carlo. Ballentine displayed 100 percent professionalism; what he would have liked to do to this walking turd was something entirely different. Ballentine grinded on Watson until the wee hours of Wednesday, when the interview ended at 12:45 a.m. Schechterle had watched every minute on the monitor.

The gaunt meth girlfriend, Jena Sedillo, who'd been given up by her mother, took the hot seat under Ballentine's glare just before 3 a.m. A fellow cop was dead: His brethren would not sleep until they had more answers.

The girlfriend wore a little pink shirt and sweatpants, her body showing the skinny and sunken-eyed ravages of methamphetamine, a drug especially effective at destroying its users. As he watched the proceedings, Schechterle's eyes were red and stinging because he hadn't been able to remove his contact lenses. Other than his eye troubles, there weren't any health issues that would keep Schechterle from doing the job.

The witness told Ballentine that when she heard a cop had been shot, the first name that popped into her head was Donnie Delahanty, who for the past three days had been saying that if they got pulled over in this car, "the cop wouldn't even have a chance to get out of his car, that he was going to shoot him because [Delahanty] didn't have anything to live for."

Just before 4 a.m., she was able to identify everyone in the Denny's photographs. After the interview, Sergeant Kotecki told his lead investigators to go home and get some sleep, but in unison they all shook him off.

Next on the list was getting better photographs of Delahanty and Wilson, because the grainy video captures were not clear enough to circulate. To that end, they ventured off to track down Wilson's mom. Later, back at 620, Ballentine asked Schechterle to visit Delahanty's parents on Wednesday morning near I-17 and West Thunderbird Road.

"You have to stay neutral and professional," Schechterle said. "You also have to respect what the parents are going through. They did not pull the trigger, and they may lose their son if he chooses to go out in a blaze of glory." The swirl of emotions also included darker thoughts: *The shitbag you raised just killed one of my friends.*

Tom Delahanty told Schechterle that he'd last spoken to his son on the phone just hours after Uribe was gunned down. The son had told his father he was playing video games, and nothing had sounded amiss. Other detectives tracked down Delahanty's brother Nick, who said he saw his brother in the Monte Carlo with friends the morning of the murder. Witness tips continued pouring into the station. After Schechterle left the Delahantys' house, Ballentine called and asked him to go to David Uribe's autopsy, which was not something Schechterle wanted to do. But in this job, a detective did what had to be done.

"Yes, sir, of course," Schechterle said, but his stomach dropped. He did not want to see what he was about to see at the Maricopa Medical Examiner's office at Jefferson and Seventh Avenue, just a stone's throw from Phoenix Police headquarters. Typically the case agent or crime-scene detective would attend the cut, but the topsy-turvy investigation was anything but routine.

Schechterle walked into the long hallway, with rooms on either side behind glass partitions. The doctor wore a headset and spoke as he worked; if Schechterle had a question he could ask it via a phone on the wall. Ballentine joined Schechterle for the solemn proceeding. Up and down the hallway every day, various autopsies were being conducted simultaneously. Any unnatural death in Maricopa County required an autopsy: Die at work. Fall down a flight of stairs. Get killed by a tree branch. Suicide. Go to the hospital with pneumonia and die from it. Drug overdose. They all ended up here under the harsh fluorescent lights and oddly unique smell.

After they had worked the case for thirty-six hours straight with no sleep, Kotecki demanded his squad get some rest. Grudgingly, the detectives finally acquiesced and headed to their respective homes after 2 a.m. They were all back at headquarters by seven o'clock Thursday morning. They debriefed and came up with a game plan: go back to Delahanty's parents to press them for their son's whereabouts.

Delahanty's father repeated what he'd told Schechterle the day before: His son had denied any knowledge of the policeman's shooting. Then the father suggested that maybe his son had taken off for Tucson or California.

"I'm not trying to hide anything, OK?" the father told detectives.

Femenia took the mother to the kitchen, asking that her husband leave them alone. She said she'd chosen not to speak with her son when he called, and feared that he was going to commit suicide. After an hour of questioning, the detectives left. Schechterle, however, couldn't hide the raw emotions as they walked to Femenia's truck.

"Anything you wanted to ask them?" Femenia asked Schechterle.

Schechterle, as the newbie, had to tread carefully: His squadmates had decades and decades of police and investigative experience.

"Come on, man," Femenia said, his voice rising. "Give it up. Don't keep this shit to yourself."

"I thought we came out here to press him about the trailer," Schechterle said. "We didn't ask shit about the trailer."

"You want to ask about the trailer?" Femenia said. "Let's do it! C'mon! Let's go!"

Back inside, the detectives brought up Chris Schneider's mobile trailer home, a name and location that had come up through the investigation. The father said yeah, he knew about the trailer, because his son's car had been stolen from there months before. But he shook off the detective's theory: no way his son would hide out in the trailer, because it was in a subdivision for senior citizens where a young kid would not blend.

Hot, angry, and working on little sleep, Femenia moved into the father's personal space, intentionally, and asked why he'd withheld this crucial information. Femenia continued to press, and eventually the father gave it up: He'd seen his son the night before and had given him a prepaid cellphone during a short rendezvous at a convenience store. Then another name popped up that detectives had heard but not yet checked out: Dave York. Schechterle's intuition and insistence had proved valuable.

At 4:30 p.m., the case broke wide open when a 911 caller told the dispatcher he needed to speak to the detective in charge of the Uribe case. When asked, the caller gave his name: Donnie Delahanty. Though skeptical, the 911 operator patched the call straight to Jack Ballentine in his office at 620.

"Hi, buddy, how're you doing?" the detective asked.

"What the fuck is going on?!" Donnie shot back.

"Well, you tell me."

"Sir, I had nothing to do with this, sir… so I am not going to go down for something I did not do."

"Well, you're not going down for anything right now."

Delahanty promised to come forward when police found the "real" cop-killer. Instead, Ballentine gave Delahanty an option: surrender, and Ballentine would arrange to have Delahanty's father meet his son at the downtown police station.

"You have my word on that," Ballentine said.

Meanwhile, just before 5 p.m., Femenia and Schechterle were still at the Delahantys' house. The stress of the investigation was palpable for everyone involved.

"It was our squad that was assigned the homicide case," said Schechterle. "We had a huge responsibility to get this done."

As Femenia pressed the father for more information, Delahanty's mother came running down the hall with a cellphone in her hand, yelling, "He's going to kill himself!"

The father screamed into the phone: "Don't do it! Don't do it!" Then he handed the phone to Femenia. "Please, talk to him."

Schechterle used his phone to call Ballentine and started running a play-by-play as Femenia tried to talk the murder suspect off the ledge. *Stay calm. Don't do this to them. Don't go out like this. Be a man. Come out and let's talk. The dog won't bite you.*

One of Delahanty's fears was being ripped apart by a K-9 dog as the Phoenix police SWAT team surrounded the trailer near Fifty-First Avenue south of I-10. The rat was trapped in a corner.

"I wasn't there," Schechterle said. "But I bet there were a hundred officers on site."

Eerily, Femenia, Schechterle, and the mother and father watched the mobile-home-park scene unfold on the Delahantys' television via a media helicopter live feed. At the academy, instructors had told Schechterle and his classmates that as police officers their greatest weapon was not their gun or brute strength, but their mouths. The art of communication, which Schechterle was about to see in action: The seasoned professional Femenia persuaded Donnie Delahanty to walk into the middle of the street and surrender. His parents watched on live television as police yelled commands, proned him out, and then swarmed their son without incident. Five minutes later, suspect number two, Chris Wilson, stepped from the trailer and was similarly taken into custody without incident.

"I remember Alex hanging up the phone and saying, 'He's in custody,'" Schechterle said. A third suspect who'd come up in the investigation, "Backseat Johnny," was soon in custody after turning himself in to police.

At 620, the officers transporting Wilson and Delahanty in two separate patrol cars used the basement-ramp entrance to headquarters, off Sixth Avenue, to avoid the cluster of media awaiting their arrival. The car transporting Delahanty went in first and dipped out of sight down the ramp. The officer driving the second car, however, didn't realize that the three steel security pop-ups had redeployed. The patrol car slammed into the immovable low pillars, which catapulted Wilson into the mesh cage and opened a nasty gash on his forehead. No one at police headquarters would shed a tear for Wilson's unfortunate injury. Sergeant Kotecki even made light of the Keystone Kops mishap by saying it was a new interrogation technique that softened up suspects for questioning. But the injury added a new wrinkle to the investigation.

"Jack Ballentine told me to escort him to county hospital in a patrol car," Schechterle said; he'd just settled in to watch Ballentine interview Delahanty. During the three-hour stitch job at the hospital, Schechterle and Wilson never uttered a word to each other. Then he drove the suspect back to 620 to be interviewed by Ballentine. It was Thursday night approaching midnight, which meant the squad had been working the case almost nonstop since midday Tuesday.

"I missed the interview with the shooter," said Schechterle. "But I was very proud of the task I was given."

On May 17, more than seven thousand people attended Officer Uribe's funeral at Radiant Church in Surprise, a Phoenix suburb. Afterward, the funeral procession proceeded to the Greenwood Memory Lawn at Twenty-Third Avenue and Van Buren Street. At the end, the sound of the dispatcher's voice filled the air with the traditional last call.

"This is the last call for Officer David Uribe, 4276," she said. "923 Bravo. 923 Bravo. 10-7. Good night, sir. You will be deeply missed. Frequency closed."

Two weeks after Uribe's murder, Schechterle took a flight to Medford, Oregon, and drove to a small town in Northern California. A witness there had been visiting Phoenix and had seen the shooting, so Schechterle went to do a photo lineup at the man's house. Once inside, Schechterle placed five similar photographs on the kitchen table, read a statement from a card with specific instructions, and watched as the man picked out the driver, Chris Wilson. Schechterle retrieved the photographs, packed up, and thanked the man for his time. Procedure did not allow Schechterle to tell the man that he'd correctly identified one of the suspects. Schechterle's critical task was a five-minute procedure sandwiched between twenty-four hours of travel.

Johnny Armendariz, who was in the back seat of the vehicle, was not charged. In 2005 David York, a former Arizona Department of Corrections officer, was sentenced to three and a half years in prison for his role in hiding a gun (not the murder weapon) and burning the two prime suspects' clothes. Christopher Wilson pleaded guilty to second-degree murder in 2006 and agreed to testify against Delahanty.

In May 2009, Delahanty, 22, was found guilty of first-degree murder for the shooting death of Phoenix Police Officer David Uribe during the traffic stop in May 2005. A Maricopa County Superior Court jury later agreed to the death penalty. In April 2011, the Arizona Supreme Court denied Delahanty's appeal and upheld his death penalty conviction.

CHAPTER 25

Lead Homicide Investigator

ON A SWELTERING JULY AFTERNOON in 2005, Eduardo Beltran got into a fender-bender in Phoenix. There was damage to his vehicle, but both parties agreed to settle up without calling the police. Instead, the driver of the vehicle who hit Beltran agreed to meet him at an auto body repair shop the next day with $1,500 to pay for the damage. It seemed a reasonable and equitable solution. The next day, July 25, around 5 p.m., Beltran met the other driver as planned. The vehicle pulled up with two men inside and, instead of paying Beltran, one of the men fired a single shot into Beltran's chest before fleeing. Beltran collapsed onto the hot pavement and soon died from the wound.

The case landed on the C-32 homicide squad. Deciding who would be lead detective, Sergeant Kotecki had a dilemma: All his senior people were deep in caseloads or going out of town. Schechterle, at home and speaking to his sergeant by telephone, immediately began his pitch: He had the time, energy, and enough experience now to be the case detective.

"Sir, please let me lead this investigation," Schechterle said. "I can do this."

Kotecki had to weigh these decisions carefully. Down the road a defense attorney would be poring over the investigation packet looking for any reasonable doubt, as *unreasonable* as most of the defense theories were, to spring the accused. A rookie homicide detective working his first case as lead investigator was just the sort of thing that made defense attorneys salivate.

Kotecki made his call: "OK, it's yours." The accompanying unspoken admonition was equally clear: *Do not screw up, Schechterle.*

Working the case with Schechterle were detectives Tom D'Aguanno and Darrell Branch. Speaking Spanish, Branch called each number dialed from the cellphone number they'd found at the scene. Using the ploy that he'd found the phone and was calling to return it, Branch asked each person he called if he or she knew who owned the phone. One of the people he called gave a name, Arturo, and the name of his ex-girlfriend, Maria. Schechterle and Branch headed out to talk to Maria. When Schechterle told her the story, Maria dropped a helpful tidbit.

"It's not the real name for that guy," she said while sitting in an unmarked car being interviewed. "He's Rodolfo. He shot my boyfriend last year."

"Talk about striking gold as a detective," Schechterle said. Now he had a name and could start the search for a usable photograph—plus the possibility that the suspect had committed an unsolved aggravated assault one year before.

Back at 620, Schechterle worked the case until four o'clock the next morning. He went home for a few hours to sleep and then was back at it. He ran the name through the computer and came up with a hit: Rodolfo Gutierrez. *Now, why had the victim been killed, and by whom?* He tracked the perpetrator through phone records and various false names. Schechterle dug through the files and went to meet with the assault detective who'd worked the boyfriend-shooting case the year before. Armed with an address from the ex-girlfriend, Schechterle went to her house.

"Where did this happen?"

She led him into a bedroom and pointed. At the top of the wall near the ceiling was a small hole. The first thing Schechterle did was check the interior wall: no exit hole on the other side. That meant there might be some valuable evidence awaiting his discovery inside the wall. He went to his truck, retrieved his toolbox, and called a crime-scene specialist to come take photographs.

"I had to get her permission to cut her wall," Schechterle said.

Schechterle used a drywall saw to cut a small hole to see if the wall was hollow, which it was. He then knelt to the floor and cut from stud to stud, popped out the piece of drywall, and grabbed his flashlight. His heart rate quickened when he saw a dusty chunk of cold lead from the year before, which had been conveniently awaiting his arrival in this case.

"Everything I did was a perfectly fitting piece of the puzzle," Schechterle said. "It was the ultimate dream homicide case for me."

Back at Phoenix PD, Schechterle impounded the evidence. Upstairs at his computer, he typed a crime lab supplement request to have the recovered bullet compared to the bullet from the body of Beltran. It didn't take long for ballistics tests to give Schechterle a match: the bullet in the wall had been fired from the same gun that murdered Beltran.

Working past 7 p.m., Schechterle had his packet together and was ready to pick up the suspect. He had strong probable cause to arrest for the current murder and, from the shooting one year before, aggravated assault. The packet included a photograph, last known address, known family, friends, and associates, and other relevant details. He called the sergeant with the SWAT unit, all of whom were the best of the best. They were the fittest, best shooters and best tactical people on the force, who'd passed rigorous testing and endured regular drills.

"If you could get him for me, I'd appreciate it," Schechterle said—the handoff was contrary to detectives on cop shows in nice suits doing the dirty work themselves and kicking down doors.

"We'll spend all day tomorrow looking for him," the SWAT team member said.

There were indescribable amounts of paperwork involved with each homicide case. Just as Kotecki had considered, over each investigation loomed the future presence of some determined defense attorney poring over the case records trying to uncover missteps, mistakes, or any little detail that might help stir up reasonable doubt. Defense attorneys did not have to prove a single fact; they only had to raise questions, point fingers at the police, and take shots at the prosecutor's case. For Schechterle and every other detective, therefore, documentation and attention to detail were paramount. Obsessive-compulsive disorder wasn't a job requirement to be a police officer, but it was a trait that certainly served cops and detectives well. An hour after Schechterle had submitted his packet to the SWAT team, the phone rang.

"We got him."

From the time of the murder, it had taken nine days to make the arrest, with all the various moving parts. The SWAT team member had driven to the last known address, solo, and saw the suspect standing on a long balcony smoking a cigarette. The balcony was accessible to anyone by stairs.

Again, contrary to what's normally portrayed on television and in films, there was no tactical van full of helmeted and armored soldiers punching down doors; and no red laser beams crisscrossing through falling dust. Just one guy dressed in plain clothes with the look of a common street turd. He casually walked up to the balcony, moved behind the suspect, grabbed his arms, and handcuffed him before he knew what hit him.

Bang: Suspect in custody without incident.

Back at 620, Spanish-speaking detective John Shallue led the interview, with Schechterle watching via monitor. Bryan Chapman sat in with Schechterle to translate Spanish. The detective crafted the interview around the original, one-year-old aggravated assault case rather than the immediate murder. He played good cop for almost two hours before even bringing up the murder.

"It killed me not to be able to do that interview," Schechterle said. "As far as prosecutors or juries would have been concerned, we had nothing," Schechterle said. "We needed Rodolfo Gutierrez to tell us the story. We needed a confession."

Gutierrez admitted to the killing, but said his accomplice Moreno told him to pull the trigger. By August 12, 2005, both suspects had been arrested. Deputy Maricopa County Attorney Noel Levy took the case.

"You can't help but view a case like this as but a terrible travesty," Levy said on camera for the television show *The First 48*, which was documenting Schechterle's turn as lead detective. The show's crew was embedded with the C-32 squad for an entire year, with four cases being profiled including the Beltran murder: "A nice family man who's never been in trouble, and now he's blown away."

Armed with the confession, Levy took the case to a grand jury, for which Schechterle testified. The case never went to trial.

"I really hoped the case would go to trial," Schechterle said. "I didn't want them to plead out."

In early 2007, both defendants pleaded guilty to a charge of murder. Rodolfo Gutierrez pleaded guilty to first-degree murder and received a sentence of life in prison. Esteban Moreno Morales pleaded guilty to second-degree murder and received twenty-two years in prison.

"That was my defining moment as to every reason I wanted to be a homicide detective," Schechterle said. "He shot and killed somebody over a minor traffic accident. Working that case is one of my all-time great memories."

FARTHER afield during 2005, there were five more Ford Crown Victoria Police Interceptor collisions, explosions, and fires involving law enforcement officers. In four of the incidents—in Colorado, Washington, and two in Texas—the officers survived the fire as Schechterle had. Officer John Wheeler of the San Antonio Police Department, however, was not so lucky during his Crown Victoria incident.

On October 14, 2005, Wheeler was running radar on Loop 410 when, at 2 a.m., a drunk driver rear-ended his Crown Victoria. Wheeler's wife was the dispatcher on duty at the time of the crash. Patrolman Wheeler managed to send a distress signal from his radio after the collision, but was trapped in the Crown Victoria per the macabre and repeating pattern. Unable to respond to dispatch, Wheeler burned alive. The other driver, who had a blood-alcohol content over twice the legal limit, also died. Like Schechterle, Wheeler was a U.S. Air Force veteran.

CHAPTER 26

End of Watch

IN DECEMBER 2005, following the fiery death of a New York City cab driver in a Crown Victoria taxi, U.S. Senator Charles Schumer, D-New York, was advocating for protection to owners and dealers of the Crown Victoria platform. Ford officials were not admitting any wrongdoing, related to any possible defects. despite calls by advocacy groups and government officials to do otherwise.

For Schechterle, the larger fight against Ford and the Crown Victoria issue faded as his eyesight issues worsened. As much as he loved his job, his time as a homicide detective was about to run out for good.

On a balmy night in April 2006, just after midnight, he was wrapping up an investigation on a murder case in Maryvale. When his phone rang and he saw that it was Sergeant Kotecki, he knew without answering he'd not be going home any time soon. Instead, fifteen minutes later, he was driving through the shimmering city lights to an outlying suburb of Phoenix called Ahwatukee. Once there, he'd begin a new murder investigation.

EARLY on the morning of April 15, 2006, the phone rang at the home of married couple Grace Pianka and Adam Kostewicz. Pianka answered and heard a female voice ask for her husband. After the call, the husband dressed quickly and hurried to his car. Suspicious, the wife followed and saw her husband get into a car driven by a woman. He returned home that evening.

When Schechterle arrived on scene in Ahwatukee there was one body, that of the husband Adam Kostewicz. Schechterle waited for the signed search warrant and then worked through the night diagramming the crime scene. Around ten o'clock the next morning Jack Ballentine walked up.

"Jason, your eye is bleeding," he said.

Schechterle had no idea. He'd been wearing his contact lenses for thirty-six hours straight. Though not verbalized at the time, it was the beginning of his realization that he was going to have to give up his dream job. A day later, he went to see Dr. Bill MacLeish, the eye surgeon, who was less than pleased when he heard about Schechterle's long hours. Schechterle's eyes, he'd repeatedly told him, would forever need extra time to rest and heal, every day. He stitched the left eye shut to allow that healing time.

"The reality started creeping into my mind very slowly," Schechterle said. "What would I do if I retired?"

From that point forward, the inner struggle was a daily battle. He finally had the greatest job in the world, a job he'd dreamed of since he was a boy. He knew that once a police officer quit, the state-required certification lapsed quickly. If he quit and wanted to come back, he'd have to go back to the academy and recertify. But for Schechterle, that would never again be an option, because once he left the force he'd never qualify to return to patrol. The gun issue would come back into play, as would his physical limitations and hand dexterity.

The case he'd caught that elicited blood from his eye turned out to be a classic lovers' triangle. Kostewicz did, in fact, have a girlfriend, Virginia "Jen" McIntyre, but she was absolved of any criminal wrongdoing. It was McIntyre who'd called 911 upon finding her married lover Kostewicz dead. The wife, Pianka, was found guilty of second-degree murder in March 2009 in her second trial in Maricopa County Superior Court after the first ended in a hung jury. She received a sentence of thirteen years.

In June 2006, Schechterle said to Jack Ballentine, "I need to talk to you about something."

"You're thinking about retiring."

"I am."

Ballentine was very helpful in discussing the pros and cons. He was also concerned about his protégé's health and, if pressed, thought retirement was the right decision. Schechterle thanked him and took a few more weeks to mull things over with Suzie and his dad. The extra time was less about making the decision, which was already made, and more about finding his own acceptance. He'd be walking away from everything he'd ever hoped to achieve. And in his condition there would be no going back. He just had to let it sit to be certain he was doing the right thing.

"When Jason Schechterle first came to us in homicide, he didn't want to go out in public," Ballentine said. "He would not walk into a restaurant until I got there. It was a process to get him to put himself out there and become more comfortable in his new body. Over time he did, and it was an amazing thing to watch."

Finally, on the appointed day, Schechterle walked into the office of his sergeant, Pat Kotecki, and just came straight out and said, "I think I'm going to retire."

There was silence and a shocked look. Then Kotecki said, "Really? We need to go upstairs."

Literally and figuratively, the two marched up the chain of command and talked to one of the assistant chiefs, who displayed equal shock. All cops had a system, which started with "identify the problem." Arrive on scene, whether chaotic or calm, and the first order is always: identify the problem. Then cops solve the problem.

For Schechterle it was pretty easy to do. His declining health, and more specifically his eyesight, was 90 percent of the problem. The other 10 percent was his inability to requalify with his duty weapon. But, clearly, had his eyesight not been an issue he'd still be working as a homicide detective today. The gun issue alone wouldn't have been enough to forever derail his dream.

"Being a homicide detective was the greatest job in the world," he said. "If a genie came out of a bottle right now and said, 'Jason, you can be anything you want, anywhere you want,' I'd say, 'Homicide detective, Phoenix Police Department.' There was nothing I didn't get to see or do as a homicide detective." During his relatively short stint on the job, he'd helped investigate fifty or so murders.

On his last official day, August 19, 2006, Schechterle did what homicide detectives do: work insane hours and take bad people to jail. Said Schechterle, "The last thing I did was arrest a woman the night before for the murder of her infant." The baby, 3, who weighed just fourteen pounds, had died of malnutrition. Bryan Brooks, who'd been first on scene the night of March 26, 2001, shared a meal and some good laughs with Schechterle before he went and made the arrest—the jarring mixture of tragedy and camaraderie typical of police work. Then Schechterle worked until 2 a.m. finishing the case paperwork.

"That was my send-off," he said.

He collected all his personal effects and took one last look around the C-32 homicide squad work area, now in a quiet lull for a few precious hours before the detectives started filing in around 6 a.m. Schechterle was exhausted, both immediately and in the larger sense, and wanted to go to bed. He knew when he awoke it would be the first day of the rest of his life, the one in which he would not put on his badge and go to work as a patrol officer or detective. There was a brief moment of quiet reflection as he looked around the office, but no tears. For some reason he had a vivid flashback to the academy and his physical conditioning shorts that had faded and were considerably higher and tighter than on Day One. His new pals Chapman and Tuchfarber wondered why Sprinkles made it so easy, but that didn't mean they eased up for one second:

You smuggling grapes there, Sprinkles?

Looks like the forecast calls for another cold morning at the academy, with a high probability of shrinkage.

Bumble Bee tuna: Your balls are showing.

John Stockton called: He wants his shorts back.

"Schechter Shorts" laughed to himself, turned, and walked out of the police department for the last time as a certified peace officer. He went to his truck and drove home. In the vernacular of the college football world he loved, he had left absolutely everything on the field, including a fair amount of his own skin. No one could ever say Jason Schechterle did not go all out, every minute, of every shift. That's who he was and how he operated.

"I always wanted to be a homicide detective," he said. "That was my version of the professional leagues. Once you touch your dream, that can never be taken away."

LESS than one month before Schechterle's retirement party, two more police officers, Dale Holcomb and Joshua Risner, together with a civilian, died at the scene of another exploding Crown Victoria Police Interceptor, in Ohio. Both officers worked for the State Highway Patrol, the agency that had been Bryan Chapman's ultimate dream. Holcomb, in fact, had joined the force in 1985, which meant he was already employed with the agency when Chapman was making his two failed attempts to join. Holcomb and Risner were killed near the intersection of Jackson Pike and Mitchell Road, in Gallia, when their patrol car went out of control on the rain-slick surface and collided with another vehicle.

On October 27, 2006, there was a retirement banquet for Schechterle at the Arizona Grand Resort. There were some five hundred people in attendance for the paid event, which after covering costs created a fund for a scholarship program.

"It turned out to be quite an event," said Schechterle, who went by limousine with his family. At the dinner, Schechterle was too nervous to eat much. Chief Jack Harris gave Schechterle a framed collection of his various badges from his career. New Times writer Paul Rubin gave Schechterle a collage of the stories he'd written about the C-32 squad.

The most emotional gift and presentation was the one from Bryan Chapman. He gave Schechterle the uniform shirt he'd been wearing at the moment of impact on March 26, 2001, neatly framed on an Arizona flag. Chapman had taken the time to find the uniform, which still had Schechterle's badge pinned to it and was tinged with soot. Schechterle had not been aware the shirt had survived the night and had been stowed for safekeeping. Schechterle tried, but he could not hold back the tears when Chapman handed over the heavy frame.

Finally, there was a video of people congratulating Schechterle, including crime-fighting television personality John Walsh, rocker Alice Cooper, and others.

"I was very proud and honored by the turnout," Schechterle said. "I was sad, too, and excited that I was starting a new chapter. At the time, my plan was to play a lot of golf and relax."

IN the end, Schechterle had spent more time trying to become a cop—eleven years—than he had served. His law enforcement career, from the start of the police academy in late September 1999 to retirement in early October 2006, was almost exactly seven years. Tragedy, suffering, and all, he still saw his time behind the badge as the best seven years of his life. The absolute finality of the end, however, would take some time to process: no more physical agility tests, polygraph examinations, annual shooting qualifications, crazy hot calls, lights and siren, dead bodies, reports and forms, bloody crime scenes, ongoing training, or any of the bizarre standardized tests—*My soul sometimes leaves my body.*

For Jason Schechterle, the dream career was 100 percent officially over and done, and once again he was simply a civilian. Except now he had earned something incalculably special from the noble career he had pursued: a lifetime of law enforcement memories to sift through and recall for the next—he hoped—fifty years.

CHAPTER 27

Moving Forward

JASON SCHECHTERLE will live the night of March 26, 2001, every day for the rest of his life. Finally, after fifty-two surgeries as of April 2013, Schechterle was no longer in bodily pain and didn't have any major health issues internally. However, he will forever battle eyesight issues, as the fire caused irreparable damage. In May 2013, after ongoing pain and issues with his contact lenses, Dr. Bill MacLeish sewed Schechterle's right eye shut to let it heal. On May 16, the doctor surgically reconstructed Schechterle's right eyelid. Twelve years after the night that changed everything, Schechterle had just undergone surgery number fifty-three. A week later he woke up and the stitches had ripped out. This is his new life.

"I feel very good all the time," he says. He does feel more aches and pains, but he attributes that to turning 40 in 2012. "Other than my eye issues, there's nothing lasting from the night of the accident that comes up. I don't even get the flu or anything else. I stay very healthy. When I wake up I'm energetic, and it lasts all day."

His lower legs weren't injured but, as the source of most of his skin grafts, are discolored and scarred. He's never been much of a runner, but he still plays golf and lifts weights. Son Zane is a big motivator to get Dad to the gym.

Wherever Schechterle goes, in hat and sunglasses, the stares follow. Most are from curious kids, but adults are not immune. He won't go to a restaurant by himself. He goes to the same grocery store where he knows the staff. He is comfortable enough now to go the beach and will go to the movies. He will never, however, go to Disneyland Park again—primarily because he doesn't want to take away from some young child's experience by traumatizing the boy or girl with his appearance.

"Over the years I've created my own bubble as to what I'm comfortable with," he says. "Some days I handle it better than others."

Schechterle especially, to this day, hates airports. He walks with his head down to avoid eye contact with people. Those minor annoyances aside, there is only one major challenge that is a daily hurdle and concerns Schechterle going forward: his eyes.

Each night he pops out his hard contact lenses, a task he has learned to do solo with reconstructed hands and a special mini-plunger. To keep his eyes moist while he sleeps, he winds Saran Wrap around his head to act as temporary eyelids. When he tears away the plastic in the morning and the air hits his eyeballs, it stings like the blast of pepper spray he suffered at the academy. Then the routine begins: saline solution, eye wash, and hard lenses. Long-term, he wonders how, and if, his eyesight will hold up. Not having vision would take away golf and seeing his family, both of which would be cataclysmic. It's a nagging concern he'll live with forever.

Since settling his case with Ford Motor Company in June 2004, Schechterle has watched helplessly as another eight police officers have died inside burning Crown Victoria Police Interceptors. In five other incidents, five officers survived with burn injuries. If there is a definition of "madness" for Schechterle, the ongoing death and trauma inside these Ford police vehicles certainly fits. But he has continued the fight. As a result of Schechterle's lobbying, in 2010 the Arizona state Legislature passed a bill to create a fund for law enforcement agencies to draw on to purchase fire protection for vehicles.

ALONG with his own unique challenges, Schechterle faces the same hazards of living as everyone else. On February 15, 2011, Schechterle's beloved Grandpa George died at age 86 in a hospital. His health had been declining as he battled the virulent staph infection MRSA. Suzie had called her husband and said, "It's going to be pretty soon."

Schechterle left a meeting to be at his grandfather's hospital bed. His grandfather was wearing a breathing mask and could not speak, but he was conscious. Grandpa tapped his watch and did a roller-coaster motion with his hand. He had never struck it rich, but he saved up and bought a Rolex.

Schechterle's academy alumnus Shayne Tuchfarber, who'd grown close to George after Schechterle's collision, was in the room, too. He got the reference.

"Is it time for you to go, George?" Tuchfarber said.

Grandpa nodded.

The doctors and nurses said they had done all they could, and that George was comfortable. His grandson nodded and said it was time to turn off the machines. He and Shayne and Suzie gathered quietly around the bed. Fifteen minutes later, Grandpa slipped away. The nurse came back in, checked his pulse, and nodded solemnly.

Eventually, Schechterle was the last one sitting there, alone, both crying and smiling. His mother came in and asked if he was OK. He nodded and smiled at her. His grandmother had died in 2001 when Schechterle was in surgery after his crash. He wasn't able to be there with her when she died.

"This made everything OK," he said. "Being with my grandfather when he passed was the most beautiful experience I've ever been through. Just to be with him. It brought things full circle with my grandmother. I finally had closure."

LIFE today is about giving back. One way Jason's story continues to give back is through the annual ball started by Jack Ballentine in 2006.

"The whole idea was to honor Jason in his retirement and start a scholarship in his name," Ballentine says. That first year there were five hundred people at the event, which raised $50,000 with the 100 Club as sponsor.

Originally, the Jason Schechterle Scholarship benefited children of officers or firefighters critically injured. The spouses and families of those tragically killed in the line of duty are typically well cared for by municipality pensions and life insurance. Those critically injured, however, often get nothing. The event, however, has grown to include other scholarships. By 2012, the attendance had almost tripled to 1,300 people, with $325,000 donated through scholarships.

"It's very humbling," said Schechterle. "It means a lot to me, because nothing's ever been done for kids whose parents are severely injured."

Schechterle also shares his wrenching and inspiring story of human triumph in a well-crafted, for-hire, forty-five-minute presentation. He started giving the speech in 2003 and was sometimes doing two or three a week. As of 2013 he's given the speech more than 300 times; his largest audience to date is 1,000 people at a corporate leadership summit. He's polished and perfected his delivery along the way. He's also narrowed the scope of his specific audience.

At one of his early speeches at an elementary school, Schechterle concluded by asking if any of the children had questions. A little boy raised his hand and said, "I think you're going to give me nightmares."

"That boy made me think about who can handle my story and who can't," Schechterle says. Speeches for high-school audiences comprise the youngest demographic now.

Invariably when his speeches conclude people want to come up, shake his hand, and share stories. After one speech at a firefighter's convention in Arizona, the crowd wanting to meet Schechterle waited in a long line. About fifteen people back, he noticed a New York City firefighter in his dress uniform, which stood out.

"Firefighters are obviously close to my heart," Schechterle says. At the time he was thinking, *Wow, this guy came all the way out here from New York.*

When the firefighter introduced himself, he was in tears. He told Schechterle about being at Ground Zero on 9/11. He talked about going through a divorce. Then he said, "But you changed my life today."

Schechterle was so choked up and unable to process all his emotions that all that came out was, "Thank you." Then the firefighter walked away and out of the room.

"I wish I could have a second chance to talk to him," Schechterle says. "He truly inspired me, and I didn't even get his name."

That was the profound moment, in 2010, that solidified Schechterle's new mission in life. "That's when I decided I wanted to be a public speaker the rest of my life," he says.

This from the shy freshman Karate Kid who had broken up with the stunning Kim McQuistion in a panic a week after she had agreed to be his girlfriend. The jumble of nerves who had to spend five horribly anxious minutes telling his academy class 333 brethren "How to Bake a Cake." The nervous academy graduate who had to call his new pal Bryan Chapman for reassurance: *Can I do this job?* The grotesquely disfigured man who abhorred being in public and once hid in the dark shadows of his own living room.

"I can't tell you why Jason's appearance never bothered me, but I've never missed how he looked before the night of March 26, 2001," Suzie says. "I didn't marry the face: I married the man. He's the same human being."

That human being has now traveled further than he'd ever imagined, in ways he could not have conjured that day in 1999 when he watched Phoenix Police Officer Marc Atkinson's funeral procession, the day he fully heeded his own call to wear the same uniform.

TO keep his spirits up, Suzie and Jason's other family, friends, and fellow cops continue to find refuge and relief in dark humor. If Schechterle is winning at poker against Kevin Chadwick—the officer who cut him free of the burning car that night—Chadwick will joke that he should have left Schechterle in the car longer.

Asking Schechterle to give someone the middle finger elicits great laughter, since he has no such configuration or dexterity. When Suzie yells for her husband to hurry up, Schechterle says he might be able to get ready faster if he still had ten fingers.

If Schechterle bumps his knee on a table standing up and cries, "Ouch," Bryan Chapman responds with, "Oh, great, another lawsuit." Of course, friends tell Schechterle he'll eventually get a discount on cremation when he dies: He's already three-fourths done. Schechterle himself takes self-deprecating jabs: One afternoon at home with his wife and parents he said that as a former smoker he could always get a job doing cigarette commercials about the dangers of smoking in bed. Humor works because he's survived the worst and now just wants to be treated like everyone else. No better, no worse. Just blend in and be a regular guy. One of the boys.

"Being a cop is a brotherhood that will always last," Schechterle says. "Even bigger, now that I understand the full power of the human spirit. There's nothing you can't overcome with a positive attitude. The sun rises, life goes on, and you can either be part of it or not. It's that simple."

Simple, perhaps, if one is made of the rare stuff of Jason Schechterle.

"No matter what I did, if Jason didn't have the inner strength he has, then nothing would have worked," Suzie says. "We were meant to be together. We're soul mates."

CHAPTER 28

Am I Dreaming?

THE MOMENT IS NOT DIVIDED from the whole. Destiny knows no such distinction. The warm spring night is in full city shimmer when the hot call pops. A full moon silvers the sky. Every time, in every scenario, he answers up. There can be no other way.

The officer worked and trained for this; he is living the dream and following the higher calling. He is the new centurion, the line between order and anarchy. He feels the adrenaline surge of anticipation as he listens to the female dispatcher. This is where the action begins, where the life is lived, the moment when the officer reaches to respond and puts it all on the line. It may be yet another paper call in a lifetime of paper calls. It may be another non-event in a long shift and career of non-events. Or it may put life and limb at risk and call all the training into demand in the flash and fury of seconds. He may be called to sacrifice his own life; he may be forced to take the life of another.

He is there so that we may all rest easy, on 24/7, around-the-clock vigil as we move through our days and nights. He and his brethren will answer each call so that we *never* have to carry that burden. They are our keepers.

He steers with one hand, leans forward, and instinctively reaches for the black mic just in case proximity and providence are about to clash and—perhaps—he saves a life. Stops a crime. Helps a child. Eases someone's fear in her worst moment. Backs down a bully, shackles him up, and takes the bad guy to cool out in jail.

"Unknown trouble," the dispatcher says. "All available units."

Bingo on action. Code 3: lights and siren.

He is minutes away: He knows the numbered streets and avenues as the map unfolds in his head. He rolls through an intersection and will likely be first on scene. The adrenaline is pumping now, all focus locked. Anyone who has ever served in dark blue knows there is no greater moment than this one.

Jason Schechterle goes cop mode: "Five-thirteen Henry. I'll start up."

Epilogue

MICHAEL ADAMS, Schechterle's brother, lives in Aspen, Colorado. He retired from the Phoenix Police Department in 2011 after a twenty-two-year career as a patrol officer and detective. He is now director of security at two Westin Resort properties in Aspen.

In June 2007, **JACK BALLENTINE** retired from the Phoenix Police Department after twenty-nine years. In 2009, he published a captivating book about his undercover-hit-man exploits (*Murder for Hire*, Thomas Dunne Books / St. Martin's Griffin), which he wrote himself without the assistance of a ghostwriter. After retiring from the police department, he joined the Phoenix Fire Department, where he is fire marshal and oversees 140 employees investigating criminal arson cases and enforcing Phoenix fire code. His son Geoff Ballentine followed in his footsteps, joined the Phoenix Police Department in 2000, and is now an officer with the Air Support Unit.

DARREN BOYCE, who worked the jump line the night of March 26, 2001, started his career as a firefighter in 1991 with Rural/Metro Fire Department. He joined the Phoenix Fire Department in 1997, where he promoted to engineer in 2002. Today he works Engine 1, C shift.

BRYAN BROOKS, who was first officer on scene March 26, 2001, and helped pull Jason Schechterle from the burning cruiser, worked as a patrol officer in Central City Precinct until 2005. From 2005 to 2008, he was part of a plainclothes-detail Neighborhood Enforcement Team. In 2008 he promoted to detective and joined the Family Investigations Bureau, domestic violence unit, where he works with partner Shayne Tuchfarber.

KEVIN CHADWICK, who cut Jason Schechterle's seat belt on March 26, 2001, and helped pull him from the burning car, worked as a Phoenix patrol officer from 1997 to 2005, including time as a field training officer. In 2005, he joined the Drug Enforcement Bureau as an undercover narcotics detective, where he worked until 2011. His next assignment was with a Neighborhood Enforcement Team for Central City Precinct, where he continues to work. The actual knife he used to cut Schechterle's seat belt on March 26, 2001, sits in a framed shadow box in Jason's poker room.

BRYAN CHAPMAN celebrated his fourteen-year service anniversary with the Phoenix Police Department in 2013. After working as a field training officer in Central City Precinct from 2001 to 2003, he promoted to night homicide detective (2003 to 2006), promoted again to sergeant as a patrol supervisor, and in 2008, joined the Family Investigations Bureau as supervising sergeant. There, he headed the Missing and Unidentified Persons Unit, overseeing a squad of nine detectives. In 2013 he promoted to lieutenant and a new post on graveyard shift.

REBECCA JOY, who was driving Engine 5 the night of March 26, 2001, started her firefighting career in 1981 as a reserve with Rural/Metro Fire Department in Sun City, Arizona. She joined the Phoenix Fire Department in 1983, promoted to engineer in 1990, and retired in 2009.

After being a trial lawyer for more than four decades, **PATRICK J. MCGRODER** has cut back from seven days a week to six days a week. As of 2013, he has garnered settlements and jury verdicts on behalf of his clients in excess of $500 million. In 2013 his two oldest children, Caroline and Patrick, joined the same firm of Gallagher & Kennedy in the Biltmore area of Phoenix.

HENRY NARVAEZ, who helped pull Schechterle from the burning car the night of March 26, 2001, left Phoenix Fire Department in 2008, and became a firefighter in California.

After thirty-plus years with the Phoenix Fire Department, **MICHAEL ORE**—who made the critical radio call the night of March 26, 2001—retired in 2008.

After forty-six years as a trial lawyer, **DAVID PERRY** and his wife Rene, a former district judge, officially closed their law firm, Perry & Haas, in 2013. They now divide their time between Corpus Christi, Texas; Durango, Colorado; and several other places where their four daughters and ten grandchildren reside. During his legal career, Perry accumulated more than $1 billion in verdicts and settlements for individual personal clients (not class-action lawsuits).

KAREN and **FRED SCHECHTERLE,** Jason's parents—along with his sister Alissa Felker—all live within a mile of Schechterle in Phoenix, Arizona. Schechterle and his father play golf once a week or more.

After earning her bachelor's degree in elementary education from University of Phoenix, **SUZIE SCHECHTERLE** began her new teaching career in 2012. Today she teaches fourth grade in Phoenix, Arizona, and plans to pursue a master's degree in reading intervention.

SHAYNE TUCHFARBER transferred to Central City Precinct in 2002 and worked patrol until 2009. He said working 51 Frank put him among the greatest assembly of police officers he had ever seen in his life. In 2009, he promoted to detective with the Family Investigations Bureau, domestic violence unit, where he works with partner Bryan Brooks.

After manufacturing and defending the design of the **FORD CROWN VICTORIA POLICE INTERCEPTOR** since 1979, in 2011 company executives at Ford discontinued the model. The replacement model is the Ford Police Interceptor, available in both sedan and sport-utility versions, which was announced in March 2010. On September 15, 2011, the last Crown Victoria rolled out of the Saint Thomas plant in Canada. With that, manufacture of the Ford Crown Victoria Police Interceptor was officially done.

Was dropping the Crown Victoria—in both name and design platform—a long-awaited response to the dark series of fiery deaths and years of costly litigation and settlements? Or, after more than three decades, was it simply time for a complete reboot of the vehicle, given today's technology? Either way, a heinous chapter appears to have closed. Law enforcement agency decision-makers across the nation can choose the new Ford as well as Chevrolet or Dodge police vehicles.

Whatever Ford executives or engineers want to publicly admit or not admit—*no comment*—the lawyers Pat McGroder and David Perry celebrated the news of the Crown Victoria's death as victory and vindication in the long campaign on behalf of those injured and killed. Jason Schechterle, too, summed it up in one word: "Finally." The Crown Victoria may be no more, but Schechterle will live, breathe, and fight against the damage and disfigurement it left behind for the rest of his days.

Interestingly, engineers put the 2011 Ford Police Interceptor on a front-wheel drive unibody platform (with optional all-wheel drive). The new chassis bore no relation to the rear-wheel, body-on-frame Panther platform that underpinned the Crown Victoria, a platform McGroder, Perry, and other advocates had identified as fatally flawed.

Also of note, Ford engineers added a large steel crossbar support to the new-model Police Interceptor. Positioned under the back seat, the extra steel bulk is purportedly rated to allow car and officer to survive a 75-mile-per-hour rear-end collision. Perhaps those inside the walls in Dearborn, Michigan, had finally been moved to action.

Here was the official company stance in a statement released September 13, 2012, by Ford executives: "To develop the all-new Police Interceptor, Ford engineers worked hand-in-hand with Ford's police advisory board of law enforcement professionals, who provided input on key vehicle attributes such as safety, performance, durability, driver comfort, and functionality."

From the same statement: "Building on Ford's safety leadership, Police Interceptor is engineered to pass 75-mph rear-end crash testing." The latter is good news to law enforcement officers patrolling in the new Police Interceptors. The former—Ford's safety leadership—might be up for debate given the all-too-frequently exploding Crown Victoria.

Other than stating its capacity of nineteen gallons, there was no other mention in the company statement about fuel tank design or positioning, or the addition of any fire-prevention design specifications into the new-model Police Interceptor. The optional automatic fire suppression system and special trunk packs introduced in 2005—designed to prevent cargo from penetrating the fuel tank in a collision—are still available as an optional add-on.

Acknowledgments

- To my wife, Suzie: We have seen enough highs and lows to last several lifetimes. I am forever grateful that you chose to spend your life with me. I love you more than you'll ever know—more than words can express—and I look forward to the rest of our story.

- For Kiley, Zane, and Masen: Of all my accomplishments I am most proud of you kids; your mom and I love you more than anything.

- Thank you to my mom, dad, sister, and brother for all the support and love.

- Thank you to the first responders who, on the night of March 26, 2001, pulled me from the burning car and got me to County.

- Thank you to the dozens of doctors, nurses, and medical staff who worked in, on, and around my body to bring me back from the dead and keep me around all these years since 2001.

- Thank you to Pat McGroder and David Perry, who took up the fight against Ford and won.

- Thank you to Russ Stallman, retired Phoenix cop, who inspired me to tell my story.

- Thank you to our design, editorial, and production team at Avery Press for a job beautifully done.

- Thank you to Bryan Chapman and Shayne Tuchfarber—Big Head and Fatty—who have always been there.

- Thank you to Landon J. Napoleon. I believe fate, patience, and our respective purposes brought us together, and you alone were meant to write this book. Your sincere love and respect for me and my family grew with this project, and I am eternally grateful for your talents and, now, friendship. It is an honor to have you create, author, and help me share my story.

- And thank you to every cop in this great nation who rolls out on patrol 24/7 to protect and serve: You are our keepers.

LANDON J. NAPOLEON is the award-winning and critically acclaimed author of fiction and nonfiction books. His debut novel *ZigZag* received widespread praise, was a Barnes & Noble "Discover Great New Writers" 1999 finalist, and went on to become a feature film. He is a graduate of Arizona State University and the University of Glasgow in Scotland. He lives in Arizona with his family.

www.landonjnapoleon.com